DATE DUE

THE UNRAVELING ARCHIVE

Sylvia Plath, Wellesley, January 1951.
*(Photo courtesy Mortimer Rare Book Room,
Smith College, ©Aurelia Schober Plath.)*

The Unraveling Archive

ESSAYS ON SYLVIA PLATH

Edited by Anita Helle

THE UNIVERSITY OF MICHIGAN PRESS

Ann Arbor

Copyright © by the University of Michigan 2007
All rights reserved
Published in the United States of America by
The University of Michigan Press
Manufactured in the United States of America
♾ Printed on acid-free paper

2010   2009   2008   2007   4   3   2   1

A CIP catalog record for this book is available from the British Library.

Library of Congress Cataloging-in-Publication Data

The unraveling archive : essays on Sylvia Plath / edited by Anita
    Helle.
      p.   cm.
    A collection of eleven essays on Plath's writing with the archive
as its informing matrix.
    Including bibliographical references.
    ISBN-13: 978-0-472-09927-6 (acid-free paper)
    ISBN-10: 0-472-09927-2 (acid-free paper)
    ISBN-13: 978-0-472-06927-9 (pbk. : acid-free paper)
    ISBN-10: 0-472-06927-6 (pbk. : acid-free paper)
    1. Plath, Sylvia—Criticism and interpretation.   2. Plath,
Sylvia—Archives.   3. Plath, Sylvia—Manuscripts.   I. Helle, Anita,
1948–
PS3566.L27Z946   2007
811'.54—dc22   2006021883

ACKNOWLEDGMENTS

Many colleagues, friends, and associates helped to bring this volume about. For collegial support and exchange, as well as advice when it was needed, I wish to thank Elizabeth Abel, Sally Bayley, Mary Braun, Christine Britzolakis, Kay Campbell and John Maul, Tracy Daugherty, Mary DeShazer, Lisa Ede, Cheryl Glenn, Gary Glisson, Susan Gubar, Heidi Brayman Hackel, Elinor Langer, Diane Middlebrook, Suzanne Raitt, David Robinson, Marjorie Sandor, Carolyn Steedman, Peter Steinberg, and Rebecca Warner. I owe large debts of gratitude for research support to directors, archivists, and curatorial assistants at primary collections, especially Karen V. Kukil and Barbara Blumenthal, Mortimer Rare Book Room, William Neilson Library at Smith College, Northampton, Massachusetts; Rebecca Cape, Lilly Library at Indiana University, Bloomington, Indiana; Stephen Enniss, Naomi Nelson, and Kathleen Shoemaker, Robert W. Woodruff Manuscript, Archives, and Rare Book Library, Emory University, Atlanta, Georgia. For assistance in answering questions at various stages in the production of this book, I thank John Hodge, Washington University Libraries in St. Louis; Simon Rooks at the British Broadcasting Corporation; Jonathan Summers at the British Sound Archives, the British Library, London, UK. I gratefully acknowledge the Everett Helm Fellowships Program at Indiana University for support of my research at the Lilly Library, the OSU Library Research Fellowship Program, and the Oregon State University Center for the Humanities for release from administrative and teaching responsibilities in 2004. For opportunities to present material on the Plath archive, I am grateful to colleagues at the OSU Center for the Humanities, to my students at Oregon State University, and to organizers of the Pacific University MFA program, who gave me the opportunity to share ideas about the archive with practicing writers. For photographs I am especially grateful for kind permissions of Susan Plath Winston, Elizabeth Gilmore, and Peter K. Steinberg. Closer to home, Cheryl McLean's editorial assistance in the late stages of this project and the support of my colleagues in the English department have been essential. I thank my editor, LeAnn Fields, at the University of Michigan Press and her assistant, Rebecca Mostov, for their professionalism and support; the anonymous reviewers for their incisive and helpful readings; and Marcia LaBrenz and the copyeditors for their keen eyes. Plath scholars have been unfailingly generous in their contributions to this volume, and their energies, talents, commitments, and patience have made the project worthwhile. Writing on Plath, one never writes alone; in assembling these essays I have often been reminded of the inspiration provided by the scholarship of Steven Gould Axelrod, Susan R. Van Dyne, Marjorie Perloff, Mary Lynn Broe, Langdon Hammer, Jo Gill, Tim Kendall, Helen Vendler, and many other remarkable Plath scholars whose work has marked new stages of intellectual discovery all along the way. Mary DeShazer, Lue Helle, Peter Sears, and Rivers Sears know how much my work ongoingly depends on them.

We are grateful to the following for permission to reproduce copyrighted material, unpublished manuscripts, photographs, and visual art.

Ladies' Home Journal® magazine for page 143 of the December 1958 *Ladies' Home Journal*. Used with permission of the publisher.

University of Wisconsin Press for Lynda K. Bundtzen, "Poetic Arson and Sylvia Plath's 'Burning the Letters,'" *Contemporary Literature* 39, no. 3: 434–51. Reprinted and formatted by permission of the author and the University of Wisconsin Press.

John Hodge, Washington University in St. Louis, for citations from Lee Anderson autograph book and transcripts for the Estate of Lee Anderson in Kate Moses, "Plath's Voice, Annotated."

Indiana University Press for Robin Peel, "The Political Education of Sylvia Plath, expanded from "The Ideological Apprenticeship of Sylvia Plath," *Journal of Modern Literature* 27, no. 4: 49–72. Reprinted in an expanded version by permission of the author and Indiana University Press.

Faber and Faber, Ltd., and the Sylvia Plath Estate, UK, for extracts of Plath's curricular materials and citations from published work in Robin Peel, "The Political Education of Sylvia Plath."

Lines from "Nick and the Candlestick" and "Temper of Time" from *The Collected Poems of Sylvia Plath*, ed. Ted Hughes; copyright © 1960, 1965, 1971, 1981 by the Estate of Sylvia Plath. Editorial material copyright © 1981 by Ted Hughes and excerpts from *Letters Home by Sylvia Plath: Correspondence 1950–63* by Aurelia Schober Plath. Copyright © 1975 by Aurelia Schober Plath in Robin Peel, "The Political Education of Sylvia Plath." Reprinted by permission of HarperCollins.

Viking Penguin, a division of Penguin Group (USA), Inc., for Diane Middlebrook, "Creative Partnership: Sources for 'The Rabbit Catcher,'" from *Her Husband: Plath and Hughes—A Marriage* by Diane Middlebrook. Used by permission of the author and Viking Penguin, a division of Penguin Group (USA), Inc., and Time Warner/Book Group (UK).

Estate of Aurelia Plath, for photographs in Anita Helle, "Reading Plath Photographs." Used by permission of Susan Plath Winston, © the Estate of Aurelia Plath, and the Estate of Otto E. Plath.

The Sylvia Plath Estate, UK, for visual art of Sylvia Plath, *Nine Female Figures* and *Two Women Reading* © Estate of Sylvia Plath, with kind permission of Frieda Hughes, in Kathleen Connor's, "Visual Art in the Life of Sylvia Plath."

The Sylvia Plath Estate, UK, for extracts of unpublished cards, juvenilia, and letters by Sylvia Plath in the Lilly Library Sylvia Plath Collection, in Kathleen Connors, "Visual Art in the Life of Sylvia Plath: Mining Riches in the Lilly and Smith Archives," © Estate of Sylvia Plath, with kind permission of Frieda Hughes.

W.W. Norton & Co. (USA) and the Trident Media Group (UK) for "On the Beach with Sylvia Plath," from *Death's Door: Modern Dying and the Ways We Grieve,* copyright © Sandra M. Gilbert. Reprinted and reformatted by permission of the author, W. W. Norton, and Ellen Levine Literary Agency / Trident Media Group (UK).

The Faultless Starch/Bon Ami Company for an advertisement, "You'll Fly Through Housework," in the October 1957 *Ladies' Home Journal*. Reproduced by permission of Bon Ami® in Marsha Bryant, "Ariel's Kitchen: Plath, the *Ladies' Home Journal,* and the Domestic Surreal."

Riviana Foods, Inc., for excerpt from Carolina Rice/River Rice advertisement, "Easy Does It!" in March 1955 *Ladies' Home Journal,* p. 148. Reproduced by permission of the Riviana Foods, Inc.®.

Elizabeth Gilmore for frontispiece photo of Plath at the south entrance of Notre Dame, April 1956, for the Gordon Lameyer Estate.

Peter K. Steinberg for photographs of Point Shirley, in Anita Helle, "Reading Plath Photographs."

ABBREVIATIONS AND COLLECTIONS

As designated in chapters, pagination refers to the following editions. Unless otherwise specified, U.S. editions are used. *The Collected Poems of Sylvia Plath* is the primary reference for Plath poems unless otherwise noted.

Ariel   *Ariel.* London: Faber and Faber, 1965; New York: Harper and Row, 1966.

AR   *Ariel: The Restored Edition,* Foreword by Frieda Hughes, London: Faber and Faber, 2004.

BJ   *The Bell Jar.* London: Heinemann, 1963 (Victoria Lucas); Faber and Faber, 1966. New York: Harper and Row, 1971 (Sylvia Plath).

BL   *Birthday Letters,* Ted Hughes. New York: Farrar, Straus and Giroux, 1998.

COP   *The Colossus and Other Poems.* London: Heinemann, 1960; New York: Knopf 1962.

CP   *Collected Poems.* Ed. Ted Hughes. New York: Harper and Row, 1981.

CW   *Crossing the Water.* London: Faber and Faber; New York: Harper and Row, 1971.

J   *The Journals of Sylvia Plath.* Ed. Francis McCullough. Ted Hughes, consulting ed. New York: Dial, 1982.

JP   *Johnny Panic and the Bible of Dreams and Other Prose Writings.* Introduction by Ted Hughes. London: Faber and Faber, 1977; New York: Harper and Row, 1970.

UJ   *The Unabridged Journals of Sylvia Plath,* New York: Anchor, 2000: published in UK as *Journals of Sylvia Plath: 1950–62;* London: Faber and Faber, 2000.

LH   *Letters Home: Correspondence, 1950–1963.* Ed. Aurelia Schober Plath. New York: Harper and Row, 1975.

WT   *Winter Trees*. London: Faber and Faber, 1971.

THCP   Ted Hughes. *Collected Poems*. Ed. Paul Keegan. New York: Farrar, Straus and Giroux, 2003.

British Library (SA)   The National Sound Archive, The British Library, London.

British Library (M)   The Department of Manuscripts, The British Library, London.

Emory   Manuscript, Archive, and Rare Book Library, Robert W. Woodruff Library, Emory Unversity, Atlanta, Georgia.

Lilly   Sylvia Plath Collection, The Lilly Library, Indiana University, Bloomington, Indiana.

Smith   Sylvia Plath Collection, Mortimer Rare Book Room, Smith College, Northhampton, Massachusetts.

CONTENTS

ANITA HELLE

Introduction

ARCHIVAL MATTERS

⊞

The eleven essays in *The Unraveling Archive* were written during a period in which literary scholarship on Sylvia Plath has yielded new depth and excitement. Organized around themes of archives and memory (as well as different kinds of memory), the essays demonstrate the relevance of diverse source materials to the increasingly varied and multifaceted strands of Plath's legacy and writing. Ultimately, the collection aims to enlarge and enrich the contexts of Plath's writing with the archive as its informing matrix, unraveling tangled connections backward to the middle decades of the twentieth century and forward to issues raised by contemporary literary and cultural criticism.

The unraveling is of histories, temporalities, narratives, contingencies. In "On Deck," a poem written by Plath in the months following the transatlantic journey she and Ted Hughes took to England in 1959 on the SS *United States,* Plath uses the reflexive mirror of the sea to capture movement in time and space.

> Midnight in the mid-Atlantic. On deck.
> Wrapped in themselves as in thick veiling
> . . . .
> Some few passengers keep track
> Of the old star-map on the ceiling.
> . . . .
> Tiny, and far, a single ship
>
> Lit like a two-tiered wedding cake
> Carries its candles slowly off.[1]

Plath's poem is marked visually and technologically as a mid-century event: hints of surveillance, the broadcasting voice ("You Are There: Midnight in the Mid-Atlantic"). The essays in this collection, written by scholars of different generations on both sides of the Atlantic, are situated along a different temporal and literary horizon. Recently that horizon has been reconfigured by an abundance of new material on Plath and by theoretical and methodological challenges of approaching the material from new directions. In our era, Plath is less than ever the product of any singular map, movement, aesthetic, or affiliation; this collection opens her work to a variety of critical persuasions, theories, and languages of canonicity, to multiple audiences and sites of reception. The essays capture a transition in Plath studies, as previous representations of Plath are disturbed, new questions posed, and familiar ones revisited. Refusing totalizing narratives of suicidal extremity, each chapter pursues one or more of the following, often overlapping, trajectories: expanding and revising our understanding of the political contexts of Plath's postwar writing (primarily poetry, but also prose and journal writing); broadening the twentieth-century cultural and interdisciplinary contexts to which her work belongs (including women's magazines, geography, travel, gender and genre, and visual culture); elaborating problems of textual editing and textual criticism; and reconsidering Plath's sources and borrowings in relation to contemporaries.

In the diversity of materials and the range of Plath's writing considered, these essays mark a second stage of debate around Plath's canonicity, and the terms we use to describe it. One generation of scholarly and critical activity, in the wake of the *Collected Poems,* framed Plath's major and minor poems around a set of issues and references, establishing discursive boundaries of "juvenilia" and "mature" work. The present transition and regrounding of Plath studies in what I have generally termed "archival matters" coincides with the turn toward historiographic textual and material research; there has been a growing recognition that much of what we thought we knew—and didn't know—about Plath has gradually come to be part of a wider conversation about culture, history, and memory for which archival material and expanded definitions of the archive provide support.

The present stage of Plath's reception has been prepared for, in part, by well-publicized "events": the acclaim garnered by *Birthday Letters* that brought with it renewed interest in Plath; a "restored" edition of *Ariel* poems; and a round of remarkable exhibitions, readings, dramatic performances, and symposia. At the same time, significant primary documents, such as art notebooks, published and unpublished artworks, journals, and drafts of Plath's poems and prose, have been more widely available in libraries or in published book form. Of crucial importance has been the publication of primary source materials on Plath: *The Journals of Sylvia Plath, 1950–1962 (The Unabridged Journals of Sylvia Plath* in the American edition), edited by Karen V. Kukil, and *Ariel: The Restored Edition,* edited by Frieda Hughes. In addition, notes and poems published in Paul Keegan's edition of *The Collected Poems of Ted Hughes,* as well as Diane Middlebrook's *Her Husband: Hughes and Plath—A Marriage,* have opened new avenues for understanding Ted Hughes's engagement in Plath's creative life, as more extensive, complex, and sustained than was previously thought.[2] Responding to these developments, scholars have traveled to archives or to other sites of significance to Plath's writing; they have appraised "evidence," however problematic; and they have incorporated arguments from an ever-expanding body of criticism.

In one influential formulation, the association of *archive* with *source* and *origin* comes to us from the Greek: *arkheion:* a house (the house of the magistrate, or *archon*), domicile, address, ark, a shelter for embodied memory.[3] Every literary archive has its history and topography, and much has been written about the idiosyncrasies of Plath's archive in particular.[4] Scholars have pored over editions and introductions, and have speculated about source materials lost, suppressed, or destroyed.[5] But not enough has been said about what threads of controversy about Plath's archive and reception have to do with Plath's place in modern cultural traditions, especially those that personalize the writer's archive as a place of singular embodiment and intention.[6] The historical problems with the Plath archive and its modernist legacy, as Jacqueline Rose has observed, are in some ways a case study—aided and enlarged by the means that confessionalism in the 1950s and 1960s furnishes—of a problem of modern authorship that arises from identifying the textual remains of the writer with the preservation of the literal body of the private individual, in *propria persona.*[7] Even if one might presume that archives of individual authors are set up, in part, to compensate for the decay of the literal body, a writer's archives consists of more than "deposits": they also consist of the discursive transactions surrounding them, the particularities in the material of which they are composed, the dispersal of materials across different sites, and the modes of retrieval by which these objects and texts become individually and collectively available in display or publication. That is to say, beyond a simple archaeology of "things," I would argue that literary archives—Plath's among them—necessarily decompose in the sense that the processes of dissemination and study invariably reconfigure the hierarchical fields of what is to be valued.

As a writer and a historical subject, Plath emerged at a point when twentieth-century figures such as Auden, Eliot, Frost, Spender, and Stevens, were becoming absorbed into modern Anglo-American canons and were arranging to preserve their own bodies of work. Even if it were not for Plath's suicide, it is not surprising, given the preoccupation with monumentality, that Robert Lowell's near-breathless foreword to *Ariel* in 1965 would propel Plath into history by fully identifying the literal and figurative dimensions of a writing "life" with a universalized perspective ("her art's immortality is life's disintegration").[8] What is particular to the discourse of the Plath archive, characteristically present in the foreword to the first *Ariel* edition, is the repeated figuration of a woman buried in her manuscripts—a structure of representation that perpetually crosses corpse and corpus, the body of the woman and the body of the writing. This is one of the most persistent and problematic, yet often retrospectively useful, threads of Plath's historical reception, and it is a structure that continues to circulate.[9] At one extreme, for example, in a *New York Times* review of the Christine Jeffs and John Brownlow film, *Sylvia* (2003), a publicity photo of Plath/Paltrow, reviewing a copy of the Cambridge magazine, *St. Botolph's Review*, is accompanied by the caption, "A Poet's Death/A Death's Poetry."[10] The caption, like the photograph, opens and forecloses on a cultural obsession. But the phototext might be taken as a parable for the politics of knowledge associated with the Plath archive, a structure that has too often denied complexity, variability, heterogeneity, and playfulness.

There is a long running dialogue about where controversies about the Plath archive began. The first textual representations of the Plath archive appear in Robert Penn Warren's dust-jacket endorsement in the first edition of *Ariel*, and in Robert Lowell's "Foreword" to that volume. Their impressions are of materials that are strikingly undomiciled, *hors d'archive*. Lowell's tone is ironic, the gaze belated, as he plucks an image from bibliographic antiquity, apostrophizing the scribes who slave over funerary stelae on the pain of death: "Oh for the humble copyist, those millennia of Egyptian artists repeating their lofty set patterns!"[11] Of course, Lowell and Warren were telescoping the history of writing to signal Plath's newness. But the uneasy praise also suggests that Plath's writing troubled the very idea of the archive as a settled place, an ordered system of retrievals. In Warren's dust-jacket blurb from the first edition, *Ariel* is at first barely recognizable as poetry *book:* he writes, *Ariel* is "unique," "scarcely a book at all," more like something painfully scattered through a broken window, "as though somebody had knocked out a window pane on a brilliant night."[12]

Was that first edition the fatal "mythologizing moment"? Perhaps. Or can the scattering beyond be understood as something else—an opening onto history? Even a myth has its history of rewriting. Now that Saskia Hamilton's edition of *The Letters of Robert Lowell* has been published, we are able to appreciate that in the decade or so following the publication of *Ariel*, Lowell was troubled by his role ushering Plath into print ("love, mockery, awe," he puts it in one letter). Inveterate reviser, he returns to this composition and its occasion ("agonizing") repeatedly, reviewing details of its composition in letters to his and Plath's contemporaries.[13] His letters encircle the scene of the foreword, suggesting a vortex of ambivalence around his dual mentoring (teacherly) and curatorial (conserving and canonizing) roles—the before and after of the Plath archive. In retrospect, the letters inadvertently disclose another persistent thread of Plath's reception, as well: having so often situated Plath and her writing at dangerous borders, Plath's readers have often cast themselves—or too often have been cast—as trespassers or transgressive intermediaries in the business of smuggling knowledge from the intimate spaces of a crypt.[14]

In addition to an interest in material textuality, a number of these essays consider archival research in terms of narrative and encounter. Archival histories consist of tales we tell about the archive, and of tales the archive tells. Plath's poetic corpus is indeed housed, according to our inherited notions of the archive, in rare book rooms or listening spaces, and on view at exhibitions; and beyond the institution, in the spaces of virtuality—but not in the way Lowell imagined the scriptorium of the "humble copyist," cloistered from everyday life. Inasmuch as archives are conceived of as repositories of embodied memory, we are more than ever aware of the frames through which we encounter these materials, from visual art to voice recordings, scrapbooks, drafts and holographs, annotations, and ephemera of the writing process. Outside "official" archives, digital images pile up on Internet websites, and things that "official" archives haven't collected are amassed in unsuspected online locations—images of all the places Plath ever lived, for example, or of all the book jackets of her publications.[15] To the extent that acts of collecting, individually and institutionally, are intrinsic to the cultural history of archivization, the mélange of stuff collected in Plath sites on the Web confirms narratologist Mieke Bal's performative premise—just as there are many kinds of things to be collected, there are many narratives produced by the reordering of objects within a collection.[16] Yet the current archival environment and the opening up of multiple points of access have not made manuscript sourcing and cross-referencing of materials in and beyond the rare book room any less demanding or exciting. Contributions to this collection also have been enabled by cooperation and collaboration among research libraries and institutions through the mounting of exhibits and symposia and the opportunities they provide for public viewing and debate: in particular, the Sylvia Plath 70th Year Commemoration and Literary Symposium in Bloomington, Indiana, which brought together Smith College and Lilly Library collections, and the 2005 Grolier Club exhibit, "'No Other Appetite': Sylvia Plath, Ted Hughes, and 'The Blood Jet of Poetry,'" which gathered artifacts from both Hughes and Plath collections around the theme of their intertwined creative lives. If Plath's writing continues to be provocative, if scholars and readers are still construing her materials with passionate intensity, it is striking that less and less of what passes across the border of the rare book room reverberates with scandal and revelation, and more resonates with textures of unexpected depth and cultural variation.

Since the publication of Jacqueline Rose's *The Haunting of Sylvia Plath*, it continues to be important to consider what is being produced when the Plath archive is not defined as a particular place, an institutional site, but as a mirror for cultural anxieties provoked by a writer who "worries and fascinates desire."[17] Rose broke new ground by approaching the problem of the Plath archive as a cultural imaginary in which liminal anxieties are evoked and reproduced. Her provocative figure for the archive, the *corps morcele,* or the body-in-bits-and-pieces, was plucked from the psychoanalytic narrative of the ego prior to the mirror stage, before the fantasy of corporeal unity is sutured to material presence.[18] Etymologically the *eaten* body, the body consumed by culture, Rose's image of the archive serves a diagnostic purpose for the production of real and phantasmagoric identifications. But if the figure of the body-in-bits-and-pieces can be read as a shattering of an intimate space or reality, the archive can also be understood as a mirror that has already scattered and broken, especially when we take materiality more on its own terms. A critical genealogy of the Plath archive in an era in which paradigms of confessionalism are under revision might thus consider a revised paradigm of the Plath archive on the model of collage composition, where disparate media and styles border each other and objects are held in tension around differential values. Such an alternative conception of the modern archive has been suggested by the arts of modernism, but it is an especially compelling model given Plath's own interest, across several decades of her work, in surrealism and the arts of collage.

What unravels, then, is the myth of monolithic memory. Rebalanced, with a wider perspective on culture and signifying practices, Plath's legacy is rendered more than a single-noted tragedy. We no longer have Plath's poetic without the intertwining histories of sound and silence, orality and writing; Plath the rigorously observant poet without her absorption of cultural influences; Plath the high culture icon without the contentious history of her readership and reception; the "overawed" shock of *Ariel* without its history of tangled lines. The historiographic turn in literary and cultural studies has made us aware of the archive as mélange—in Foucault's terms, the "mass of things, spoken and unspoken in culture, conserved, valorized, re-used, repeated and transformed."[19] Feminist and poststructuralist methodologies have also emphasized the usefulness of the fragment and the palimpsest as tools for critical incision.[20] Poststructuralist methodologies, such as reading from the margin and the peripheral detail, and investigating the role of the researcher in cultural locations have made research in the Plath archive more complex, more problematic—and ultimately, I argue, more richly reflexive about cultural mediations.

Part I, "The Plath Archive," thus returns to the compelling questions Jacqueline Rose raised in her exploration of the body-in-bits-and-pieces, but from a perspective that accepts the palimpsest, the fragment, as a contingency of situated knowledge: What is the corpus? What is the body of her writing? What are its politics—within and outside the writing? We are advantaged in the present moment because these questions, so fundamental from one perspective, have, until recently, been difficult to approach. This section is particularly concerned with newly published, underutilized, and underrepresented material, with gaps, exclusions, or omissions.

Revisiting the canonical position critics have taken with regard to *Ariel*, Tracy Brain in "Unstable Manuscripts: The Indeterminacy of the Plath Canon" considers what is both revealed and obscured in *Ariel: The Restored Edition*—that is, hesitations and aversions to finality that are typical of Plath's composing practices. Robin Peel's "The Political Education of Sylvia Plath" and Kathleen Connors's "Visual Art in the Life of Sylvia Plath: Mining Riches in the Lilly and Smith Archives" each press for the relevance to the Plath canon of materials composed prior to 1956, exceeding the discursive limit established by the *Collected Poems*. Peel examines Plath's annotations in curricular and extracurricular materials to argue for an "ideological apprenticeship" in politics and intellectual history, an apprenticeship that Plath returns to and revises in her later work. Connors surveys the interplay of picturing and composing, the "eye" and the "I" in Plath's aesthetic development. Drawing upon her experience as curator of a Plath visual arts and manuscripts exhibition, she cross-references word and image to reveal visual strategies that link Plath's juvenilia formally and thematically to later poems. Kate Moses, in "Sylvia Plath's Voice, Annotated," offers a detailed guide—both description and cultural explanation—of the contexts of some difficult-to-access and familiar Plath recordings from the public and private perspectives encouraged by a concept of "close listening." Supplementing this essay, Moses's appendix of annotations to Plath voice recordings, a catalogue of poems and recordings, updates Stephen Tabor's *Sylvia Plath: An Analytic Bibliography* (1987) and recognizes the increasing importance of Plath's oral archives to modern sound histories.

Part II, "Culture and the Politics of Memory," reflects the opening up of critical approaches to Plath and also the explosion of the canon—a movement inward and down, to works that have received less critical attention, and outward to a heightened awareness of the contexts and settings that have mediated our understanding of Plath's multiple identities. Sandra Gilbert's essay, "On the Beach with Sylvia Plath," opens this section. With its emphasis on bringing materials from Plath's *Unabridged Journals* together with analysis of an often neglected long poem, "Berck-Plage," against the backdrop of a French

coastal town with powerful literary, geographical, and aesthetic historical resonance for Plath, Gilbert's essay sets many of the themes for
reading Plath in cultural and historical contexts. Gilbert concludes
that "Berck-Plage" "lays the foundations" for twentieth-century public
as well as private features of mourning through a "gravity of lamentation" that exclusive focus on "family elegies" might overlook. Continuing the theme of genre and history, Ann Keniston's essay, "The Holocaust Again: Sylvia Plath, Belatedness, and the Limits of Lyric Figure,"
revises the vexed subject of Plath and Holocaust memory by drawing
upon Plath's dictionary annotations, as well as upon recent work in
trauma studies: her essay examines the distinctively lyric techniques
used by Plath to represent the Holocaust's disruptions of history and
memory. A cluster of essays by Janet Badia, Anita Helle, and Marsha
Bryant expands the perimeters of the Plath archive with cultural
research, unsettling the high/low culture binaries that have been persistently problematic in Plath's reception. Badia's "The 'Priestess' and
Her 'Cult': Plath's Confessional Poetics and the Mythology of Women
Readers" analyzes the construction of the Plath reader represented in
popular film and the literary reception of Plath's works. In "Reading
Plath Photographs: In and Out of the Museum," I explore the
neglected topic of Plath photographs as image events. Mieke Bal's
exploration of the photograph as a "telling object" serves as a frame-
work for considering the display of public/private artifacts in formal
exhibition and in a photo album. Marsha Bryant's "Ariel's Kitchen:
Plath, *Ladies' Home Journal,* and the Domestic Surreal" uses Henri
Lefebvre's theory of the everyday to examine a "missing page" of
Plath's archive, analyzing the plural meanings of postwar domesticity
through the magazine's poetry, advertising, and journalistic features.
Since recent Plath scholarship has so often emphasized what Heather
Clark has recently described as the "contradictory messages" that
Plath and Hughes sent about their "collaborative relationship,"[21] it is
fitting that this collection concludes with essays that tease out literal
and figurative dimensions of Plath texts as a kind of shared archive.
Lynda Bundtzen's and Diane Middlebrook's essays are cornerstones of
an interpretive tradition that analyzes Plath's and Hughes's mutual
poetic influence in relation to Plath's creative life and manuscript practices; each of their essays looks closely at a major poem that, for various reasons, falls outside the first *Ariel* edition. Bundtzen's essay,
"Poetic Arson and Sylvia Plath's 'Burning the Letters,'" enlarges the

contexts in which Plath's manuscripts and patterns of composing participate in acts of textual violence, analyzing Plath's habit of "bleeding through" manuscript pages and their figurative implications. Middlebrook's "Creative Partnership: Sources for 'The Rabbit Catcher'" gives a thick description of the source material for a poem that makes a poetic statement about the "place of force" in Plath's creative life. Middlebrook's essay also offers a compressed instance of Hughes's hand in the archives long after Plath's death, a hand still attached to the thread of her memory.

In this volume's claim to embrace different sites of archival knowledge is an implicit invitation to dialogue. A range of possible conceptions of the archive is assumed—the archive as a problem, a site, a theme, a cultural encounter, and a figure for memory. The linear ordering of the essays does not adequately capture the effect, at times, of a colloquy of voices that converge and also disagree in debates about many of the same texts. The points of divergence gesture toward persistent issues in Plath criticism, brought into new focus by recent opportunities to reexamine the record. No one would have predicted, for example, that Plath's maternity would continue to produce new cluster studies of poems, with "Morning Song" or "Nick and The Candlestick" referred to in these pages almost as frequently as the canonical "Ariel" and "Daddy"; nor would one have predicted that the very same poems that have marked Plath's canonization in Palgrave's *Golden Treasury of the Best Songs and Lyrical Poems in the English Language*[22] would, for this volume's contributors, inspire ongoing debate about discrepant versions of modern maternity (Brain, Moses, Middlebrook). The fact that Plath's poetic has long been predominantly associated with confessional traditions makes the life-writing materials from *The Journals of Sylvia Plath, 1950–1962,* a companion for most new scholarship: yet it is striking, too, that in these essays the coded status of Plath's journals hovers ambiguously between performed "fiction" and "document." Another set of dialogues and debates in these pages resonates along the lines of high modernism's antipathy for mass culture (a persistently vexed issue for Plath), with what it means to explore the many possible points of reference between the archived and the domestic (Bryant, Helle). Finally, while the purpose of this collection has not been explicitly to challenge confessional paradigms, a number of essays redescribe or revisit them, including traditional, poststructuralist, and narrative criticism.

There is often confusion about why books and critical essays on Plath are published. These essays are intended for scholarship and teaching, and as stimulus to further research and the exchange of ideas. Accordingly, the use of materials in these essays corresponds to guidelines and principles published by the Society of Authors and the Library of Congress. The conventions by which scholars use their good sense to determine extent of quotation of copyrighted material are well known. An abundance of biographical material, some of it recent, has been published on Plath (and Hughes). Given that the purpose is not to disturb the privacy of individuals, biographical detail has been included when corroborated by already established biographies, and in cases where Plath's well known affinity for the egotistical sublime—a tradition closely linking life and art—warrants these connections. Lines between the "strictly literary" and the cultural have blurred in recent years, rendering the relationship of literature to periodical culture, political culture, and popular culture increasingly relevant. Archival material is thus not strictly or always intended to refer to Plath's archive alone.

Of course, there have been ghosts in the room—more than one, in fact. One ghost is that of Jacques Derrida, especially the Derrida of *Archive Fever* (*Mal d'Archive*). Derrida reminds us that the desire that fuels archival fever is potentially melancholic, fueled by the passion for what inevitably slips away.[23] This is a desire dependent on looking, and since Plath is one of the most looked at female authors in the past century, I would argue that the dangers of merely reproducing certain gazes obligates scholars from time to time to reflect on the kind of knowledge that is made. Research on Plath is not conducted merely to produce new academic commodities—it is conducted out of love for her writing and a desire to do justice to the complexity of her art. Another ghost is that of Plath herself, whose poems include wry, ekphrastic jokes and droll reflections on the literal and metaphorical significance of archives and museums. Her perspective reminds us that archives are, in part, social constructions. They swell, even as we write about them.

Plath's surprising strangeness, the "good dangerousness" of her ferocious linguistic confrontations with the forbidden, is still with us.[24] A commitment to including a wider range of her own signifying practices and to recontextualizing fragments of evidence as active and mobile expressions has required devotion, patience, and respect for the difficulties her legacy entails. In this volume, we have wanted not merely to track "old star maps" but to begin new conversations, from outside and within the rare book room. Consistent with the archeology of the fragment, yet not locked into the inward gaze, such conversations acknowledge the power of writing to revisit and recode the scene of knowledge as the essence of critical practice.

NOTES

I wish to thank Elizabeth Abel and Suzanne Raitt for their commentary on earlier versions of this essay.

1. *CP,* 142. Paul Giles's excellent reading of Plath's transnationalism in *Virtual Americas* (Durham: Duke University Press, 2002) relates such reflexive moments to trajectories of transnationalism among post-World War II poets; in this instance memory is localized in the perception of entropy and drift.

2. See Susan R. Van Dyne, "The Problem of Biography," in *The Cambridge Companion to Sylvia Plath,* ed. Jo Gill (Cambridge: Cambridge University Press, 2006), 3–20; and Sally Bayley and Kathleen Connors, eds., *Eye Rhymes: Sylvia Plath's Art of the Visual* (Oxford University Press, 2007), for the comprehensive view of art work that this volume does not attempt.

3. Jacques Derrida, *Archive Fever: A Freudian Impression,* trans. Eric Pernowitz (Chicago: University of Chicago Press, 1995), 2.

4. Ibid.

5. For a summary, see Sarah Churchwell, "Ted Hughes and the Corpus of Sylvia Plath," *Criticism* 40 (1997): 99–133; Christine Britzolakis, *Sylvia Plath and the Theatre of Mourning* (Oxford: Clarendon Press, 1999), 1–2; Lynda K. Bundtzen, *The Other Ariel* (Amherst: University of Massachusetts Press, 2002), 6–14; see also Tracy Brain's chapter, "Unstable Manuscripts: The Indeterminacy of the Plath Canon," in this volume.

6. I am grateful to Ben Alexander and to panelists in the recent "Archive and Intention" session of the Modernist Studies Association 2004 for the suggestion.

7. See Jacqueline Rose, *The Haunting of Sylvia Plath* (Cambridge: Harvard University Press, 1991), 80–81.

8. Robert Lowell, foreword to *Ariel* (New York: Harper and Row, 1966), x. For a commentary on the related problem of autobiography and the "universalist" perspective in the 1950s, see Deborah Nelson, "Plath, History, and Politics," in *The Cambridge Companion to Sylvia Plath,* ed. Jo Gill (Cambridge: Cambridge University Press, 2006), 22.

9. Discussion following an MLA Session 2004 arranged by Ann Keniston with Lynda K. Bundtzen and Diane Middlebrook considered related themes.

10. A. O. Scott, "A Poet's Death/Death's Poetry," *New York Times,* October 17, 2003.

11. Lowell, foreword, x.

12. Robert Penn Warren, *Ariel,* dust jacket (Harper & Row 1966 edition).

13. Robert Lowell, *The Letters of Robert Lowell,* ed. Saskia Hamilton (New York:

Farrar, Straus and Giroux, 2005): on "love mockery awe" see 631; also 424, 467, 476, 595, 601, 603.

14. Lowell's situation is not unlike that of feminist scholars in the anxiety and interest aroused by trespass. "Trespass" vision was an important term in Tillie Olsen's afterword to Rebecca Harding Davis's *Life in the Iron-Mills* (New York: Feminist Press, 1972); for recent accounts of "transgression" and the Plath archive see Britzolakis, *Theatre of Mourning*, 1–2; and Richard Anderson's bio-fiction, *Little Fugue* (New York: Random House, 2004).

15. See Peter Steinberg's www.sylviaplathinfo.com (accessed November 2005). The Sylvia Plath Forum (www.sylviaplathforum.com), an online discussion forum that logged ten thousand hits in its first six months, illustrates the prominent role that citizen-readers have had in reconsidering archival material shaping Plath's recent reception (accessed November 2005).

16. See also Mieke Bal, "Telling Objects: A Narrative Perspective on Collecting," in *The Cultures of Collecting*, ed. John Elsner and Roger Cardinal (Cambridge: Harvard University Press), 1994.

17. Rose, *Haunting*, 72.

18. Julia Kristeva, *Powers of Horror: An Essay on Abjection*, trans. Leon S. Roudiez (New York: Columbia University Press, 1982), 1.

19. Michael Foucault, *Essential Works of Foucault, 1954–1984*, ed. Paul Rabinow, 3 vols. (New York: New Press, 1997–2000), 2:289, quoted in Thomas R. Flynn, *Sartre, Foucault and Historical Reason: A Poststructuralist Mapping of History* (Chicago: University of Chicago Press, 2005), 147.

20. The point is widely made in poststructuralist and feminist cultural critiques—e.g., Linda A. Kinnahan, *Lyric Interventions: Feminism, Experimental Poetry, and Contemporary Discourse* (Iowa City: University of Iowa Press, 2004), 41–47; Elizabeth Frost, *The Feminine Avant-Garde in Poetry* (Iowa City: University of Iowa Press, 2003); Rachel Blau DuPlessis, "Manifests," *Diacritics* 26 (1996): 31–53; and Lynn Keller and Cristanne Miller, *Feminist Measures: Soundings in Poetry and Theory* (Ann Arbor: University of Michigan Press, 1994).

21. Heather Clark, "Tracking the Thought-Fox: Sylvia Plath's Revision of Ted Hughes," *Journal of Modern Literature* 28 (2006): 100.

22. *The Golden Treasury of the Best Songs and Lyrical Poems in the English Language*, ed. Francis Turner Palgrave, 6th ed. (Oxford: Oxford University Press, 1996).

23. Derrida, *Archive Fever*, 91.

24. For Plath's "good dangerousness," I am indebted to a comment by Holly Laird from our Modernist Studies Association Seminar, 2005.

PART ONE

The Plath Archive

TRACY BRAIN

Unstable Manuscripts

THE INDETERMINACY OF
THE PLATH CANON

⸬

The publication, late in 2004, of *Ariel: The Restored Edition,* will do much in the coming years to familiarize a larger readership with the difficulties in establishing complete, authoritative, and final versions of Sylvia Plath's writings. This new edition—which follows the typescript of *Ariel* that Plath left on her desk just before her death—is very different from the *Ariel* that Ted Hughes published in 1965.[1] Hughes omitted some of the poems Plath included in her *Ariel* typescript (e.g., "The Rabbit Catcher" and "The Detective") and inserted others that she did not (e.g., "Edge" and "Words"). Perhaps most infamously, he changed the sequence of the poems in the typescript. In so doing, he helped to shape the still-prevalent idea that *Ariel* was the poetic confession of a suicidal depressive, rather than the narrative of female regeneration and emergence that Marjorie Perloff argues Plath intended.[2] The restored edition certainly gives readers an *Ariel* that is closer to Plath's own vision of her book than the edition Hughes published in 1965. Yet Plath's vision still cannot be perfectly ascertained and then reproduced. The new *Ariel* reveals—but also obscures—the ongoing and difficult decisions Plath made while writing and editing her work. It not only reinstates Plath's own selection and arrangement of the poems, but also provides a facsimile of Plath's full *Ariel* typescript, thereby allowing readers a glimpse into a writing process that continued until her death. Readers can see how Plath changed her mind about the book's title, scoring out *The Rival, A Birthday Present, The Rabbit Catcher,* and *Daddy* on two different pages, before typing *Ariel* on a fresh sheet of paper.[3] The titles of poems themselves are under review until the last, so that on the contents page, "The Courage of Quietness" becomes "The Courage of Shutting-Up."[4]

Questions about what poems to include also persist to the last *Ariel* typescript. There is a duplicate of the typed contents page that Plath used to make notes about where poems had been variously submitted, accepted, or published. On it, there is the handwritten insertion "Death & Co." between "Ariel" and "Magi." On the original title page, she types "Death & Co." in the same position and draws an arrow to indicate that it is to be placed between "Ariel" and "Magi." Such apparently last-minute changes of mind are also visible to us in the parentheses Plath places around the poem "The Swarm" on the contents page, indicating that she decided to omit it from the collection—a decision she confirmed by removing the poem from the typescript. Tiny adjustments of punctuation and spelling also appear throughout Plath's typescript. Some of Plath's choices, for instance when she chooses to lose the American spellings of "appall," "distills," and "gray" and replaces them with the English spellings, "appal," "distils," and "grey,"[5] are nonetheless interesting. So, too, is her decision to move in the other direction—that is, from English to American usage—when she exchanges "Paralysing" for "Paralyzing."[6] Such choices are symptomatic of Plath's continuing awareness of even the subtlest national and cultural tensions between Americanness and Englishness.[7]

Many of Plath's late alterations of spelling and punctuation were not followed in *The Collected Poems*. At the back of the new edition of *Ariel*, "Notes" by David Semanki make it clear to readers who might not have previously realized it that the versions of Plath's poems most commonly found in the public domain—in other words, in *The Collected Poems*—do not follow Plath's own changes to her latest *Ariel* typescript and contain a number of transcription errors. Typically, these discrepancies are of only one letter, yet they can have a great impact on the sense of the poems, for instance when "stalacmites" is given as "stalactites" in "Nick and the Candlestick," or "cooker" substitutes for "cocker" in "Amnesiac," or "flies" for "plies" in "Purdah."[8]

The new edition of *Ariel* provides readers with facsimiles of Plath's handwritten drafts and typescripts of the collection's title poem. Now, at least in the case of the poem "Ariel," readers can see this for themselves and get a sense of the poetic choices Plath was constantly making as she reenvisioned her work through her revisions.

But what can we not see? What remains obscured despite the publication of *Ariel: The Restored Edition?*

I ask this question despite the fact that reconsiderations and restorations can only ever be partial. The Plath "archive" largely consists of materials in the Lilly Library at Indiana University and the Mortimer Rare Book Room at Smith College. But the archive is a dispersed thing, with smaller holdings in other libraries around the world, and a good deal of Plath material mixed with Ted Hughes's papers at Emory University. As Carolyn Steedman tells us, the archive "is not potentially made up of *everything.*"[9] Rather, it has been constructed posthumously and piecemeal—even haphazardly—from materials that have been donated or sold by those who are willing to part with them; but many more materials are not there and have instead been lost or discarded or retained in private hands. Considering the very nature of the archive, Steedman writes, "there will be something left unread, unnoted, untranscribed."[10]

The more we try to establish the "right" Plath text, the more we find that it eludes us—in part, that is the nature of the work scholars do with manuscripts in archives. We seize upon evidence that is consistent, in principle, with the best reading text at our disposal. Sometimes we narrativize the circumstances surrounding a given text so that it legitimates what we want to do with it or say about it—even if it means turning a blind eye to inconclusive or contradictory versions of that text. For these reasons, my goal is not to establish a new basis for an authoritative or final, correct version of any Plath text. Rather, it is to bring to light some of the reasons why the unstable texts of *Ariel* might lead to possibilities for placing poems alongside one another in alternative configurations. And this brings me back to the more specific question of what remains hidden, whether buried or in plain sight, or merely inaccessible, despite the publication of *Ariel: The Restored Edition*—and my attempt to provide a partial answer.

For one thing, the facsimile drafts of "Ariel" are only a taster. They let the reader observe the process of Plath's composition, but do so for just one poem. For another, the choice of "Ariel" as the only poem reproduced in facsimile is, at least in one respect, an unfortunate one, for, as Susan R. Van Dyne points out, "Ariel" was "composed on fresh memo paper rather than on the *Bell Jar* manuscript that had been exhausted a few days earlier."[11] As interesting, and prominent, as it is to the formation of the Plath canon, "Ariel" is one of the few *Ariel* poems that does not allow the reader to see the relationship between what happens on both sides of the page. Plath "recycled" paper by drafting new work on the back of old, often entering into a dialogue with this earlier writing. Possibly she did this for economic reasons—to save money and conserve paper. Possibly she did this as the result of postwar thrift and a puritan upbringing. Probably she did this because it helped inspire her to write. It certainly became an integral part of her working method. These "back drafts" include earlier poems by Plath and Ted Hughes, pieces of correspondence, and typescript pages from *The Bell Jar* (many of which are scored with Plath's handwritten edits).

Another fact that the publication of the restored *Ariel* will not rectify is that many of Plath's non-*Ariel* poems, for which the reader must still rely on *The Collected Poems,* remain corrupted by small errors that have not yet been brought to light. "Lyonnesse" is a good example of the local instance in which textual editing is significant. Here we are told to "Take a look at the white, high berg *on* his forehead,"[12] so that the berg is made to seem a sort of boil or growth. Plath's manuscripts tell us that the line should read, the "berg *of* his forehead,"[13] so that the berg is the jutting shape of the forgetful man's forehead, as well as of Lyonnesse itself.

This amendment brings geography and historical topography to a reference that might have appeared merely personal. Further, the error-strewn *Collected Poems* is not a collected poems in the proper sense, in that it does not contain all of Plath's extant poems. If we take into account the many sound recordings of her poems that Plath made, especially the ones for the BBC in the autumn of 1962—although this will not be the primary focus of this essay—it becomes clear that written manuscripts do not necessarily reflect the most up-to-date versions of her writing. The existence of sound recordings of *Ariel* poems that differ from the versions of Plath's last known typescript, the circumstance that Plath did not actually send *Ariel* to a publisher, the fact that there are small corrections dotted throughout the manuscript, the practice of continuous editing that is evident throughout Plath's papers—all these might suggest that, had she lived, Plath would have done more work to *Ariel.*[14] The *Ariel* that we have, as polished as it is, should only be regarded as Plath's latest draft. Indeterminacy—and I use the word to stand in for doubts, hesitations, ambiguities, and discontinuities of various kinds—comes into play with Plath to an extent that doesn't apply to most writers because, with the exception of *The*

Colossus and *The Bell Jar,* she simply wasn't around to review proofs, negotiate with the publisher, and make final decisions.

I want to argue for the indeterminacy of the Plath canon by focusing on the ways her manuscripts (and one sound recording of particular relevance to *Ariel*) put in doubt any notion of a finished object or complete and self-contained poem. I want to put this indeterminacy in the perspective not only of Plath's habits of editing and composition, but in terms of one possible principle for editorial decision making—her practices of arrangement, dating, and noting submissions of her poems. In doing so, I challenge many of our assumptions about the connections between poems (that have largely been treated as discrete) and invite us to look again at the sequencing of Plath's work, especially of her last poems. To do this is to question the prevailing consensus about what Plath's final poetic words actually were and reexamine the very textual particularities of the canon and its archival significance.

Ted Hughes wrote that Plath's "separate poems build up into one long poem."[15] While I would not say this unilaterally of all of Plath's poems, there are occasions when the *Ariel* collection and the texts written during its composition need to be thought of as connected, as longer works, clusters and sequences composed of two or more texts, rather than as numerous individual ones. Three poems that Plath wrote over a four-day period at the end of February 1961 look at different experiences of women's reproductive lives. Although quite different in their verse forms, "Morning Song" (February 19), "Barren Woman" (February 21), and "Heavy Women" (February 22)[16] all operate through references to statues, museums, and paintings. Together, they form a sort of rehearsal for the radio play Plath was to write a year later, *Three Women* (March 1962).

"Morning Song" is spoken by a mother to her baby. The mother breast-feeds the child in the middle of the night and refers to the baby as a "New statue" in the world's "drafty museum."[17] Plath's next poem, which she wrote two days later, was "Barren Woman," which looks back at its immediate predecessor and recasts its images of statues and museums as frames of references for affective and structural conditions of fullness and emptiness. Here, the eponymous speaker's position, summed up by the poem's title, provides a wry contrast with the privileged position of the mother in "Morning Song," whose speaker has the relative luck of possessing what the speaker of "Barren Woman" wants but cannot have: a baby. The "Barren Woman," unlike the "cow-heavy" lactating speaker of "Morning Song" with her "New statue," regards her body as a "Museum without statues,"[18] empty of the thing she most desires.

The day after writing "Barren Woman," Plath wrote "Heavy Women," a poem that observes the insufferable pride and placidity of the hugely pregnant. The clear-sighted, pained and envious narrator of "Heavy Women" (who never inserts herself into the poem—and the fecund world of the heavy women—with the word "I") ironically seems to see things as the "barren woman" would. To the narrator of "Heavy Women," the self-absorbed pregnant women resemble the Venus "pedestaled on a half-shell" of Botticelli's late-fifteenth-century painting *The Birth of Venus*. They also resemble countless paintings of "beautifully smug"[19] Madonnas in "Mary-blue." It is as if "Barren Woman" and "Heavy Women" are spoken by the same narrator, with the first poem concentrating on the pain of her infertility and her failing body and the second upon the distress she feels when confronted with pregnant women.

"Paralytic" and "Gigolo," both written on January 29, 1963, are also strongly linked. Both are written in quatrains. Both are spoken by solipsistic male narrators. Each of these narrators experiences a crisis in which his masculinity is troubled and challenged—even feminized—by his own weakness: the paralytic by his physical and sexual helplessness as he lies in his hospital bed, immobile and unable even to breathe for himself; the gigolo by the economic and sexual helplessness that makes him a male prostitute, forcing him into a profession more commonly associated with women. Each of these narrators is enraged by the dependence on women that his powerlessness necessitates and rails ineffectually against his impotence.

"Mystic," "Kindness," and "Words" were all written on February 1, 1963. Like the other "sets" of poems, these three revisit the same question and theme from different points of view, and, like many of the *Ariel* poems, are preoccupied with motherhood and children. "Mystic," "Kindness," and "Words" are each given a one-word title. Each is written in five-line stanzas. In each of the three poems, the first-person voice appears to be the same, asking in three different ways how to deal with despair. "What is the remedy?" for those who have been "used, / Used utterly," is the question "Mystic" repeats twice. Christianity is not a solution ("the pill of the Communion tablet"). Nor is "Memory"[20] a solace. While "Mystic" runs through the options for how the sufferer might deal with his or her own despair, "Kindness" looks at the ways outsiders respond to someone else's troubles. "Kindness" mocks the rituals that human beings engage in when faced with someone else's distress, and the platitudes people deploy as useless antidotes against dejection. But although the "smiles" and "sugar" and "cup[s] of tea"[21] in "Kindness" are ineffectual and false, "Kindness" and "Mystic" do agree that one thing successfully dissipates the sadness they explore; they find the same answer to the question that "Mystic" poses: "What is the remedy?"

The "remedy" is found, in the end, in children (and flowers). These are the last three lines of "Mystic":

> The children leap in their cots.
> The sun blooms, it is a geranium.
>
> The heart has not stopped.[22]

These are the last three lines of "Kindness":

> The blood jet is poetry,
> There is no stopping it.
> You hand me two children, two roses.[23]

In both poems, children are what draw the speaker away from death and sadness. In both poems, also, there is a proximity between children and flowers. And in the last lines of both poems, the speaker experiences a late-dawning awareness of the physical force of the human body—a force that defies dejection as hearts and blood beat and flow on regardless.

The speaker of "Words," unlike that of "Mystic" and "Kindness," finds no "remedy" for the emptiness that surrounds him or her. There are no children. There is no corporeal body—stubbornly alive—with beating heart or spurting blood.[24] There is only "sap" that "wells like tears" and a "rock" like a "white skull." While the speakers of "Mystic" and "Kindness" find something real and central and physically tangible—that is, children—everything is endlessly deferred and remote in "Words." The "Mystic"/"Kindness"/"Edge" trilogy seems to end on a note of despondency, yet if we consider not just the connections between the three poems, but their sequencing, too, our reading of them as discrete productions—and this despondency—can be challenged.

Both the English and American editions of *The Collected Poems* arrange "Mystic," "Kindness," and "Words" in the order in which I have just listed them. But what we do not know is the order in which Plath wrote them, or how *she* would have arranged them herself. They were written after her own version of *Ariel*, so she did not include them in her own ordering of the book.[25] Certainly the confidence of a Plath scholar such as Tim Kendall in the "thoroughness and chronological arrangement"[26] of *The Collected Poems* is misplaced (we see this, for instance, in the incorrect dating of "Heavy Women," above, and "Waking in Winter" and "Nick and the Candlestick," below, as well as in the omission of numerous poems). If Plath wrote "Words" first, or intended to place it before or even between "Mystic" and "Kindness," our sense of the three poems as a linked sequence will be of progression rather than regression, of a victory against hopelessness and death rather than surrender to them.

Such a reversal of the customary trajectory that sees everything in Plath as sinking towards death can be made not just by attending to the sequencing of the poems as part of a larger whole, but also of the lines *within* each of the parts of this whole. The most famous lines from "Kindness" are

> The blood jet is poetry,
> There is no stopping it.

For many readers, these lines have come to represent the poet herself, bleeding to death for the sake of her art. Many critics—Tim Kendall for instance—halt their citations from "Kindness" with "There is no stopping it," and do not go on to quote the poem's last line, a single, self-contained sentence: "You hand me two children, two roses."[27] After the rush of the blood jet lines, "Kindness" concludes calmly, with a moment of loving, wondrous contemplation and appreciation of the two children who are likened to roses (in their beauty and fragility) as well as to poems.

Nor does the more teleological reading of the cluster of poems of "Mystic," "Kindness," and "Words" as life story necessarily support the "denouement" of Plath's last poems. Lynda K. Bundtzen's excellent *The*

Other Ariel is distinguished by its awareness of the publication history of Plath's last poems. She writes of "Edge" and "Words":

> Together these two poems constitute a farewell to life and to writing. . . . "Words," composed on February 1, 1963, and "Edge," composed on February 5, 1963, also her last poem, together form a tragic denouement.[28]

As far as I can see, the strongest connection between "Words" and "Edge" is that, unlike "Mystic" and "Kindness," there is little in them to redeem the speaker against despair. Ted Hughes secures the connection between "Words" and "Edge" by placing them as the last two poems in an anthology of Plath's poetry[29] and in his own ordering of *Ariel*. Bundtzen notes that "Edge" was composed four days after "Words." There is, however, a poem that was composed the same day as "Edge." That poem is "Balloons," and as such, may make a better pairing with "Edge." And if "Balloons" and "Edge" were written on the same day, how do we know that "Edge" was Plath's "last poem"? Why do we assume that "Words" and "Edge" are the "tragic denouement," or end of the story (and, by extension, that Plath knew she was going to kill herself when she wrote them)?

Many poetry anthologies place "Balloons" and "Edge" as the last two poems offered to the reader in their selections of Plath's poems. Most, when they elect to print "Edge," give it the dubious privilege of being the *very* last poem.[30] Although Hughes's *Ariel* reverses the chronological—and more typical order—by making "Edge" (February 5, 1963) the penultimate poem and "Words" (February 1, 1963) the last, he nonetheless chooses to close his *Ariel* with two of Plath's saddest poems, rather than with some of the more hopeful poems that she was writing on those two days. Anne Stevenson's and Paul Alexander's biographies contain the identical sentence, "'Edge' was possibly the last poem Sylvia Plath wrote."[31] For Stevenson, it is Plath's "own dead body there on stage" in "Edge," where she is "both heroine and author."[32] In a similar vein, Ronald Hayman rather absurdly concludes that "Balloons" "says a reluctant farewell to the children," while "Edge" is not only Plath's "last poem" but also shows that "she had been intending to kill the children when she killed herself."[33] Yet not everybody approaches the poems as crudely as Stevenson and Hayman.

Diane Middlebrook shows caution in stating that "Edge" "*appears* to be the last poem Plath ever wrote."[34] Susan Bassnett recognizes that "the woman who wrote 'Edge' also wrote the beautiful 'Balloons' on the same day. . . . Two such different poems."[35]

Certainly Plath's own notes raise questions about the order in which she wrote the poems and the sequence(s) she intended for them. It may be that the best we will ever be able to say of "Edge" and "Balloons" is that any order we choose for them can only be random. If we place "Balloons" after "Edge" (instead of in the order that *The Collected Poems* and so many anthologies place them),[36] then Plath's last word to us as a poet is not a celebration of the death of a woman and her children. If we reverse the customary order and place "Balloons" after "Edge," we end instead with a mother's complicated observation of her baby son's hope and disappointment as he looks at "a world clear as water" from the vantage point of the burst balloon's "red / Shred in his little fist."[37]

Is there any evidence that might help us to fine-tune our knowledge of the sequencing of these last poems? To account for Plath's work properly, to understand the important relationship of her texts to one another and the historical contexts that informed them, we need accurate information about when they were written. It is worth turning to the manuscripts that Smith College holds to see if they reveal anything about the sequence of Plath's composition, or her intended ordering of the poems she wrote on February 1 and 5. Robin Peel contributes in important ways to the ongoing project of uncovering sequences by attending to the page numbers on *The Bell Jar* typescripts that appear on the reverse sides of some of the poems. He notices that these page numbers drop "with each successive piece of work."[38] Using this evidence, he comes up with the plausible theory that "Waking in Winter" was not written in 1960, which is the date that *The Collected Poems* gives it, but just after "New Year on Dartmoor," early in 1962. Through this redating, and by looking at material from early drafts of the poems, Peel argues persuasively for a new relationship between "New Year on Dartmoor," "Fever 103," and "Waking in Winter," which, together, "document the last month of pregnancy, the birth of the child, and its first outing."[39]

In attempting to think about the sequence of Plath's last poems, it seems worthwhile to try Peel's method. In the list that Plath kept of where she was submitting her poems and the dates of submission, Plath types a few titles (a tiny amount of a crowded page) under the heading, *The New Yorker,* February 4, in the following order: "Kindness," "Mystic" (underlined), "Words," "Edge," "Balloons," and "Contusion" (handwritten).[40]

This list does not help much in terms of Plath's establishment of any authoritative sequence and chronology. First, Plath's own dating is uncharacteristically inexact here. She notes that the poems were all submitted to the *New Yorker* on "Feb. 4," but "Edge" and "Balloons" were not written until the following day (unless she intentionally misdated them), so at least some of them were probably sent slightly later than February 4. Nor is Plath especially concerned with chronological order here. "Contusion," added by hand to the end of the list, is the only poem that Plath dated February 4, the day before "Edge" and "Balloons," though "Edge" and "Balloons" precede "Contusion" on the list.

One possibility that few have considered is that Plath intentionally misdated her manuscripts, even if only by a few days. The daughter of a field biologist who appeared in the *Dictionary of Scientific Biography* and who kept meticulous charts and records of his progress and achievements for posterity, Plath was shrewd about the fact that her papers could end up in literary archives. She notes in a letter to her mother of November 20, 1961, that she sold "about 130 pages of poetry manuscript," and that the papers will go to Indiana University[41] (to which her mother was to sell the very letter in which she writes this). Van Dyne points out that from the time Plath sold these papers, she "saved and scrupulously dated her drafts and revisions."[42] Perhaps Plath wished to create an impression of concentrated intensity in her late manuscripts, and therefore inscribed all the drafts of a poem with the date on which she arrived at a more complete version. Perhaps she wanted the dates to tell a compelling story, when she had in fact been writing over a longer period—even if only a few days rather than one— or at least in her head for some time. It is important to bear in mind that the above list forms a sort of memorandum Plath made for herself to keep track of where her poems were, but not a record of the order in which the texts were written. Yet this does not preclude the possibility that Plath simultaneously used the list as a quick test of a sequence, a sort of rehearsal through proleptic memory.

The poems that Plath identifies in the list as her February 4 cluster were composed on reverse sides of poems and papers that Plath wrote in October and November 1962. In an attempt to discern a pattern, I began by listing the poems in the chronological order of the material on their reverse sides. One handwritten page of "Edge" (February 5, 1963) was drafted on the back of a typescript from "Wintering" (October 9, 1962).[43] One handwritten page of "Balloons" (February 5, 1963) was drafted on the back of a handwritten draft page from "Thalidomide" (November 8, 1962).[44] Two handwritten pages of "Mystic" (February 1, 1963) were drafted on the back of typescript pages from "Death & Co." (November 14, 1962).[45] One typescript page of "Words" (February 1, 1963) was written on the back of a typescript page from "Mary's Song" (November 19, 1962).[46] One handwritten page of "Kindness" (February 1, 1963) was drafted on the back of advertisements for Mother's Helpers that Plath copied. A typescript page of "Kindness" appears on the reverse side of the draft of a letter from Plath to Karl Miller (November 29, 1962).[47]

It might help to see this more clearly in a tabular form.

Reverse Side of Paper & Date		*February Poem & Date*	
"Wintering"	Oct. 9, 1962	"Edge"	Feb. 5, 1963
"Thalidomide"	Nov. 8, 1962	"Balloons"	Feb. 5, 1963
"Death & Co."	Nov. 14, 1962	"Mystic"	Feb. 1, 1963
"Mary's Song"	Nov. 19, 1962	"Words"	Feb. 1, 1963
Mother's Helper ads	Not dated	"Kindness"	Feb. 1, 1963
Letter to Karl Miller	Nov. 29, 1962	"Kindness"	Feb. 1, 1963

But what are we to make of all this? It is possible that Plath put scrap papers (discarded versions of her correspondence, no-longer-needed carbon copies, and previous drafts of poems) into a stack as she finished with them. Hence, more recent papers from later dates would be at the top of the pile, and earlier pages further down. If this were the case, then the sequence in which Plath wrote the February 1 poems would be "Kindness" (November 29), "Words" (November 19), "Mystic" (November 14).[48] "Contusion" was the only poem that Plath dated February 4. If we were to apply the same logic to the February 5 poems, their sequence would be "Balloons" (November 8) and then "Edge" (October 9).

In *Dust: the Archive and Cultural History,* Carolyn Steedman argues that archival research "is to do with wanting things that are put together, collected, collated, named in lists and indices; a place where a whole world, a social order, may be imagined by the recurrence of a name in a register, through a scrap of paper, or some other little piece of flotsam."[49] Steedman warns of the scholarly impulse to make narratives out of archival discoveries: "as stuff, it just sits there until it is read, and used, and narrativized."[50] The opposite is also true; we can search for materials in the archive in an attempt to legitimate our narratives, to substantiate our theories. As Steedman puts it, the stuff of archives, "reordered, remade, then emerges—some would say like a memory—when someone needs to find it, or just simply needs it, for new and current purposes."[51] In terms of my arguments for a less death-and-doom-driven reading of "Kindness," "Words," and "Mystic"—or rather, in terms of my desire to construct and give credence to a juxtaposition that would reveal an alternative reading through archival materialism—the new arrangement lent by the dates on the reverse sides of the pages responds to my desire for a different narrative. It does nothing to advance my wish to rethink whether "Balloons" or "Edge" is truly Plath's last word.

How much credence should a different order be given? Although the evidence for a new ordering of these late poems is powerful, it is by no means authoritative and may well be informed by mere coincidence. Robin Peel points out that "paper in a scrap pile is likely to be mixed up, particularly if there are young children in the house."[52] While it appears that papers from within a few months of each other were put in the scrap pile adjacent to one another, their ordering in a reverse chronological sequence may never have been exact. There may have been instances where Plath needed to retain papers for reference or action, and then eventually put them onto the pile, so that the top papers were not invariably the most recent ones. It is also likely that Plath sometimes searched through her scrap pile with intent, to look specifically for an earlier manuscript or document that she wanted to write a new poem on the back of, and so deliberately chose what would appear on the reverse side of a new piece. On other occasions she may have sifted through it in the hopes of coming across something that would inspire her. Van Dyne speculates that one of Plath's motives for using early manuscripts of *The Bell Jar* in this way was a "desire for sympathetic magic,"[53] a sort of writer's superstition that a previously completed and successfully placed piece of writing will seep through the page to benefit one's current work. There is no definitive answer about the sequence of these last poems, but the evidence is powerful enough to render a strong challenge to any assumptions readers and editors may have about any story such an ordering may tell to the exclusion of others.

If we can challenge the Plath canon by rethinking any assumptions that the poems are discrete and definitely ordered, we can also challenge it by questioning the authority held by any given version of a single poem. We see this with "Fever 103," "Stopped Dead," "Lady Lazarus," and "Medusa," to name but a few examples. Among the many questions to be raised about the Plath archives is whether a poem was finished or has a "final" form. This question of "final form" is certainly a problem with "Nick and the Candlestick." Elsewhere, I have discussed Plath's original conception of "Lyonnesse" and "Amnesiac" not as separate poems, but as parts 1 and 2 of a single poem.[54] Van Dyne reveals that Plath initially had a similar plan for "Nick and the Candlestick," which was to follow "By Candlelight" (October 24, 1962) in a two-part poem. Only later in the drafting process did the two poems become separate: "the same images coexisted in both for a time."[55]

"Nick and the Candlestick" is fourteen stanzas long. The first seven tercets are more opaque than the last seven. In them, we overhear the speaker as she watches the nursery candle drip and sees her baby's room as a chilly cave lit by a blue-burning light. Miners used to watch their lamps for a blue halo over the flame, because the halo indicated the presence of methane gas, and the attendant danger of explosion or suffocation.[56] What the last seven tercets of "Nick and the Candlestick" share with "By Candlelight" are a coherence and clarity and charm that result from a mother's direct and tender address to her baby. When the candle "recovers its small altitude," and strengthens from cold blue to warm yellow, the atmosphere transforms, too, moving away from the abstraction and ice of the poem's first half to the solidity of the child as the speaker talks to him directly for the first time: "O love, how did you get here?" Warmth, color ("the blood blooms clean / In you, ruby") and domestic objects ("soft rugs") replace the blue and white ("Even the newts are white")[57] of the chill cave's "stalacmites" and "calcium icicles."[58]

But what Plath was never to resolve about "Nick and the Candlestick," once she separated it from "By Candlelight," was the question of where the poem should end. Plath crossed out eight entire stanzas, over a third of the poem, when she finished her written manuscript,[59] but restored these six days later when she recorded the poem for the BBC.[60] In the print versions, "Nick and the Candlestick" ends with three lines that emphasize the unity of spirit and flesh:

> You are the one
> Solid the spaces lean on, envious.
> You are the baby in the barn.[61]

In the published recording, and in a holograph cited by Christine Britzolakis, Plath gives us another ending:

> The brass Atlas you inherited
> Is hefting his milk pillar.
> He kneels
>
> Head bent,
> A panther head on a panther pelt
> . . . .
>
> Each incisor a wide, bright horn,
> The panther mane
> . . . a million
>
> Gold worms down his back.

As Plath continues, extended description of Atlas is supplemented by return of the gaze between mother and child:

> A bearded Greek!
> Under the gold
>
> Bowl of his navel
> Where his phallus and balls should be—
> A panther claw!
>
> I leave you the mystery.
> It is not the firmament
> That makes him look so sick,
>
> This philosopher.
> . . . .

The beastly lobotomy!

The mirror floats us at one candle power.
We smile and stare.
That's you! That's me![62]

With the exception of the final tercet, what gives these stanzas their own coherence—but also a difference from the rest of the poem—is their central image of the candlestick of the poem's title, a brass statue of Atlas holding the world on his shoulders.[63] It is the same "little brassy Atlas"[64] to which "By Candlelight" refers, but "Nick and the Candlestick" uses the image less compactly and assuredly than "By Candlelight,"[65] where the statue is integrated smoothly into the poem, and doesn't disrupt its tone.

When Plath reads "Nick and the Candlestick" aloud for her radio recording, there is a vocal hesitation, a pause after the line, "You are the baby in the barn." It seems that she was going to conclude her reading at that point. It is surprising, almost as if she is beginning a new poem, when she continues, "The brass Atlas you inherited." That delay between "barn" and "The brass" seems a writerly one, a space where Plath pauses to consider whether to add those eight stanzas even as the tape recorder whirs. Was she uncomfortable with the reference to Atlas's "phallus and balls"? Was the object, the brass Atlas, too private and particular, and not made sufficiently accessible to the reader? Without these extra stanzas, the poem's fourteen tercets are well balanced, dividing almost in the poem's middle between the speaker's visions of the cavelike cave and the domestic cave. The extra stanzas spoil this balance, tipping the poem's already challenging frame of reference into a mixed-up set of images and taking the focus away from the baby. Even the one instance of a direct second-person address in these extras lines, "I leave you the mystery," seems too knowing and ironic to be addressed to a child; the tone is not quite right.

I prefer the poem without the extra stanzas, but for the very last one, which, had the choice been mine, I would have retained for its charm; for the way it returns to the poem's central images of the child, the candle, and the mother; for its refrain of the connection between spirit and flesh; and for the way it insists that the poem must be read as the mother speaking *to* her baby:

> The mirror floats us at one candle power.
> We smile and stare.
> That's you! That's me!⁶⁶

The first of these lines does not just suggest the wavering reflection of the mother and baby in the mirror, but also returns us to the idea of Atlas, where the candle is Atlas holding up the speaker and the child, or "floating" them as if they were the world. It is as if the mother and child constitute an air balloon kept aloft by the candle's flame.

The three lines together return to what is implicit in the last stanza of the published version of the poem:

> You are the one
> Solid the spaces lean on, envious.
> You are the baby in the barn.

The role of Atlas circulates. Here, the child is Atlas (or Hercules), the one "solid" who acts as a support even for empty space. However, we can only see Atlas here through the context of the spoken lines, or in the poem's canceled relation to "By Candlelight." Without one or the other of these, there is no Atlas in the published version.

In these last three lines of the spoken version, the mother holds her baby so they can look in the mirror and talk and point. In these lines, there is a sense that it is the baby's physical presence in his mother's arms that prompts what she says to him and positions her as Atlas holding him as if he were the world. In the published version, the mother is not necessarily holding the baby. Rather, she may be watching him from a small distance as he sleeps in his cot. In the published version's concluding three lines, Plath inserts a line break between "one" and "Solid," so that the words "You are the one" can be read as a finished sentence. If read with such emphasis, when the mother tells her baby, "You are the one," she tells him that he is the only thing that matters, the most important baby in the world. It is another way of saying, "You are the baby in the barn," which is uttered tenderly and in marked contrast to the cynical and playful references to Christianity—to "holy Joes" and "Christ!" in the poem's first half.

Is there anything wrong with my urge to play with the poem, to retain the one stanza that stays with me while I throw away the seven that don't? We cannot easily resolve the matter by concluding that the *Ariel* typescript should have the final say because it contained what were probably the latest versions of these poems.[67] The extra lines that Plath restores for the BBC reading do not appear in the *Ariel* typescript. Do we, or should we, prioritize later versions over earlier ones, or written evidence over oral? Even if *Ariel's* typescript was indeed the last version Plath produced, we cannot discount her vacillation. Her death was very close to those moments of indecision. As Hughes observed, "She was forever shuffling the poems in her typescripts—looking for different connections, better sequences. She knew there were always new possibilities, all fluid."[68] The *Ariel* typescript reflects Plath's continued aversion to "finality."

The paradox that scholars face in seeking a reading text of *Ariel* poems—acknowledging the desire for stable text, alongside Plath's aversion to finality; noting her habit of composing in clusters and sequences; accepting the variability of written and recorded versions of poems—is one we will continue to live with. But this instability raises the question, too, about more synoptic or, eventually, hypertextual editions of Plath's work. Such editions would capture the patterns of continuous revision and the idiosyncrasies of Plath's composition processes, especially the multiple, underlying strata that link *Ariel* poems to other poems through back drafts of earlier pieces of writing. Such a representation of Plath's work would find a way of providing her cuts and variants, perhaps in footnotes, or in a lighter, italicized font. Thereby the reader would have access to the published version of a poem or piece of prose, as well as the material Plath found difficult to excise, or lines she abandoned but are nonetheless worth reading. Admittedly, such a project would not be simple. Hughes was right to observe that it would be a massive undertaking to publish everything ("printing them all would have made a huge volume")[69]—a comment that anybody who has seen the quantity of paper that comprises the manuscripts for Plath's late poems would understand. Plath's handwritten drafts and typescripts for the sixty-seven of her late poems that are held in Smith College's Mortimer Rare Book Room fill seven box files, each three inches thick and stuffed to the brim.

The conclusion that these difficulties lead me to is this: reading Plath doesn't mean reading her only once. When editing and interpreting Plath's texts, and trying to establish any sort of Plath "canon," there is a way of reading that comes back to the poem or story or novel again and again, experimenting with different versions and orders and connections. Reading Plath involves a long-term relationship with her work and its multiple, indeterminate versions. Rather than viewing acts of versioning as an insurmountable problem, we may consider these versions as underscoring the contingencies of practice and differential shaping of text and context.[70] Such a reading relationship makes the poems less melodramatic and distances them from her life. If there is anything that readers—and many critics—cling to with respect to Plath, it's melodrama. But what Plath's writing asks for is a business not of melodrama, but of loving, careful attention. It's a business that welcomes the instabilities of her manuscripts, a business that doesn't shrink from the difficulties and challenges her writings present, and a business that must continually foreground the knowledge that the Plath canon is dependent upon an archive that is limited, partial, and ceaselessly in need of emendation. For me, to read Plath with any real engagement—and pleasure—is to become part of an ongoing dialogue about the principles of the archive's formation, reception, and continuing evolution.

NOTES

1. Susan R. Van Dyne, Marjorie Perloff, Jacqueline Rose, and Lynda Bundtzen have analyzed the difficult publication history of Plath's work, in particular Hughes's departure from the plans Plath left for *Ariel*. See Van Dyne, *Revising Life: Sylvia Plath's Ariel Poems* (Chapel Hill: University of North Carolina Press, 1993); Perloff, "The Two *Ariels*: The (Re)making of the Sylvia Plath Canon," *American Poetry Review*, November–December 1984, 10–18; Rose, *The Haunting of Sylvia Plath* (London: Virago, 1991); and Bundtzen, *The Other Ariel* (Amherst: University of Massachusetts Press, 2001).

2. Perloff, "The Two *Ariels*."

3. Smith: Box: Plath—Ariel Poems—Typescript, Notes, Proofs; Folder: Ariel Poems, Final Typescript.

4. *AR*. Pages of *Ariel* facsimile not numbered.

5. In, respectively, "The Arrival of the Bee Box," "Morning Song," and "The Couriers" (*CP*, 212, 156, 247).

6. "Medusa," *CP*, 224.

7. On Plath's midatlanticism, see Tracy Brain, *The Other Sylvia Plath* (London: Pearson Education, 2001).

8. Ibid.

9. Carolyn Steedman, *Dust: The Archive and Cultural History* (Manchester: Manchester University Press, 2001), 68.

10. Ibid., 18.

11. Van Dyne, *Revising Life*, 119.

12. *CP*, 232; emphasis added.

13. Smith: Box: Plath—Ariel Poems, Amnesiac—Berck-Plage; Folders: Ariel Poems, "Amnesiac," Drafts 1–3, Typed Copies 1–4.

14. As outraged as scholars have been by Hughes's changes to Plath's last known plans for *Ariel,* it is not inconceivable that she herself would have added some of the later poems that Hughes included.

15. Hughes, "Notes on the Chronological Order of Sylvia Plath's Poems," *Tri-Quarterly* 7 (Fall 1966): 81.

16. Van Dyne, *Revising Life,* 160.

17. *CP*, 157.

18. Ibid.

19. Ibid., 158. "Childless Woman," a poem from late 1962 spoken by an infertile narrator and built around a conceit of the female body as a landscape, seems to revisit "Barren Woman." There is a progression indicated in the movement of the titles, in which Plath shifts from cause—and the disparaging adjective, "Barren"—to effect, and the more sympathetic adjective, "Childless."

20. Ibid., 268.

21. Ibid., 269.

22. Ibid.

23. Ibid., 270.

24. "Contusion," the only poem of Plath's in the public domain that is dated February 4, is centrally about how the physical body shuts down and fades away—the vivid bruise that, by the poem's end, can be read forensically as a death blow or fatal injury that sucks color into itself and out of the rest of the body.

25. *CP*, 295.

26. Tim Kendall, "Famous Nearly Last Words," *Times Literary Supplement,* November 26, 2004, 6.

27. See for instance Bundtzen, *The Other Ariel,* 181; and Tim Kendall, *Sylvia Plath: A Critical Study* (London: Faber and Faber, 2001), 189.

28. Bundtzen, 105. For "Edge," see also *Anthony & Cleopatra* (5.2.307–8).

29. *Sylvia Plath,* Poems, selected by Ted Hughes (London: Farrar, Straus and Giroux, 1985, 2000), 70–71.

30. See, for instance, Jeni Couzen, ed., *The Bloodaxe Book of Contemporary Women Poets* (Newcastle upon Tyne: Bloodaxe, 1985), 164. Many biographers and critics also assume that "Edge" is Plath's last poem. See, for example, Linda Wagner-Martin, *Sylvia Plath: A Literary Life* (London: Macmillan, 1999), 104.

31. Anne Stevenson, *Bitter Fame: A Life of Sylvia Plath* (London: Viking, 1989), 300; Paul Alexander, *Rough Magic: A Biography of Sylvia Plath* (New York: Viking, 1991), 323.

32. Stevenson, *Bitter Fame,* 298.

33. Ronald Hayman, *The Death and Life of Sylvia Plath* (New York: Birch Lane, 1991), 193.

34. Diane Middlebrook, *Her Husband: Hughes and Plath—A Marriage* (London: Little Brown, 2003), 227; emphasis added.

35. Susan Bassnett, *Sylvia Plath* (London: Macmillan, 1987), 146.

36. See for instance Fleur Adcock, ed., *The Faber Book of Contemporary Women's Poetry* (London: Faber and Faber, 1987), 250–51; and Diane Wood Middlebrook, ed., *Sylvia Plath* (New York: Alfred A. Knopf, 1998), 236–38.

37. *CP*, 272.

38. Robin Peel, *Writing Back: Sylvia Plath and Cold War Politics* (London: Associated University Presses, 2002), 124.

39. Ibid., 126.

40. Smith: Sylvia Plath Collection, Writings, Poems (fragment of a long list).

41. *LH*, 437.

42. Van Dyne, *Revising Life*, 8.

43. Smith: "Edge," Item 1: Holograph, February 5, 1963.

44. Ibid., "Balloons."

45. Smith: The manuscripts of "Mystic" are not itemized by the Mortimer Rare Book Room.

46. Smith: The manuscripts of "Words" are not itemized.

47. Smith: The manuscripts of "Kindness" are not itemized. The letter to Miller concerns a review of *Lord Bryon's Wife* that Plath wrote for the *New Statesman*.

48. The dates within parentheses are for what appears on the poems' reverse sides.

49. Steedman, *Dust*, 81.

50. Ibid., 68.

51. Ibid.

52. Peel, *Writing Back*, 132.

53. Susan R. Van Dyne, "'More Terrible Than She Ever Was': The Manuscripts of Sylvia Plath's Bee Poems," in *Critical Essays on Sylvia Plath*, ed. Linda W. Wagner (Boston: G. K. Hall, 1984), 5.

54. See Brain, *The Other Sylvia Plath*, 24.

55. Van Dyne, *Revising Life*, 161.

56. See Bill Johnstone, "Let There Be Light," first featured in *Discovery*, 1997, accessible online at http://www.royalbcmuseum.bc.ca/mh_papers/lettherebelight.html. See also Bassam Z. Shakhashiri, "Chemical of the Week: Methane," online at http://scifun.chem.wisc.edu/chemweek/METHANE/Methane.html (accessed December 8, 2004). Shakhashiri writes, "Methane is combustible, and mixtures of about 5 to 15 percent in air are explosive. Methane is not toxic when inhaled, but it can produce suffocation by reducing the concentration of oxygen inhaled."

57. Plath's reading at the time she wrote "Nick and the Candlestick" might shed light on the mining and caving and scientific references within the poem. It is one of many moments when the missing late journals might have provided cultural references.

58. *CP*, 241. I am following the "stalacmites" of the *AR*, 47.

59. Plath's own manuscripts date the poem's composition as October 24, though *The Collected Poems* gives the date of October 29. See Smith: Ariel Poems, Nick and the Candlestick, Typed Copy 7 (Revised).

60. Peter Orr, *Plath Reads Plath* (Cambridge: Credo Records, 1975).

61. *CP*, 242.

62. Qtd. Christine Britzolakis, *Sylvia Plath and the Theatre of Mourning* (Oxford: University of Oxford Press, 1999), 76; this second ending appears in two published audiotape recordings, *Plath Reads Plath* (Credo, 1975) and *The Voice of the Poet: Sylvia Plath*, ed. J. D. McClatchy (Random House, 1999).

63. The references to the "panther mane" and "panther pelt" make me wonder if

the statue was of Hercules standing in for Atlas during the eleventh of Hercules' labors, when he persuaded Atlas to fetch the golden apples of the Hesperides. Hercules wore the pelt of the Nemean lion that he killed during the first of his twelve labors. (See "The Labors of Hercules"online at *The Perseus Project* website: http://www.perseus.tufts.edu/Herakles/labors.html; accessed December 6, 2004.)

64. *CP,* 237.

65. Ibid. From "By Candlelight": "While the brass man / Kneels, back bent, as best he can / Hefting his white pillar with the light / . . . / At his heels a pile of five brass cannonballs, / No child, no wife. / Five balls! Five bright brass balls! / To juggle with, my love, when the sky falls."

66. Smith: Box: Plath—Ariel Poems, Nick and the Candlestick, Typed Copy 7 (Revised).

67. *CP,* 14. This latest version was "some time around Christmas 1962," when Plath "gathered" and "arranged" the poems "in a black spring binder," according to Hughes.

68. Hughes, "Art of Poetry," 79.

69. *CP,* 17.

70. See also Jerome McGann's seminal discussion of the problem of an authorial "final intention" in *A Critique of Modern Textual Criticism* (Charlottesville: University Press of Virginia, 1983), esp. 81–94; and George Bornstein, *Representing Modernist Texts* (Ann Arbor: University of Michigan Press, 1991), 1–16, on instability in modernist manuscripts more generally.

ROBIN PEEL

The Political Education
of Sylvia Plath

I may have barren spells, times of despair, as when I consider the
possibilities of another war (I am an ardent pacifist).

For even as I am a product of the twentieth century, so am I a victim of
the popular fallacies; I have unconsciously assimilated the ideas and
catchwords that are "in the air" everywhere.

The influence on Plath's writing of her prolonged literary education
has been carefully traced by a number of critics.[1] Important and central
as this education is, there is another education experienced by everyone growing up in the Cold War period from 1946 to 1962, which
someone who was a student in both America and England experienced
in a very particular way. This was an education in the new threat of
Armageddon promised by all future international power confrontations, a threat haunted by the images of nuclear war.

A recognition of the existence and legacy of Sylvia Plath's political
education and her anxieties about world events contributes to a more
informed reading of her final work, particularly the *Ariel* poems. Critics have tended to take Plath's poetry out of the politics, but as Jacqueline Rose's feared, they have also "taken the politics out of the poems."[2]
The battle with the "Other" that is enacted in the later poems is seen
primarily as a gender or personal battle, ignoring the political legacy of
Cold War McCarthyism, in which the enemy is internalized, and the
Other is within America as well as outside. The Rosenbergs' execution,

with which *The Bell Jar* opens, is merely the most obvious metaphor for the process in which public events work on the private imagination.

Sylvia Plath's final poetry provides similarly explicit glimpses of a Cold War and nuclear war awareness, as in "Fever 103" with its ghostly images of "radiation" and "Hiroshima ash."[3] She learned to see America better from the global perspective offered by her later experience. But this awareness, though deliberately disguised or concealed in most of her imaginative work, had been part of her consciousness since childhood. As a twelve-year-old, Plath recorded in her diary the news of the dropping of the atomic bomb on Hiroshima. Five years later she coauthored a published article protesting the decision of the United States to continue research into nuclear weapons. Later she corresponded with her admirer Eddie Cohen, whose long letters expressed anxieties about international events.[4] As the Korean War unfolded, she saw men in uniforms on the Smith campus and read of the escalation of the war in newspapers and journals. During her college years she encountered a range of political ideas, in her classes and from talks given by guest speakers at Smith, that raised political questions that were to be asked more urgently and directly when she moved to England.

Ted Hughes's 1963 comparison of Plath with Emily Dickinson ignores this dialogue with politics and international, principally Cold War, events.[5] Throughout her life, Plath's artistic ambitions competed with her desire to engage with the wider world, and this dialogue was strongly reexpressed in the poetry that follows her separation from Hughes, a point I have argued in *Writing Back*.[6] The extent and question of Plath as a Cold War writer hinges on the relatively unexplored matter of her political education, an issue I wish to return to here. In concentrating on the early, pre-1956 years of Plath's induction into politics, I will be drawing heavily on the archive of early Plath materials held at the Lilly Library. This archive includes small personal diaries Plath kept as a young girl, hard-backed notebooks in which Plath made notes for her Smith courses, secretarial-type notepads on which she made journalist notes from talks given by visiting speakers, and her own copies of college textbooks, some of which are annotated very heavily in bold ink in the manner characteristic of students eager to learn. Rather than claiming, as I did previously, that Plath's political education underwent a sudden acceleration in England in 1960, I will be arguing here that her post-1960 experience involved a reassessment, revival, and restoration of a dormant political engagement, culminating in the *Ariel* sequence.

There is, however, an important difference in the relationship between her politics and art in the post- and pre-1960 phase. It is only after 1960 that we see the effective fusion of politics and art in, for example, such imaginative writing as *The Bell Jar* and the poems of 1962 and 1963. Plath's earlier knowledge of politics was more developed than has generally been acknowledged, as I intend to show, but it remained in a separate box from her poetry and short story writing, reflecting the separation of politics from "culture" in the dominant New Critical aesthetic theory of the time. Nevertheless I wish to argue that, however divorced from her creative ambition it may have been, the broad American college curriculum that led to the acquiring of that knowledge constituted an important, hitherto unacknowledged, ideological apprenticeship.

The Individual and the Crowd: Reading Plath's Annotations

Plath's strong faith in individualism and the independence of art from society was cultivated by her upbringing and reinforced by her reading.[7] Three significant influences on Plath's version of individualism are Friedrich Nietzsche, José Ortega y Gasset, and D. H. Lawrence, and her dialogue with these writers can be traced in her notes and essays made at Smith and Newnham College, Cambridge. These sources are assimilated in the context of her precollege experience, as a 1940s daughter, school student, and member of an Emersonian Unitarian church. Parental ambition, school competitiveness, and spiritual introspection combined to foster in Plath an American individualism ready to be taken further by these three European writers.

Brought up with tolerant Unitarian beliefs, Plath's intellectual development was not circumscribed by any narrow religious dogma. In the essay written in May 1952 for Religion 14 at Smith College, Plath advances what the teacher's annotation describes as "a reasonably clear and forceful statement of Humanist position." Plath summarizes her core beliefs as follows:

I believe that man is born without purpose in a neutral universe. . . . I do not think that man has an inborn conscience or
preconceived moral standards; he is really indoctrinated with
the particular man-made laws and moral customs particular to
his own area and environment.[8]

In the completed essay,[9] Plath cites approvingly Nietzsche's celebration of power, will, and strength, and her discovery of Nietzsche
became for a time the dominant influence on her worldview. In an
assignment for a History of Europe course, Plath acknowledges
Zarathustra "as our bible of individualism at the moment."[10] The essay
concludes with an underlined quotation that indicates the appeal for
the writer-artist of Nietzschean nonconformity:

Our favorite Nietzschean epigraph will close this paper. "<u>One
must still have chaos in one to give birth to a dancing star</u>."[11]

Plath's own copy of *Thus Spake Zarathustra*, part of the Smith College collection,[12] is much annotated, and its importance for her creative work[13] is shown in her 1955 poem "Notes on Zarathustra's Prologue":

Look to the lightning for tongues of pain
Steep are the stairs to the Superman

Go. . . .
And strip the shroud from coward's back

Till the womb of chaos sprouts with fire
And hatches Nietzsche's dancing star.[14]

There is a seam of Nietzscheanism in much of Plath's writing, and it
surfaces starkly here.

Plath's admiration for Nietzsche and her celebration of artistic
individualism spirited her away from a belief in the need to connect
collective political involvement with the practice of art. To strengthen
the assertion in her history essay that "Man" passively accepts his role
as an automaton, she quotes from Auden's "September 1st 1939"[15] and
reports approvingly Fromm's argument that we suffer from an "opti-

mistic delusion that as soon as external threats are eliminated [e.g., Communism today] all will be right with the world." Although this belief prevented her from becoming a victim of the anti-Communist hysteria of the period, it drew her away from political enquiry.

The corollary of this celebration of the individual, whether that individual is seen as artist, intellectual, or part of an aristocratic elite, is that American notions of democracy were undercut by a suspicious disdain for the majority. This is sometimes exposed strikingly in Plath's later writing. The mass of people become the mob, the "stinking people" she sees in Yankee Stadium,[16] the potato people that Plath refers to in her later correspondence from Devon, or the "peanut-crunching crowd" who come to watch a striptease of the performer in "Lady Lazarus."[17] Her student reading of Ortega's *The Revolt of the Masses*, published in its English translation in 1932, encouraged such an attitude. One important concern was population explosion, which, he observed, had several important consequences. These included overcrowding and intrusion, but there is a third consequence of the plebeian occupation of places reserved previously for the privileged few that was particularly alarming for Ortega. This was the growing influence of the populace, by which he meant the indiscriminate nature of the material ambitions of the majority, ambitions that threatened to suffocate the individual artist. John Carey describes Ortega's sequence of thought as follows, starting with the growth of the masses:

> [One] consequence is the dictatorship of the mass. . . . The triumph of "hyperdemocracy" has created a modern state, which Ortega sees as the gravest danger threatening civilization. The masses believe in the state as a machine for obtaining the material pleasures they desire, but it will crush the individual.[18]

Plath has heavily underlined and annotated her own 1951 edition. An early section of Ortega's argument has met with her approval:

> As they say in the United States: "to be different is to be indecent." The mass crushes beneath it everything that is different, everything that is excellent, individual, qualified and select.

Anybody who is not the everybody runs the risk of being eliminated.[19]

Next to this underscored section, Plath has written, "Lord yes! Observ-
able everywhere—popularity qualifications'—in college, business,
etc."[20] Ortega's description of life as a Darwinian struggle also pleases
her, endorsing as it does a Nietzschean confirmation of the need for
will, resolution, and inner strength in the creation of her idea of the
superior, *über* man or woman. Plath in her edition has partly underlined the following passage:

> All life is the struggle, the effort to be itself. The difficulties
> which I meet with in order to realise my existence are precisely
> what awakens and mobilises my activities, my capacities.[21]

In the margin Plath has written approvingly, "my *own* philosophy—
out of struggle, conflicts, hardship, comes a strong, vital creative
nature."[22] Plath carried this philosophy to England and found further
confirmation of it in the writing of D. H. Lawrence. At Newnham College she submitted an essay discussing *Fantasia of the Unconscious,
Lady Chatterley's Lover, Women in Love,* and *The Woman Who Rode
Away* to Dorothea Krook, her English tutor, in a style that is much
more mature and sophisticated than that evident in the Smith essays.[23]
She was also taught by F. R. Leavis (her Cambridge papers include a
sketch she made of him during a lecture), who was a great Lawrence
champion. What most appealed to her about Lawrence's philosophy
was the synthesis of literature and religion and the license it gave to her
own intensity of feeling, with an ability to love and hate in equal measure. In her essay she notes, "The implication is that spontaneous hate
is infinitely better than faked love."[24] But the enthusiasm for this sentiment, whose Nietzschean undertone she no doubt approved, was perhaps held in check by the margin comment of her Cambridge supervi-
sor, Dorothea Krook "Yes—but neither is *good.*" Plath admired Krook,
admired her dedication to literature, and admired even her rejection of
the social life.[25] But although Plath's spring meeting with Hughes, who
espoused a form of pastoral individualism,[26] might have reinforced the
priority given to such beliefs about will and the individual's need to
withdraw from society, it simultaneously camouflaged another Plath,

who was alert to political and institutional struggles and who had long debated them.

Politics, Government, and Society

On Wednesday August 8, 1945, when Plath was twelve years old, her diary suddenly stops its preoccupation with school life and friends and records with a certain sense of bewilderment the shocking news:

> We learned that the United States dropped the first atomic bomb on Japan and that it destroyed 60% of Hiroshima! This bomb, it is said by President Truman, can be used for constructive as well as destructive purposes. For instance, the same power may be used to cultivate and save food crops or of starvation [sic]. Also, Russia has at last declared war on Japan (the latter nation may capitulate within a few months many people hope . . .).[27]

Elsewhere in her diary for 1945, Plath records her response to the end of the war in Europe, the end of the war in Japan, and the celebration throughout America now that World War II was over. She regularly listened to the radio, as the diary references to Jack Benny and other programs reveal,[28] and the radio was her most accessible source of up-to-the minute news. Anxieties about war clearly clouded her thoughts during the postwar years. In 1948, when she was fifteen, Plath wrote a poem "Youth's Appeal for Peace" in which Youth appeals to the Four Horsemen of the Apocalypse to turn back.[29] Over these years, as she passed from being girl to young woman, her pacifist views, not yet formulated in the diary entries from the war years (which are largely silent on the conflict), became more rooted, eventually finding very public expression in 1950. In March of that year the *Christian Scientist Monitor* printed an article with the heading "Youth's Plea for World Peace."[30] Written jointly by Sylvia Plath and Perry Norton of "English 41 Wellesley Senior High School,"[31] the article is cautious and moderate in its call for peace, stopping short of condemning outright the use of nuclear weapons. Instead it quietly questions the logic of the president's direction to the Atomic Energy Commission that it continue its work on the hydrogen bomb. The short appeal ends by saying, "For those of us who deplore the systematic slaughter legalized by war, the hydrogen bomb alone is not the answer."

Plath's pre-1956 encounters with political ideas took place in privileged and career-conscious contexts. At Smith College, Plath's copious note making on political matters was either to pass a course (Government II) or to report on visiting speakers for the *Smith Review*. This selective and self-interested engagement with political ideology was continued at Cambridge University in England, where Plath joined the Labour Club largely for social reasons,[32] and seized the opportunity to attend a reception at the Soviet Embassy for Khrushchev and Bulganin so that she could later write an article about it. The politics at play here reflect 1950s gender ideologies. Plath is only invited because one of the *Varsity* editors turned to a woman reporter because the invitation extended to his nonexistent wife. The piece she wrote appeared in the *Smith Alumnae Quarterly* and is whimsical in tone. Plath's early political ideas were not challenging, and her early 1950s journals do not suggest that they were deeply pondered. The twenty-year-old Sylvia Plath was sharp but as yet uncomplicated and performed expertly the role of the all-American girl. But her later imaginative writing reveals the latent influence of an interest in profounder questions about history and politics, from Napoleon through World War I and World War II to contemporary Cold War events, especially those that occurred in the years 1960–62.

Apart from the record provided by Plath's journals and letters, her dialogue with political theory and her evolving political beliefs can also be traced in her notes and essays for courses at Smith and in her notes from talks given by visiting speakers. Unlike the journals and letters, these notes, essays, and marginalia rarely feature in critical discussions of her work.[33] They pose a particular problem, however. At Smith, for example, Plath had read Erich Fromm's *Escape from Freedom* (she has dated her own copy 1954) and next to Fromm's observation that everyone in the medieval period "was chained to his role in the social order" Plath has written, "how awful." Such a remark, standing alone, immediately raises the problem of the various voices employed by Plath. "How awful" could be an example of the throwaway irony found in Plath's journal sketches of her contemporaries. Plath offers us similar challenges in her fiction and poetry, often seeming to delight in leaving the reader uncertain how to read such lines as "I hated babies" or

"Every woman adores a Fascist." It is wise to suspect irony, but we cannot always be certain that Plath is not deftly smuggling in several political alternatives under the cloak of creative ambiguity.

Plath's more extended discussion of Fromm, a social theorist and psychologist who argued that liberation from medieval society created new anxieties that in turn encouraged people to accept a new authoritarianism, appears in an essay "The Age of Anxiety and the Escape from Freedom" for History 38b. Fromm, who in *The Sane Society* (1955) had argued in favor of communitarian socialism, extolled the virtues of humans taking individual moral action, rather than obeying authoritarian moral values. The history course, which Plath took in 1954, involved a history of thought that looked at such issues in the broader context of topics as romanticism, conservatism, and liberalism. The course examined the ideas of Carlyle, Nietzsche, Marx, Engels, key thinkers of nineteenth-century liberalism, and socialism.[34] This was her second review of Marxism—in her first year at Smith she had written a paper "Darwin, Marx, Wagner: an essay" for Mrs. Koffka's History II class.

Between the two courses, particularly in the earlier part of her Smith course before her breakdown, Plath had significant curricular contact with political ideas. The most obvious, and most sustained, is the 1951 Government II class, which had as its reading assignment *The Strategy and Tactics of World Communism*,[35] a government report as interesting for its appendices as for its findings. Plath has not marked anything in the sixty-two pages of her own copy of the report itself, held at the Lilly Library, but sections in the various supplements are heavily underlined and annotated.

Plath's reading of this report at a politically charged time when McCarthyism and Cold War hysteria were at their peak makes it doubly significant. In 1950 the invasion of South Korea by the Communist North provoked a UN/U.S. intervention, which in turn led to a combined Chinese and North Korean counterattack that by June 1951 was deep into South Korea. Plath had written to her mother in December 1950 to say how sickening it was to see all the uniforms on campus,[36] and a month before had received a letter from Eddie Cohen in which he spoke of his anxiety that with the "megalomaniac neo Prussian MacArthur' in charge there was the possibility of a terrible war escalating from Korea.[37] In that same year Julius and Ethel Rosenberg, whose execution was to become the focus of the opening of *The Bell Jar*, were tried and convicted of espionage. The House Un-American Activities Committee had been active since 1947, and the successful prosecution of Alger Hiss in 1950 had launched the career of Richard Nixon, who appears in Plath's antimilitary, antipatriarchy, and anti-Republican collage of 1960.[38] In February 1950 Joseph McCarthy, the senator from Wisconsin, had claimed that the State Department had been infiltrated by more than two hundred Communists, and such had been the fear over Korea that on December 15, 1950, Truman had declared a state of emergency that did not rule out the use of the atomic bomb.

There was no obvious political refuge for those like Plath, who were uneasy about the turn events were taking in McCarthyite America. If the right was rampant and threatening, the left in general seemed embattled and gloomy.[39] In California Theodor Adorno had begun to disseminate a Marxist analysis of culture that saw popular American culture as a symptom of bourgeois false consciousness.[40] Some of this thinking would have percolated through to Plath via her tutors, as intellectuals from both left and right saw reason to preserve the separation of art and politics, and art and popular culture. Elsewhere the American Left exerted influence through *Partisan Review,* the journal whose intellectual leaders included pacifist Dwight McDonald (and Paul Goodman and C. Wright Mills). Yet like Adorno, Macdonald believed that high art was beyond politics.

Against such an intellectual and political background, with McCarthyism in the ascendant, Plath read supplement 1 of the assigned government report, the first section of which contains *The Communist Manifesto.*[41] Plath has underlined many sentences in Marx and Engels's famous rallying cry, as she has in section 4, which contains Lenin's 1920 essay "Left Wing Communism: an infantile disorder."[42] Plath's annotations are not easy to interpret, as their brevity often makes their exact meaning uncertain. In section 5, "The Tasks of the Youth League," Plath protests with a "NO!" in capital letters next to a sentence about pre-Communist education, which she has underlined for emphasis:

> Every word was adapted to the interest of the bourgeoisie. In these schools the young generation of workers and peasants were not educated: their minds were stuffed with things that were to the interest of that bourgeoisie.[43]

Her "No!" could indicate a confident sarcasm or a dismissive rejection. Plath apparently subscribes to orthodox anti-Communist sentiments (or perhaps an anti-Sovietism) when she writes, "Let's hope so" next to Lenin's remark that "as long as Russia remains the only workers' republic . . . we shall be weaker than they, we shall be under the constant menace of attack."[44] She is dismissive of comments in an essay by Andre Zhdanov, a member of Stalin's government, heavily underlining later sections of "The International Situation." Plath's reaction to Zhdanov's claim that Anglo-American diplomacy since the war has "persistently and unswervingly striven to implement a policy that threatens peace, protects fascist elements" and persecutes "democracy in all countries" is to comment in the margin, "sweeping assertions." Yet when the argument moves to the subject of the atomic bomb, and the opposition of the United States and Great Britain to a UN resolution from the Soviet Union prohibiting the use of atomic energy for warlike purposes, Plath, mindful no doubt of her own call for peace published in the *Monitor,* offers the remark, "how annoying to have to admit the follies of one's own side."[45] Plath writes, "Sounds valid" on the following page next to a paragraph that describes the expansionist nature of American imperialism, citing specifically the "accumulation of atomic bombs," a phrase Plath has underlined. Her underlining of a passage in which Zhdanov refers to the "stifling of political resistance within the country" includes his claim that the minds of unenlightened American masses have been "poisoned"

> with the virus of chauvinism and militarism, and in stultifying the average American with the help of all the divers means of anti-Soviet and anti-Communist propaganda—the cinema, the radio, the church and the press.[46]

The underlining is by Plath, and in the margin she has written, "pot calling kettle black?" While this remark challenges the right of the Soviet Union to adopt a position of moral superiority, it acknowledges that the United States may indeed be something of a black kettle. Plath's pacifism is shocked by the reminder that "American strategists say quite openly" that the United States "is preparing bacteriological weapons," her reaction being an energetic "what!" written in the margin.[47] On the other hand, a more reflective "hmmm?" has been written on the same page against the claim that the United States is in the process of making preparation for the use of the Arctic for military aggression.

A sentence making another challenging claim is indicated below by Plath's extended underlining:

> The principal purpose of the ideological part of the American strategical plan is . . . to <u>deceive public opinion by slanderously accusing the Soviet Union and the new democracies of aggressive intentions, and thus representing the Anglo-Saxon bloc in a defensive role and absolving it of responsibility for preparing a new war.</u>[48]

In the margin Plath has written sarcastically, "That explains it! I am a victim of American propaganda!" Even if the remark is only an echo of a comment made by the teacher, Plath is clearly moved to ponder these issues, and the selfsame questions posed by this text were to reappear when she went to England, and regarded America from a distance.

Another, less provocative, book that Plath read for Government II was J. Corry's *Elements of Democratic Government*.[49] Its principal subject is the American system of government, though there are significant comparisons with other systems, and the book has been much marked by Plath. It is interesting for a number of reasons. First it provides evidence of Plath's awareness of the complementary relationship between art and society, which is here expressed in terms that contrast with the intellectual hierarchy identified by Ortega. On page 20 of Corry's book Plath has marked the following:

> At the peak of self-expression, the artist is largely dependent on others for the leisure and materials his art requires. To free the poet for his art, others must work at more prosaic tasks.

In *The Intellectuals and the Masses*[50] John Carey argues that the purpose of modernist writing was to exclude the newly educated reader by deliberately being difficult, "thus preserv[ing] the intellectual's seclusion from the 'mass.'"[51] This is an idea made explicit in Ortega's *The Dehumanization of Art*,[52] where the pure aesthetic, which excludes the element of accessible social narrative that provides human interest in art, excludes the masses who desire such human interest.

Despite Plath's reservations about the "peanut-crunching crowd," Plath was temperamentally adverse to this kind of exclusive artistic elitism. Plath's short stories in particular were directed at the mass market, the "slicks," which consisted of popular magazines for women such as *Seventeen* and *Mademoiselle,* and others such as the *Saturday Evening Post* and the *New Yorker.* Her goal in prose writing was always "human interest." It is important to see Plath's rapid and often paradoxical political adjustments (acceptance of conformist anti-Communist sentiments, flirtation with the rationale for a cultural elite, unwillingness to relinquish her own cultural capital as an investor in the "slicks" marketplace) as the natural corollary of the voracious, synthetic, and absorptive reader that she was.

The Smith-era journals, in which she makes clear her writing ambitions, also provide evidence of her belief in the primacy of the individual. Corry's set text offered much reassurance on this subject: "From the point of view of democracy, the highest value, *the ultimate for politics,* is the liberation of and respect for individual personality."[53] This view is very similar to the one endorsed by Plath and Perry Norton in a 1950 *Christian Science Monitor* review: "We wish to spread democracy and the capitalistic system since we believe that our society is more nearly ideal than any other existing at the present time."[54] Plath's limited annotations show either a rather uncritical, accepting response to Corry's anti-Communist emphasis or a lack of interest in it. There has been little underlining of the book's "Communism in Practice" section, except for the following sentence: "The essential feature of the equality is an equal subject to an all powerful government."[55]

Although other annotations suggest that Plath found Corry's book dull, she clearly learned much from Corry's text about the USSR's system of government and the British system of parliamentary government and was alert to the book's omissions. It offers, for example, a very hasty treatment of the segregation issue, and Plath has simply written "Good!" alongside Corry's passing admission that such discriminatory practices are a denial of democratic rights.[56] The approving comment may signal that she would have liked to see more on this subject. Plath had a developed sense of the importance of civil rights and the corrupting influence of discrimination, as she had shown in her 1952 short story "The Perfect Setup," which explores the corrosive effects of anti-Semitism.[57]

Plath's other notebooks from Government II[58] contain her detailed notes on Plato (one of her assignment topics was Plato's view of the current U.S. tax system), Machiavelli, Hobbes, Locke, and Rousseau. She has lecture notes on exploitation, colonialism, imperialism, and nationalism in Asia (October 9) and on "The Character of Asian Communism" (November 7), the latter given by Edwin O. Reischauer of Harvard. If Plath's notes are a fair reflection of Professor Reischauer's talk, his was another very complacent reading of Communism, which Plath's notes faithfully record as a flawed system that "doesn't have any future." She then adds, "We should play along with forces of Asia without compromising ourselves."[59] In Plath's second notebook for the course[60] she slips into using the common, but revealing, abbreviation "Commie," and her notes generally support a depiction of Communism as the enemy of liberty. There is some acknowledgment of the Communist reading of Western liberty as a false, class-interest version of liberty, however. The notes also register a recognition of the need for civil rights in America to be extended to African-American citizens. The theme of the session, led by Mr. Pierce, was "Rights, Powers and the Constitution," and Plath responded with copious notes. Her sketch in this part of the notebook of a sleeping student, however, suggests that not all found the subject particularly stimulating. On December 11, 1951, she attended Mr. Pierce's session on Marxism and made further detailed, clear notes. This was followed on December 17 by a session led by another tutor, Mr. Overstreet, and here Plath has further notes on Marxism, Leninism, and Stalinism. Her jottings illustrate a particular personal twist to the internalization of the enemy "Other" that marked the McCarthyite period. Her notes emphasize Marx and Engels's German nationality (Plath's father was German) and record that Americans ("we") are biased against the Russians, who are not the source of the Communist ideology. The unsaid corollary of this note is that Germany is guilty again, as the new ideological enemy Communism replaces the vanquished Nazism. Politics and personal genealogy become intertwined in complex ways.

In yet another solid, hard-back notebook, Plath has made many further notes for Government II for the second semester. For a lecture (though it is possibly the title of a book) called "Peace Can be Won" Plath's notes discuss the current Cold War situation and the theory of containment. Consistent with her pacifism, she rejects the proposal for universal military training.

Because the notes are so detailed and carefully recorded, at first sight they seem to provide evidence of significant, influential contact with the ideas of politics, though as suggested earlier we can sometimes suspect irony or the faithful recording of the teacher's comment. There are two further contextual points to be made, however, about the frames in which these comments should be read. The first might appear trivial, but is worth noting. Plath's notes on government are peppered with little drawings of dreamy subjects such as a tropical island with palm trees, a mermaid and a sunbathing woman, all suggesting moments of escapist reverie. Possibly more significant is the wider discursive frame in which these political ideas were encountered. Plath's upbringing may have been strongly pacifist,[61] in a culture that would have considered such beliefs quite radical, and by autumn 1952 she may have developed into the "passionate Democrat" described by Anne Stevenson.[62] In other respects her family does not seem to have been what could be described as progressive or liberal. Aurelia Plath had a career, but like most postwar American women had not seemed unwilling to sacrifice her own ambitions for those of her husband and children. Plath's appeal to her mother not to vote for Nixon suggests that she might have voted Republican.[63] The Catholicism of Sylvia Plath's Aunt Dot was accompanied by a conservatism that Plath was not eager to cross. On the other hand it is not uncommon for children to reject the politics of their parents, and Plath was well aware of her own early social conditioning.

At Smith the teaching encouraged an openness of ideas, but in the years before 1960 the majority of students, many of whom saw Smith as a kind of finishing school in preparation for an appropriate marriage, were not likely to have welcomed serious ideological challenges to the status quo. Thus the intellectual and economic climates were not conducive to radical political engagement. Yet, ironically, the excesses of McCarthyism meant that this was the most political of times. Evidence of this is to be found in other notebooks kept by Plath, which move beyond the kind of notes that the average Smith literature major might have kept. They provide evidence of nascent, if undeveloped, political journalism.

Apart from taking courses such as Religion, History, and Government, Plath also attended a number of talks on political and ethical themes given at Smith by visiting speakers. Her attendance did not reflect a straightforward interest in the subject, as she was there to provide reports of the talk for the Press Board, which distributed press releases about events at Smith to local newspapers. But her notes, kept in a spiral-bound reporters' notebook of the kind also used by 1950s secretaries, are not perfunctory or lacking in response: far from it.

Two of the sessions were unremarkable. Margaret Morrison speaking on "Christian Science: The Voice of Truth" and attendance at the monthly meeting of the Day School PTA for a discussion of child development were duly noted by Plath and duly filed. But other talks, particularly those that formed the series sponsored by the Hillel Foundation, an organization for Jewish students, with the umbrella title "Modern Thought and Religious Belief," were much more striking. One example, which provides poignant evidence of McCarthy's success in creating hysteria about subversion, was a talk given by Dirk Jan Struik, "Academic Freedom and the Trend to Conformity."[64] Struik had been a math professor for twenty-five years at MIT and had been temporarily discharged that fall for his political beliefs, the allegation being that he occasionally taught Marxism to his classes. Plath's awareness of the politics in the South was more developed than her Government II notes indicate, because she observes wryly that while fears about subversion in colleges are occupying everyone's attention, not one lyncher has been brought to justice. In a letter not included in *Letters Home* and dated March 6, 1952,[65] Plath tells her mother that she had heard Struik, who had been accused and suspended under the antianarchy law of 1919, speak on the previous Monday night. She then comments, "Really a fascinating Marxist. The Press Board took my review of it (playing down the controversial) almost verbatim!"[66] Plath also had firsthand experience of the extreme form of anti-Communist rhetoric. In a later letter to her mother, dated April 10, 1952, Plath reported that she was going to hear Senator McCarthy "tomorrow."[67] Her reaction to this talk is given in a May 1952 letter, again not included in *LH,* in which she tells her mother of a refreshingly different speaker:

> In the evening . . . went to hear the most wonderful lecturer—
> Patrick Murphy Malin—Head of the Civil Rights Commission.
> . . . As an antithesis to Senator McCarthy's "guilt by association
> and hearsay" lecture he was an example of integrity and outstanding promise.[68]

Although these discourses were received by Plath within a specific cultural and historical frame,[69] they were potentially liberating and intellectually provocative. Another talk in the Hillel series was given by a Bennington history professor. Its subject was "Marxism and Religious Beliefs," and Plath took eight pages of heavily underlined notes, clearly responding to the questions about reason and religion it raised. If we add together the government course from the beginning of her time at Smith, the history course from the final year, and the series of talks that she attended as a student reporter, this provides extensive evidence that Plath had contact with a range of political ideas, all meticulously recorded and articulated. The problem for anyone wishing to interpret this as evidence of a rigorous, stimulating political education is that these ideas were not necessarily discussed, aired, interrogated, teased out, followed up, or encouraged outside the classroom or lecture hall. Political discourse was pervasive, but circumstances were not right for Plath to experience a major shift in her reading of institutions, global politics, and the structure of society. That shift was made easier when she looked back to America from England and saw the world from the wider global perspective that experience on the other side of the Atlantic gave her. Plath's early political education was an important and necessary preliminary stage in this reassessment, however, in that it meant that she was very familiar with a range of political models and ideologies. It is not surprising, therefore, that the contradictions and paradoxes in her outlook seeped into her poetry as she became more gripped by the reporting of Cold War events and closer geographically to the political fault line along which the two major ideologies were grinding like tectonic plates.

Conflicting Discourses: The Fusion of Opposites

By 1955 Sylvia Plath was consciously seeking to enlarge her range of poetry by experimenting with verse that addressed wider political issues. On February 2 Plath sent to her mother the poem "Temper of Time," which was to be accepted by the political paper *The Nation* later in that year. In what appears to be a rather disingenuous explanation, designed to reassure her mother that she was not really too worried by world events, Plath writes:

Understand that "Temper of Time," while ominous, is done tongue in cheek, after a collection of vivid metaphors of omen from the thesaurus, which I am rapidly wearing out. It is a kind of pun on the first page of the NY *Times* which has news much like this every morning.[70]

The poem, which appears in the "Juvenilia" section of *Collected Poems*, contains the following verse:

> In the ramshackle meadow
> Where Kilroy would pass
> Lurks the sickle-shaped shadow
> Of snake in the grass.[71]

Kilroy is presumably a reference to the name of the archetypal American soldier whose name appeared on equipment and walls all over the world during World War II. The name has been traced to James J. Kilroy of Massachusetts, who wrote "Kilroy was here" on the ship parts he inspected in the Bethlehem Steel Company's Quincy shipyard, though the expression may actually predate the war. The threat from the Soviet Union, associated with snake and sickle, is the danger in the meadow, a danger that may already have destroyed America, now reduced to ramshackle plot. Plath may have been dismissive of the newspaper/thesaurus origins of this poem, but her note to her mother shows that she regularly read the front page of the *New York Times* (provided free in all the Smith Halls at this time) and took an interest in international events.

This was the period in which she was contemplating teaching at the American School in Tangier.[72] On a valentine card to Gordon Lameyer dated February 10, Plath says that she has just had the interview: "I am entranced by the coming importance of an international orientation in my life, which is what I want to have."[73] In February 1956, on the eve of her relationship with Ted Hughes, Plath wrote to her mother a letter speculating on her possible future. Again, these political references were not included in *Letters Home:* "The political frontiers here are most interesting. . . . I would like so much to work for a paper like the *Monitor*."[74] Before too long she was indeed contributing to the *Monitor*, though her sketches of Cambridge hardly reflect the "political frontiers."

Nevertheless, Plath's changing outlook was affecting her imaginative writing. In March she wrote that she was now scornful of the "coy love lyric" and other features of her earlier poetry. Now she was bringing

> the larger social world of other people into my poems. . . . Now I am making a shift. The world and the problems of an individual in this particular civilization are going to be forged into my discipline.[75]

Examining world and "self" at the intersection of global issues would enrich her understanding, and was not to be at the expense of her belief in the value, for her development as a writer, of scrupulously examining her own subjectivity. There was a clear possibility of making connections between the two: "between my private crisis and the huge crisis aroused by Britain's incredible and insane bombing of Egypt, the universe is in a state of chaos."[76] Such a belief in correspondence, traceable down through Neoplatonism and Swedenborg to Emerson, is basically the religious theory that "man" is a microcosm of the world adapted to serve an artistic practice. The immediate private crisis was the need to confess to the Fulbright Commission that she was now married. The international crisis referred not only to what Plath describes as the British arrogance over Suez, but to the British refusal to respond to the appeals coming from Hungary following the Russian occupation. The letter conveys Plath's disgust at the behavior of world leaders and expresses how much she approves of the protesting voice of newspapers and dissenting Cambridge students. It also anticipates her complex grafting of the self and global issues that came to fruition in the final poetry.

It is my contention that the meeting with Ted Hughes in 1956 arrested this progress toward political and artistic convergence,[77] and it applied a brake to any further move Plath may have been inclined to make toward activism and overt political involvement. This is not say that Plath meekly allowed herself to be dominated by Hughes, but rather that she was readily persuaded by the strength and certainty of his convictions. Hughes, with his interest in magic, astrology, and spiritualism, had a clear idea about the circumstances that assisted the creative writer. In a letter to Lucas Myers from which I am not permitted to quote, Hughes says that the only way to progress as a writer is to become a political outsider, live anonymously, and become introspective.[78]

Plath's shift in this direction was gradual, and it did not commence immediately with the first Falcon Yard meeting with Hughes in February 1956. In late March Plath was in France, and in another section cut from a letter included in *Letters Home,* Plath describes to her mother a meeting in Paris with an Italian activist:

> His name is Giovanni Perege and he writes mainly political articles, but also on artists and writers. He is ever without a doubt the nicest communist I've ever met and I've learnt so much: he is very idealistic. . . . [He] fought in the resistance during the war.[79]

Within three months of writing this letter, Plath was married to Hughes and enthusiastic about almost everything her husband believed in. Perege's passionate political commitment was forgotten. In a November 6 letter to her mother, there is rage and anger at Britain's involvement in Suez and the betrayal of Hungary as the Soviet Union began to occupy that country. But Hughes's influence is apparent in Plath's new response to the world situation. Her reaction to Suez and Hungary is to propose a move away from Europe to America and to find some corner of the world, "some island or other,"[80] where they can live the honest, creative life. It is a wish to withdraw from the world, a desire traceable in the letters by Hughes in the archive at Emory University.

This is exactly what Hughes persuaded Plath to do. In a revealing sentence omitted from the *Letters Home* version of the November 6, 1956, letter, Plath reports Ted Hughes's interpretation of the events in Suez and Hungary as, in Hughes's view, stirred up by the "opposition of the planets."[81] A profound conflict had been created. As Plath reported to her mother, Hughes believed that world events were governed by astrological events and therefore beyond the control of humans. The resistant part of her that wished to engage with the public world had taken them to Massachusetts, where she had taught in her own college[82] and worked in a hospital, and when Hughes had been homesick they had returned not to Yorkshire but to London. But then the retreat from the world was completed by the move to the "island" in Devon, away from people actively engaged in politics, away from people actively engaged in the arts, away from people engaged in academic life. The neighbors in Devon with whom she came into contact were often people who had retired from colonial service in India, Nigeria, or some other part of the former British Empire.

When Plath and Hughes went to visit one such couple they had met through the bee society in June 1962, Plath seemed to have settled for the view of life that all idealism is naive, and that individualism and self-development are the chief things in life. Her notes for a visit to the Billyealds in Winkleigh, a few miles north of North Tawton, record her impressions of George Manly, the father of Bertha Billyeald, who is more at home than his son-in-law, Major Stanley Billyeald, formerly of British Guiana.

> The old man, his father-in-law, a sort of elderly double of himself. Three things I'll tell you, he said: There is no sentiment in business. There is no honesty in politics. And self-interest makes the world go round. All right, I said. I give you those.[83]

If this grudging concession to an old man's cynicism were Plath's final or only statement on politics, then there would be little point in advancing the argument that Plath's artistic and personal ambitions competed and grappled with an equally strong altruistic engagement with political issues right up until the moment of her death. But three months later, Plath was to separate from Hughes, was to write the *Ariel* sequence of poems, and was to pack up and move to London.

After 1961 there is, unfortunately, no record in the public domain of Plath's awareness of Berlin and the Cuban Missile Crisis. These events are not mentioned in her letters. Her journals for the period are lost. But it would be very odd if her habitual monitoring of radio, magazines, and newspapers and the political awareness that her education had developed, suddenly ceased. It survived her meeting with Hughes and more than survived her parting from him. Because we know about the marriage, and the crisis in the marriage at Devon, we have been eager to unravel the personal element in the poems. But the Cold War tension continued to be high during the first three years of the 1960s and was at its most tense in the missile crisis week during which Plath wrote significant poems in the *Ariel* sequence in the Devon "cave" of

Court Green that in "Nick and the Candlestick" is both prison cell and sanctuary. Here we have the conflation of aesthetics and politics acted out at the intersection of subjectivity and global issues, leading to an ethical response. In the midst of such a political and personal crisis, religious fatalism and serenity become the only survival response, with the cave in the poem achieving the apotheosis of the nativity:

> Let the mercuric
> Atoms that cripple drip
> Into the terrible well,
>
> You are the one solid
> The spaces lean on. . . .
> You are the baby in the barn.[84]

In the end it is necessary to retreat underground, but even here there is correspondence, as the earth weeps like the candle that lights the baby's room. In the Cold War, the prayer for the survival of the baby in the shelter is a microcosm of the perilous state of the world as a whole, and correspondence is complete.

The themes of surveillance,[85] coldness, and betrayal, and the titanic clash of worldviews between two powerful former allies, now enemies, can be as suggestive of a metaphorical global collision as they can be of a domestic one, and a reading that includes a greater acknowledgment of Plath's international political awareness should encourage an acknowledgment that such are some of the meanings implicit in later works. It is time to assess the extent to which our understanding of supposedly "confessional" writers such as Plath changes when we read them politically.

ACKNOWLEDGMENTS

An Everett Helm Fellowship allowed me to visit the Lilly Library at the Indiana University to research much of this material. An abbreviated version of this essay appeared as "The Ideological Apprenticeship of Sylvia Plath" in the research report section of the *Journal of Modern Literature*, Spring 2005.

All quotations from Plath copyright material appearing in the *Journal of Modern Literature*, and reproduced in this version are copyright the Estate of Sylvia Plath and are printed with permission of Faber and Faber Ltd. and with permission of the Lilly Library.

NOTES

The epigraphs that open this chapter are from the following: Plath, "Religion as I See It," May 3, 1952, for Smith College course Religion 14 (Lilly: Plath MSS II, Box 10, Folder 8), 8; and Plath, "Darwin, Marx, Wagner: an essay." The essay is a review of the book *Darwin, Marx, Wagner* by Jacques Barzun (Boston: Little, Brown, 1941) for the Smith College History II course run by Mrs. Koffka 1951–52 (Lilly: Plath MSS II, Box 10, Folio 7).

1. See, for example, Linda Wagner-Martin, *Sylvia Plath: A Literary Life* (London: Macmillan, 1999) and specific chapters in Al Strangeways, *Sylvia Plath: The Shaping of Shadows* (London: Associated University Presses, 1998); and Tracy Brain, *The Other Sylvia Plath* (London: Pearson, 2001).

2. Jacqueline Rose, *On Not Being Able to Sleep* (London: Chatto and Windus, 2003), 53.

3. *CP*, 231.

4. See letters from Eddie Cohen to Plath (Lilly: Plath MSS II, Correspondence Box 1, 1938–51).

5. "[N]o other woman poet except Emily Dickinson can begin to be compared to her." Ted Hughes to Aurelia Plath, March 15, 1963 (Lilly: Correspondence January–June 1963), quoted in Diane Middlebrook, *Her Husband: Plath and Hughes: A Marriage* (London: Little, Brown, 2004), 218. Hughes's comment echoes the then-fashionable view of Dickinson as a visionary, unworldly poet.

6. See Robin Peel, *Writing Back: Sylvia Plath and Cold War Politics* (Madison, N.J.: Fairleigh Dickinson Press, 2002).

7. One example of this is her contact with the Christopher Movement, to which she submitted some short stories for one of its thirty-four contest prizes (she was successful). Aurelia Plath explains: "The Christopher Movement, founded in 1945, emphasized the importance of personal responsibility and individual initiative in raising the standards of government, education, literature, and labor relations" (*LH*, 153). Later that year (1955) Plath described herself as an "ethical culturist" (*LH*, 201).

8. Three-page draft of material that eventually became the essay "Religion As I See It" (Lilly: Plath MSS II, Box 10, Folder 8).

9. Plath, "Religion As I See It," May 3, 1952, essay for Religion 14, Smith College (Lilly: Plath MSS II, Box 10, Folder 8).

10. Plath, "The Age of Anxiety and the Escape from Freedom," essay reviewing Fromm's *Escape from Freedom* and Nietzsche's *Thus Spake Zarathustra* for History 38b, History of Europe in the Nineteenth Century May 27, 1954 (Lilly: Plath MSS II, Box 10, Folio 7), 7.

11. Ibid.

12. Plath's copy is held at Smith.

13. The jacket of the book has been pasted in one of her art scrapbooks.

14. Plath, "Notes on Zarathustra's prologue" (Lilly: Plath MSS II, Box 8, Folder 1).

15. Ibid. For example: "What can reach the deaf / who can speak for the dumb. / Defenceless under the night / Our world in stupor lies."

16. *LH*, 120.

17. *CP*, 245.

18. John Carey, *The Intellectuals and the Masses* (London: Faber and Faber, 1992) 3–4.

19. José Ortega y Gasset, *The Revolt of the Masses* (New York: New American Library, 1951). Plath's copy held at Lilly.

20. Ibid.

21. Ibid., 72.

22. Ibid.

23. Plath, "D. H. Lawrence: The Tree of Knowledge Versus the Tree of Knowledge" (Lilly: Plath MSS II, Box 13, Folder iv).

24. Ibid., 8.

25. See Ann Stevenson, *Bitter Fame: A Life of Sylvia Plath* (London: Penguin, 1989), 100–01.

26. See Keith Sagar, *The Art of Ted Hughes* (Cambridge: Cambridge University Press, 1975); and Middlebrook, *Her Husband,* 74–76.

27. Plath Diary 1945 (Lilly: MSS II, Box 7, Folder 1).

28. See, for example diary entry for January 2, 1944 (Lilly: Plath MSS II, Box 7, Folder 1, Diaries 1944 and 1945) .

29. Plath, "Youth's Appeal for Peace," March 27, 1948 (Lilly: Plath MSS II, Box 8, Folder 5).

30. Plath and Perry Norton, "Youth's Plea for World Peace," *Christian Science Monitor,* March 16, 1950.

31. Perry Norton was a neighbor and the same age as Plath. He was the brother of Dick Norton, whom Plath dated and who is the basis for Buddy Willard in *The Bell Jar.*

32. Plath met Mallory Wober, with whom she had a brief relationship, at a Labour Club event.

33. For a discussion of the commentary on politics revealed in Plath's journals and letters, see Peel, *Writing Back.*

34. Plath's notes for this course are kept at Lilly: Plath MSS I, Box 10, Folder 7.

35. Plath's copy of *The Strategy and Tactics of World Communism/Report/Committee on Foreign Affairs; Sub-committee No. 5/ National and International Movements 80th Congress 2nd session* (Washington, D.C.: U.S. Government Printing Office, 1948). On the cover in Plath's own hand is written "Sylvia Plath Haven House."

36. Plath letter to Aurelia Plath, December 4, 1950, *LH,* 63. In 1952 Plath was to write an antiwar story for English 220b. In the story, a girl on a train to Boston finds herself sitting opposite a Korean veteran who has lost a leg and has returned home for his sister's wedding. He is concerned about how he will be received (Lilly: Plath MSS II, Box 8, Folder 18).

37. Letter from Eddie Cohen to Plath, November 17, 1950 (Lilly: Plath MSS II, Correspondence Box 1, 1938–1951).

38. This collage was made by Plath in 1960 and is preserved at Smith and is discussed in Peel, *Writing Back.*

39. See David Harris, *From Class Struggle to the Politics of Pleasure* (London: Routledge, 1992), 16.

40. Theodore Adorno and Max Horkheimer's *Dialectic of Enlightenment* (New York: Social Science Association, 1944; Herder and Herder, 1972), as Stephen Con-

nor points out, is one of the most extreme examples of the separation of culture and politics (*Postmodern Culture* [Oxford: Blackwell, 1992], 238). This was a view shared by Queenie and F. R. Leavis, though they did not approach it from a leftist position at all; in the late fifties and sixties, when Plath was in England, a far more sympathetic view of popular culture developed, through Raymond Williams at Cambridge and the Centre for Contemporary Culture at Birmingham.

41. Marx and Engels, "The Communist Manifesto," February 1848, in *Strategy and Tactics* supplement 1, section 1, 1–27.

42. Lenin, "Left-Wing Communism: An Infantile Disorder," in *Strategy and Tactics,* supplement 1, section 4, 34–65.

43. Lenin: "The Tasks of the Youth League," October 20, 1920, in *Strategy and Tactics,* supplement 1, section 5, 67.

44. Ibid., 74.

45. Ibid., 219.

46. Ibid., 220.

47. Ibid., 221.

48. Ibid., 222.

49. J. A. Corry, *Elements of Democratic Government* (New York: Oxford University Press, 1951). Plath's copy is marked "Sylvia Plath Ex Libris" (Lilly: Plath MSS II, Box 5, No. 9).

50. Carey, *The Intellectuals.*

51. Ibid., preface.

52. José Ortega y Gasset, *The Dehumanization of Art and Other Essays on Art, Culture and Literature,* trans. Helene Weyl (Princeton, N.J.: Princeton University Press, 1968), 5–23.

53. Corry, *Elements of Democratic Government,* 27.

54. Norton and Plath, "Youth's Appeal."

55. Corry, *Elements of Democratic Government,* 57.

56. Ibid., 414.

57. *Seventeen,* October 1952.

58. Lilly: Plath MSS II, Box 11, Folder 4.

59. Ibid.

60. Lilly: Plath MSS II, Box 11, Folder 5.

61. Aurelia Plath writes, "I explained to them that their father, who felt regret when he accidentally stepped on an ant, had told me he could never bear arms" (*LH,* 31).

62. Stevenson, *Bitter Fame,* 35.

63. *LH,* 378.

64. Lilly: Plath MSS II, Box 11, Folder 6.

65. Plath to Aurelia Plath, March 6, 1952 (Lilly: MSS II, Box 2, Correspondence May 1951–September 1952).

66. Ibid.

67. *LH,* 84.

68. Plath to Aurelia Plath, April 10, 1952 (Lilly: Plath MSS II, Box 2, Correspondence May 1951–September 1952).

69. The political culture at Smith seems to have been what would be described in Europe as a liberal conservatism.

70. *LH*, 157.

71. *CP*, 336.

72. The belief in the importance of internationalism influenced both Plath and her brother. In 1956 Warren Plath spent some time in Austria as a member of the "Experiment in International Living" (*LH*, 249).

73. Plath to Gordon Lameyer, February 10, 1955 (Lilly: Lameyer MSS).

74. Plath to Aurelia Plath, February 14, 1956 (Lilly: Plath MSS II, Box 6, Correspondence 1956, Folder 1, January–February). The *Monitor* is the *Christian Science Monitor*, a serious national U.S. paper.

75. *LH*, 222.

76. Ibid., 282.

77. This is my argument in *Writing Back*. It would be wrong to conclude that the reappearance of this convergence in the autumn 1962 poems indicates that everything Plath wrote in between is constrained by Hughes. Her work benefits from his advice, encouragement, and commitment in ways that are obvious, his long written list of suggested subjects being one of the most striking. But her treatment of these subjects is her own. The reporting of Cold War events foregrounded the politics that Hughes's view of art may have caused Plath to otherwise suppress.

78. Ted Hughes to Lucas Myers (Emory: MSS 865, Box 1, Folio 4).

79. Plath to Aurelia Plath, March 26, 1956 (Lilly: Plath MSS II, Box 6, Correspondence 1956).

80. *LH*, 284.

81. Lilly: Plath MSS II, Box 6, Correspondence 1956; *LH*, 284.

82. And where she continued to meet political animals such as the poet and former Smith history teacher Peter Viereck, whose mixture of conservatism, anti-McCarthyism, and liberalism was as complex and paradoxical as her own. See *J*, 353–54; and *New Yorker*, October 24, 2005, 38–40, 42–47.

83. *J*, 661.

84. *CP*, 242.

85. The effect of the invasion of privacy brought about by Cold War surveillance is discussed in relation to Plath's poetry in Deborah Nelson's *Pursuing Privacy in Cold War America* (New York: Columbia University Press, 2002).

KATHLEEN CONNORS

Visual Art in the Life
of Sylvia Plath

MINING RICHES IN THE

LILLY AND SMITH ARCHIVES

⸭

On November 13, 1949, after abandoning her regular diary entries for
more than a year, Sylvia Plath copied a carefully composed discourse
on the "rapture of being seventeen" into a new booklet. The passage
contains key revelations that encapsulate Plath's struggle for self-
understanding and empowerment: "I want, I think, to be omniscient";
"I think I would like to call myself, 'The girl who wanted to be God'";
"I am I—I am powerful."[1]

How "The girl who wanted to be God" came to be the renowned
author of *The Bell Jar* novel and *Ariel* poems can be clearly seen in Indiana University's Lilly Library and Smith College's Mortimer Rare Book
Room. These two major collections of Plath's correspondence, visual
art, scholarly papers, memorabilia, and creative manuscripts house one
of the most extensive records of a major artist's life and works ever
assembled. By cross-referencing these various artifacts, one can trace
the course of Plath's artistic development from early childhood on. The
sheer volume of these collections makes the process exciting, for they
contain a great deal of underexplored material.

This essay considers archival works that reveal the trajectory of
Plath's creative oeuvre, with a focus on how her interdisciplinary and
cross-textual artistic experiments contributed to the visual world of
her mature poetry—in particular, poetry that touches on the relationship between the mother and child. Starting with early juvenilia, I

examine Plath's engagement with the painterly "eye" and the personal "I" of her two major disciplines, visual art and literature. I look closely at her teen years, during which she developed a strong identity as a professional artist; her first years at Smith, before she dropped her visual art training in favor of literature; and her post-Cambridge years in Boston and upstate New York, when she and her husband, Ted Hughes, quit their teaching jobs to pursue a living as writers. It was during these last two years before returning to England that Plath transited from authoring her second batch of what she called "art poems" in 1958 (which she then thought would make her name as a poet)[2] to her "Poem for a Birthday" sequence, written at the Yaddo artist colony in 1959, which many scholars see as the first real signs of the later *Ariel* voice.[3] Along with the first segment of this sequence, I will take a special look at journal entries and other poems Plath wrote while in Boston and at Yaddo that may offer a new perspective on the formation of "Edge"—a final poem written in 1963 that is generally interpreted as a suicide note.

I begin chronologically with two illustrated letters home that exemplify works used to introduce "Eye Rhymes: Visual Arts and Manuscripts of Sylvia Plath," an exhibition I produced at Indiana University in 2002.[4] The fact that these key texts were found in 1996 in the attic of the Plath family's Winthrop home only contributes to the sense of mystery and surprise many readers associate with the artist's life and works—and that I associate with mining her archives.[5] Although there is a general tendency to read Sylvia Plath's body of writing with reference to an assumed pathology and the provocative voice exhibited in many late poems, I believe her artistic portfolio deserves another context. It belongs with the research of arts advocates and cognitive development specialists who affirm the positive impact of visual learning and cross-disciplinary arts for young people, specifically on self-identity and the lifelong learning process.[6]

The Young Artist at Work

Sylvia Plath's extraordinary dedication to writing is the focus of many biographies, books, and essays written about her life and work. What is not commonly known is her serious devotion to the visual arts from a very early age. She moved between writing and art-making constantly, integrating their components with practiced ease and a great deal of pleasure. As a child she considered a poem she had written or transcribed to be incomplete without a picture, whether copied, cut out of magazines, or created from her imagination. During her teens she recorded what she called "technicolor" dreams that told complete stories, and she began making increasingly complex drawings in her diaries to illustrate her topics. Until her junior year at college, she considered the two disciplines as offering equally promising careers.

Sylvia Plath revealed her early self-consciousness as a writer and artist at age seven in two letters sent to her parents in February 1940. They were written at a difficult time, when she was staying temporarily with grandparents at their oceanfront home while her mother tended to her fatally ill father and little brother Warren. Along with these letters she included a duplicate of a colored drawing she sent to Aunt Dot and a handmade valentine. To her father she commented on something she had observed that she thought would amuse him:

> Over grandma's there were
> many ice-cakes and
> on every one sat a
> Seagull!

To her mother she explained the themes, images, and colors of the enclosed drawing she had made for Aunt Dot:

> The letter said how
> dlightful [sic] it is to fly!
> And showed a picture
> of aunt dot flying
> with a wand (which
> grandpa said was an ice-cream
> cone, or a flower.) (Ha Ha)
> . . . .
> The only colors I may use
> are yellow, purple, orange red blue.[7]

Plath's attachment to the seashore, a fascination with bright colors and images of flight, as well as a delight in humor, would stay with her throughout her life—as would the artistic dialogue with her mother.

Aurelia Plath devoted a great deal of her limited time and resources to her children's education and arts enrichment both in and out of school. Whatever the young Sylvia requested in terms of art, dance, or music lessons, art and writing supplies, or simple treats such as fresh fruit while at camp, seemed to have been provided. Plath's frequent gifts to her family were her art: drawings and poems tucked under table napkins as a surprise, letters and postcards sent home from camp, birthday and greeting cards with colorful drawings and clever poems, items made in arts, crafts, and sewing classes.

As a child Plath received a great deal of praise for her visual art as well as her writing. She loved to draw flower gardens, nature scenes, and buildings, as well as figures from fairy tales and classical myth—in some cases, well beyond the age when she was reading them. When she was twelve she made two glamorous cutout women with huge wardrobes of wildly colorful and flamboyant outfits, reflecting her interest in the 1940s film and print culture, as well as the world of fashion. She was comfortable with ink, charcoal, pastels, and tempera, and in her 1946 camp journal she noted being "thrilled" with the purchase of her first set of oil paints and canvases.[8] Plath's training as a visual artist included formal and informal instruction in a variety of settings, from the early art lessons provided by her mother in the form of art books and Boston museum visits, to near daily classes in junior high school and camp, and weekly private lessons in still life pastels with a neighbor. During her high school years at Wellesley's Bradford High School she took visual art composition and advanced painting courses, and she took weekly classes at the Star Island summer camp during the summer before her senior year.

During her adolescence she began to place colorful or emotive language in her diaries, along with animated and illustrated commentary on the more important topics. Plath's long-term interest in the uses of the subconscious as a source of inspiration was first recorded when she became a teenager. A series of vivid dreams inspired her to record her dreams in her 1946 diary, where on February 19, she recalled a storybook sequencing that appealed to her sense of visual order and narrative plot:

Last night I had five dreams. . . . The titles are (1) "Rocketship to Mars" and (2) "The Sled that Coasted Around the World."

Nine Female Figures, tempera, 18″ × 24″, by Sylvia Plath, ca. 1950–51. (© The Estate of Sylvia Plath, United Kingdom), The Lilly Library.

. . . They had very satisfactory endings because the pictures conveniently faded into each other.[9]

At this time Plath looked to models provided by career women who were writing about their experience. In a diary note dated June 20, 1946, she described one of her favorite children's book authors, Adele de Leeuw, as "exceptionally intelligent" for the "professional language" she used in stories about young women facing many career choices.[10] Plath placed herself in the category of women who would not be content with a life devoted solely to a husband and family—and those who were writing about it. She was thirteen years old at the time. Already eager to publish, she was conscious of her beginner status as a writer, and she often discussed her developing technique. The traditional tools of art, particularly pens and ink, were frequent subjects of her writing and art, as were her own hands. The act of seeing and the eye itself, the catalyst for much of her inspiration, would also become a common image in many texts. A 1946 three-page story titled "The Mummy's Tomb," for example, revolved around the image of the villain's evil eye glowing in the dark. The story is told from the perspective of a girl locked into a museum at night who manages to escape the clutches of a murderous museum stalker and bring him to justice.[11]

Plath started "Stardust," the most ambitious story of her midteen years, in the summer of 1946 and completed it a year later in June.[12] She described her "beautiful long fairy tale" in a diary entry that revealed a sophisticated understanding of story development and narrative voice:

> 2/2/47: I . . . decided that I should either make the happenings seem natural, or marvel on the impossibility of them. . . . I've decided not to make it all goody-ish, preachy, or morally, unless sometimes I make an action, seemingly innocent, take on a deeper meaning. This is quite impossible since I am not that experienced (yet!)[13]

Sylvia Plath's 1947 diary, named "My Memory Book," recorded routine activities and intimate confessionals that ran from one paragraph to a few pages, most illustrated with full-figure self-portraits, miniature landscapes, and holiday themes, as well as notes about school. She occasionally made thumbnail sketches of paintings in progress to accompany her text, and her diary characterizations at times evoked personalities she felt could be developed for stories. One such figure was her art teacher and neighbor, Miss Hazleton, among the rare teachers who did not offer her praise:

> 1/31/47: . . . She is a tiny wizened old lady. . . but . . . her voice, though sounding like staccato, bird-ish chirps, has a ring of sincerity and the tone of one who sees the big, beautiful world as it really is—not dimmed by hazes of prejudice, hate, or anything else.[14]

Plath's focus on Miss Hazelton may have inspired three other short stories featuring an elderly protagonist named Miss Minton, all of whom had similar experiences. Ten days after Plath described her art teacher, she wrote a story in her diary titled,"The Miraculous End of Miss Minton."[15] In 1949 she would write "East Wind," and in 1952 "Sunday at the Mintons" was published.

After reading a diary of noted children's book illustrator Wanda Hazel Gág at age fourteen,[16] she noted in her diary that readers might one day be interested in her own personal life. During this period she had also been engaging her diary as a confidential friend, whom she often referred to as "you":

> 1/31/47: I actually stopped reading [Wanda Hazel Gág's diary] because I felt I would rather catch up here, first, for who knows—someday you might be in print.[17]

Plath's reading as a teenager included a wide array of works, from the classic novels and poems she was studying in her advanced literature courses (where, for example, she studied *Mrs Dalloway*), to popular magazines and pulp fiction. Her reading habits and her use of daily events to further her experiments in dramatic prose are evident in one of her more romantic and humorous diary scenarios. This description of a school dance, from February 28, 1948, began with a reference to a huge rainbow Plath had drawn on three sides:

> Today was ever more colorful and dreamy than this bright rainbow border. . . . The ladies choice was the last dance, so

seeing that Dave was picked first, I chose Tommy. He kept holding me tighter and tighter until I could hardly breath. I'm just so "in love" with him that it hurts. . . . I was just in dreamland. Tommy, Tommy, Tommy!!!—if you don't say you like me (*this* year!) I shall die of thwarted love.[18]

Mixing Disciplines and Genres at Smith

Plath's successful amateur efforts at art-making and writing took on new importance once she enrolled at Smith College in 1950, and began considering how to earn a living. Many of the letters Plath wrote to her mother in her first two years at Smith reiterated her indecision on which discipline offered the more "practical" career path. While she continued submitting her writing to publishers, she also worked intensively in Art 13, a studio course on technical design, and Art 210, a class on visual expression in painting. As she had been taught in her painting and writing courses at Wellesley High School and at Smith, Plath used colors to symbolize emotional and physical states, or to develop meaning around objects in her writing and her environment. In a 1951 letter she wrote to her artist friend Ann Davidow during her freshman year, Plath joked about her art training in relation to her view of Smith's Hopkins House:

Do you realize why I have my desk facing the window? . . . Hopkins House is yellow. Yellow is a "morale-building" color (or so the higher-ups say in Art 13.)[19]

The subjects of her writing and painting courses, as well as her interest in psychology and philosophy, started to overlap in numerous forms during her first year at Smith. In 1951 she made a loosely drawn colored-ink sketch of Hopkins House on the back of her "Den of Lions" story page, where she managed to capture a philosophical equivalent of the "geometric tension" she suggested for a painting on the subject in her journal:

Hopkins House is ugly. . . . It is all awkward corners . . . red tiled roofs worn to purple . . . smeared with the year's grime, paint peeling, soiled window frames . . . Yet I love Hopkins

House. Such is the resiliency of man that he can become fascinated by ugliness which surrounds him everywhere and wish
to transform it by his art into something clinging and haunting
in it's lovely desolation. . . . I would paint in a bleak and geometric tension of color and form . . . the ugliness which by
man's sense of wishful thinking becomes a beauty touching us
all.[20]

Pictures Plath made at Smith, however, continued to focus primarily on
representations of women. Perhaps the most common subject of her
childhood and teen artwork, Plath's fascination with the female body is
evident in all genres of her artwork, from her early diary doodles of film
star glam-girls to her last dated visual piece in the archives, a 1960 collage of newspaper cuttings that places a shapely woman in a bathing suit
within commodity culture and militarism of Eisenhower's America.

One of Plath's most abstract and compelling works is a painting of
nine female figures fixed in patterned squares of bright colors, one of
many large-format temperas she made for Art 13, most likely the final
assignments of her freshman studio in 1951.[21] The painting's nearly
indistinguishable female figures are cartoonlike outlines, seated nude,
merged into the static, two-dimensional boxes that prevent them from
breaking out, highlighting their vacant eyes and sexual function.
Mostly limbless, propped in rows, their postures are defensive and vulnerable. Using a modernist placement of the female within layers of
geometric planes championed by Duchamp and Picasso, this painting
gives clear expression of the troubling midcentury cultural conditions
Plath had been addressing in all forms of texts. The double standards
for men and women's sexuality, the mind-numbing restrictions of the
traditional 1950s housewife, and the frustrations of inhabiting a
woman's body were some of Plath's more notable complaints of late
adolescence, the kind of commentary that would later cause many fem-
inists to place her squarely in their camp.

Plath represented similar conditions in literary compositions written within the same period of spring, 1951. In an usually long journal
entry she questioned whether marriage and children might "sap my
creative energy" or provide "a fuller expression in art" before noting
the "blind box houses" she passed before stopping instinctively, "like
the rat in the maze," entering her own and locking her door to "the disturbing wasteland of sleeping streets and fenceless acres of night."[22]

These images of postwar suburban sprawl also brought to mind the women who would inhabit the straight rows of houses in the "million million microscopic towns" of her 1951 poem "Geography Lesson": "Straight go the little Main Streets / Bright shine the little houses." In this poem Plath used children's literary cadence and rhyme schemes and the layout of colored maps to wryly bring home her antiwar sentiments in the poem's final lines:

> Shrill squeak the little bullets,
> Sharp bark the little shotguns,
> And now a river
> A bright red river
> Stains the lavendar [sic] part of the map.[23]

In April 1951 Plath handed in a class paper titled "The Imagery in *Patterns*," an Amy Lowell poem Plath called a "personal favorite" that again spoke to her antiwar sentiments as well as her vision of women trapped in a cruel world.[24] The six-page essay related the unique way that Lowell used imagery to convey the "sorrow and rebellion" of a woman who finds her lover has been killed in what Plath called "a pattern called war." She offered a detailed analysis of the poem's imagery, particularly the "richly dressed lady walking up and down" what Lowell described as "patterned garden paths." Plath then contrasted the sensory images of the women's skin with the "artificial stiffness" of her gown before stating her rebellion against "manmade" patterns such as a third world war.

Plath's final identification of the poem's "clear imagery" that "intensifies and answers" her own emotions demonstrates how she chose and developed her own artistic subjects. She continually created and reformed her own image in her art, trying out various personalities in self-portraits or literary works featuring female protagonists. In one of two class papers she wrote on the poetry of Edith Sitwell, dated March 1953, Plath equated the poet's vivid and sensual imagery with that of Rossetti's "Goblin Market" before commenting on how a child might better respond to it. She equated Sitwell's "acute and vivid observations" to that of a "terribly clever and technically adroit child" who awakens in "a very personal and intimate wonderland"—a child that sounds very much like the young Sylvia Plath.[25]

Plath went on to describe the other side of this "bucolic world" where the "storybook animals turn harsh and grunting and all is mired" in what Sitwell called a "heavy brutish greedy darkness." She then quoted Sitwell's lines on how "Destiny is befouled" in the darker side of nature in a stanza that ends: "the country gentlemen wander, hunting for something, hunting."[26] Once again Plath's repugnance for the male world of wars and violence against nature is set in contrast to the woman's and child's sensibilities.

Many of Plath's high school and Art 13 studio paintings offered possible alternatives to this dark vision, notably in the figures of women at their leisure, often reading or in the company of female friends. Two large-format temperas she made at Smith may be seen as foils for her painting of boxed-in women. Both were executed in the same year and used a similar expressionist palette of blues, greens, yellows, and oranges. The subjects—an engagement with women in nature and at home—are also comparable; however, none of the collision of home and woman or rigid conformity is present. In the painting of two women reading, the planes of the buildings do not meet; they float above a patch quilt of colored scenery, airy and unenclosed.[27] Sitting apart and freed from the demands and confinement of the home, the readers pursue their own interests, relaxed under a tree with a friend, drinking a glass of wine. In a clear example of recycled imagery, Plath sketched the same design in her history class notebook during her final year of high school.

The composition of this tempera may also be seen as an unconventional conflation of cubism and linear perspective, techniques Plath had been studying for years. While cubism tends to flatten geometrical objects into multidimensional fields of monochromatic colors, often presenting multiple viewpoints simultaneously, this painting places vibrant, multicolored forms of shifting dimensions within a prominent two-point perspective. The scene is positioned from the viewpoint of one woman stretched out on the lawn, whose gaze is aligned with the viewer of the painting, blurring the division between the seeing eye of the creator and her audience.

The other large-format tempera that departs from the theme of entrapment and sexual stereotyping found in *Nine Female Figures* is a picture of a woman with a halo sitting on a stool. Leaning forward, one elbow positioned in space, she floats high above a hilly, springlike landscape with houses in the distance. Her eyes are closed, as if she is indulging an inner vision. Perhaps appropriate for a saintly figure, her clothes are dowdy, her shoes are comfortable, and her hair is not stylish. This painting is interesting not only for its spiritual overtones (Plath was taking a course on religion in the spring semester of 1951), but for its resemblance to another pencil sketch she made while a senior in high school. Placed among her biology notes, this drawing has a more fashionable woman sitting outdoors on a stool, with hills in the distance, one elbow extended, yet she is holding the scales of justice.[28] These similar figures represent two major (yet often conflated) personas of Plath, that of society's high judge engaged in righting the injustice of the world—the position she mentioned taking in her 1949 diary—and the figure of the mystic or contemplative, floating high above life on earth, distancing herself from mundane affairs.

If the painting of female entrapment represents the future that Plath fears will overtake her, the two women reading and the woman with a halo, and its secular prototype, might be seen as a future that she would choose for herself—with eyes focused on a just society, the realm of literature as well as the interior spaces of the divine mind. If Plath had decided to pursue visual art, these paintings give a sense of where her famous literary themes and interest in modern art may have found shape on the canvas. Artworks she made after college, with a few exceptions, were formalist and realistic in nature, usually taken from still models that featured scenes in cities or the countryside she visited.

After making serious efforts to improve her visual art while at Smith, Plath found initially encouraging reviews were outweighed by later criticism. She expressed shock at her Art 13 year-end art review, as seen in another letter to Davidow written in May or June 1951:

> I just . . . got one of life's little blows. I took my first painting together with my last one up to be criticized. . . . Mr. Swinton's comment was hideously encouraging—thought the first was much better, more naive and free—that the last was artificial and gaudy as bad wallpaper. Made me feel I'd really accomplished something! (Now Sylvia, don't be bitter!)[29]

Bitter or not about this criticism, she was resilient; she could not give up hope for bringing her visual art skills to professional levels. Yet any progress Plath might have made in painting and drawing could not approach the incredible success of her poems and stories during her first two years out of high school. *Seventeen* magazine, responsible for forty-five of her previous rejection notices, had bought the story "And Summer Will Not Come Again" for their August 1950 issue, and the poem "Ode to a Bitten Plum" that October. The magazine also gave her a third place prize for her story "Dens of Lions" in 1951, which they published along with her stories "The Perfect Set-up" and "Initiation." She wrote "Sunday at the Mintons" soon after, published by *Mademoiselle* in August 1952 after winning one of two $500 prizes for its College Fiction Contest. Other poems published that year include "The Suitcases are Packed Again" and "Carnivale Nocturne" in *Seventeen* and "Cinderella" in *Christian Science Monitor*.

The fact that these works brought in over $750 in awards, in conjunction with Plath's rare grade of B for both semesters of sophomore art studio, likely influenced her choice of a literary career. Though she considered taking another art course at the beginning of her junior year, she decided writing was the more practical option, and declared a major in honors English with a minor in art. She would never again take formal art lessons. But even as she developed her work as a poet, essayist, and novelist, she would not abandon her trained investment in contemporary art and visual motifs—particularly in her use of color. Plath also hated to waste any of her better efforts. So while she valued drawing in particular as an enjoyable form of relaxation, she reserved her more ambitious pictures to accompany published essays. Many of these articles were inspired by her favorite drawings or featured a visual art form in their titles: "Spring Sketching in Paris," "Arts in America. 1954. Collage of a Collegian," "Sketchbook of a Spanish Summer," "Mosaics—An Afternoon of Discovery."

Plath's continuing interest in modern art during these last years at Smith may be attributed to the numerous visits she made to New York City's museums and galleries with Richard Sassoon, her cultured boyfriend, a student at Yale. Viewing the masters' works in a gallery, as Plath noted, is more exciting than seeing reproductions in books. During her senior year poetry tutorial she began writing poems based on specific works of modernist painters and sculptors. In spring 1955 she wrote a handful of poems using art at the Whitney Museum as her subject—a topic also incorporated into her "Art in America" essay, written for *Vogue* magazine's "Prix de Paris" editorial contest. In this college contest submission, Plath extended her cross-disciplinary approach in discussing how we think in terms of "synesthesia," where music is visualized and verbalized: "Our ear isn't tutored to hear music in its own terms alone; as we listen, tunes turn to color, chords vibrate into words."[30]

The relationship of the spectator to the artwork as a frame for generating a line of poetry is used in "Wayfaring at the Whitney: A Study in Sculptural Dimensions," which includes three segments that describe the sculptures of Lindsay Daen, Sahl Swarz and Hugo Robus. "Black Pine Tree in an Orange Light" is based on the painting *Pine Tree* by Gregorio Prestopino, and the first line of "Midsummer Mobile" opens with the painters' tool—"Begin by dipping your brush into clear light"—to introduce the "sky of Dufy blue," Seurat's "fleck schooner flanks" and "the mellow palette of Matisse" in sonnet form. The final couplet presents the museum visit itself as a sculpture: "Suspend this day, so singularly designed, / Like a rare Calder mobile in your mind."[31] Plath's trip to Paris in spring 1956 included many museum visits. Viewing original artwork she had studied in books inspired her to make drawings of the local sites and to write about the act of drawing, in essays, journals, and letters. On her honeymoon that June in the Spanish fishing village of Beiderdorm, she created what she described as the best sketches she'd ever done, many of which accompanied articles she sold during her lifetime, as well as limited edition collections of her poetry and prose, produced by her husband Ted Hughes in the 1970s and 1980s.

Plath's career plans after college included novel writing, freelance journalism, and the lucrative short fiction market for women's magazines. Yet after receiving her second literary degree at Cambridge in 1957, and starting a job at Smith College teaching freshmen that fall, she became frustrated by writer's block. Turning to areas that had proved fruitful in the past (including psychotherapy and exploration of the unconscious), Plath audited a course on the modernists taught by a Smith colleague in the spring semester of 1958. When *Art News* asked her for a poem on art, she got excited about the assignment and went to the library for books on her favorite artists. In a letter home dated March 22, she talked of being able to "at last burst into a spell of writing" that resulted in eight "art poems" based on paintings and etchings of Klee, Rousseau, and de Chirico. In this letter she compared her more plodding writing process with the inspired approach she could access in viewing the art of the "primitives":

I feel like an idiot who has been obediently digging up pieces of coal in an immense mine and has just realized that there is no need to do this, but that one can fly all day and night on great wings in clear blue air through brightly colored magic and weird worlds.[32]

Plath's image of this immense coal mine seems to connect to the wide range of literature she had "obediently" studied and remembered, as well as her personal self-explorations that formed the basis of so much of her writing. With her writing steeped in Jungian thought and her own experiences with psychoanalysis, she often depicted the subconscious mind and childhood memory as reflecting watery pools or lakes that she could access for her work. As Plath grew out of adolescence and looked back with nostalgia on her passing youth, she still associated these magic flights with her creative imagination and the unfettered mind of a child. In an undated journal entry written at age eighteen, she wrote of "the beautiful dark-haired child (who was you) winging through the midnight sky on a star-path in her mothers box of reels."[33] And in her 1962 essay, "Ocean 1212-W," she characterized the first nine years of her life as "a fine white, flying myth."[34]

But in 1958 it was Giorgio de Chirico's paintings and diary notes that stimulated her own visionary leanings. Plath recorded her excitement in a journal entry dated March 29 that discussed her new art poems and the intriguing de Chirico prose, which had what she called a "unique power" to move her. She noted that two of her poems, "The Disquieting Muses" and "On the Decline of Oracles," were based on his early painting, *The Enigma of the Oracle*. Plath copied some of his inspiring notes on "the hour of the enigma" that included a ruined temple (in which, de Chirico says, "the broken status of a god spoke a mysterious language"), an old ghetto that housed sweets of "exceedingly strange & metaphysical shapes," and the "revelatory song of the last, morning dream of the prophet asleep at the foot of sacred column, near the cold, white simulacrum of god."[35] Plath responded to these powerful images with her own description of this world:

And everywhere in Chirico city, the trapped rain puffing in a labyrinth of heavy arches, vaults, arcades. The statue, recumbent, of Ariadne, deserted, asleep in the center of empty mysteriously-shadowed squares. And the long shadows cast by unseen figures—human or of stone it is impossible to tell.[36]

Treasures from the Yaddo "Storehouse" and Its Aftermath

After a cross-country trip taken during the summer of 1959, Plath and Hughes spent eleven weeks at Yaddo artist's colony in Saratoga Springs, New York. Unburdened by household duties, and pregnant with her first child, she had time to read, draw, and explore the beautiful estate grounds at her leisure. The work she accomplished at Yaddo provided her with a storehouse of images and notes from which she drew for the rest of her short life and that manifested quite surprisingly in some of her most important late poetry.

Along with four poems, Plath had five articles published in the *Christian Science Monitor* in 1959, one accompanied by a new drawing and three using her favorite sketches from her Spanish honeymoon two years earlier. After selling works to the *Monitor* starting in 1950, she considered the publication "smalltime," and wrote in her Yaddo journal of having "dreams of grandeur": the *New Yorker* accepting her illustrations along with her written works—"giving sanction to my running about drawing chairs and baskets."[37] With her literary career in mind, and under pressure to produce good works, she turned to evocative images from the rich visual surroundings at Yaddo for inspiration. An intricate drawing of a greenhouse that Plath made at Yaddo, and its description in her journal, indicate how she used her habit of sketching as a way to focus her mind for the act of writing. In this case the greenhouse drawing, which she described as "an exercise begun, in grimness," had two days later turned into "a fine new thing"—the "ambitious seeds" of a birthday poem (her own coming five days later) that would be "a dwelling on madhouse, nature: meanings of tools, greenhouses, florist shops, tunnels, vivid and disjointed. An adventure. Never over. Developing. Rebirth, Despair, Old women. Block it out."[38] This same journal description of the greenhouse as "a mine of objects" formed the basis of imagery found in *Who*, the first segment of "Poem for a Birthday":

10/22/59: Drew a surgical picture of a greenhouse stove yesterday and a few flowerpots. . . .Watering cans, gourds and squashes and pumpkins. Beheaded cabbages inverted from the rafters, wormy purple outer leaves. . . . The superb identity, selfhood of things.[39]

"Who," which Plath admitted was influenced by Roethke, re-creates the spatial and visual placement of her clearly defined drawing subjects while positioning herself as the viewing eye and subject:

I. *Who*

The month of flowering's finished. . . .

. . . .

Old tools, handles and rusty tusks.
I am at home here among the dead heads.

. . . .

. . . They bloom upside down.

. . . .

Cabbageheads: wormy purple, silver-glaze . . .

. . . .

O the beauty of usage!
The orange pumpkins have no eyes.[40]

. . . .

Another set of images Plath gathered at Yaddo stimulated the development of her important poem "The Moon and the Yew Tree." Just as Plath made a journal note to "Send for diary" after mentioning her inertia in starting stories at Yaddo,[41] she likely returned to her Yaddo journals (and perhaps her astonishing visual memory) to re-create her vision of the private estate for a poem titled "Private Ground," written in February 1961. In this poem she applied her favored technique of giving natural or inanimate objects an emotional life, as seen in the last two lines of the poem's third stanza of four: "Flatten the doped snakes to ribbons. In here, the grasses / Unload their griefs on my shoes."[42] Eight months later Plath felt the concept of grieving grasses was good enough to reuse in "The Moon and the Yew Tree," which had the image slightly reformulated and placed significantly in the poem's third line: "The grasses unload their griefs on my feet as if I were God."[43]

"The Moon and the Yew Tree" was written in October 1961, five days before her twenty-ninth birthday—always a productive month for Plath. In this poem, a cool landscape of blue and black took dominance in the poem's second line and last stanza, where blue was aligned with the sky, the heavens and the saints—in contrast to black:

> This is the light of the mind, cold and planetary.
> The trees of the mind are black. The light is blue.
> . . . .
> I have fallen a long way. Clouds are flowering
> Blue and mystical over the face of the stars.
> Inside the church, the saints will all be blue, . . .
>
> And the message of the yew tree is blackness,
>   blackness and silence.[44]

But perhaps the most significant use Plath made of her Yaddo experience was to surface in "Edge," the poem that may be the last she wrote before committing suicide:

> The woman is perfected.
> . . . .
> Each dead child coiled, a white serpent,
> . . . .
> Pitcher of milk, . . .
>
> . . . into her body as petals
> Of a rose close when the garden
>
> Stiffens.[45]

The seeds of "Edge" can be discovered in a journal entry dated November 11, 1959, which begins the description of "stiffened" frost on the plants and grass, the "dead" petals of the roses, and the white statues that were being covered for the winter season:

Frost stiffened and outlines the grassblades with white, and the whorls and rosettes of leaves and weeds. The rose garden shone in the sun, the thorny stems, with dead red leaves, bound together. The white statues are all encased in little wooden huts.[46]

These objects provided the visual setting for the first lines of "Private Ground," written fifteen months later:

First frost, and I walk among the rose-fruit, the marble toes
Of the Greek beauties you brought
Off Europe's relic heap.

The acceptance or inevitability of death expressed in "Edge" (also found in the last lines of "Private Ground") has caused many readers to see this final Plath poem as pointedly autobiographical in detailing the death of the "woman perfected" so close to her own suicide. But the connection between dead children and serpents, one of the poem's most provocative images, may be related not to Plath's own story of loss, but to the fate of Katrina Trask, Yaddo's mistress, as well as the dead snakes (including the "dead baby snake") Plath had written about seeing on the estate grounds.[47] In her early Yaddo journal notes she also mentioned "Medallion" as the "one good poem" she had written since her arrival, and described it as "an imagist piece on the dead snake."[48] Indeed, "Medallion" contains many words and concepts found in "Edge." It features a dead snake with a "rose-colored tongue" whose opaque belly recalled "milk glass" around which "white maggots coil."[49] And the final lines present the laugh of the snake as being "perfected" in death, just the first line of "Edge" offers a woman perfected in death. And where the "throats" of roses bleed sweetness in "Edge," it is the white statues in "Private Ground" that serve to "sweeten the neck" of the woods.

The Yaddo grounds are known for their magnificent and extensive rose gardens, as well as a collection of imported statues. Plath had shown a keen interest in the huge manor house and its furnishings, which she drew and described in her journals. A draft of "Private Ground" includes a reference to a painting by Fuseli at the estate, though she did not comment on the numerous portraits of the Trask family that likely evoked their tragic story.[50] All four of the Trask children died from diphtheria while young, and the Trasks dedicated the artist colony (named by their daughter) and one of its statues, to their memory. The fact that Mrs. Trask was interred in a rose-adorned grave on the estate, and that the pregnant Plath had expressed worry about birthing a healthy child, may also be significant to the female figure of "Edge." One might look again to the de Chirico prose and art Plath wrote of in 1958—in particular, the painter's notes on the dream of the prophet "asleep at the foot of the sacred column, near the cold, white simulacrum of god"—as well as hers: "The statue, recumbent, of Ariadne, deserted, asleep in the center of empty mysteriously-shadowed squares. And the long shadows cast by unseen figures—human or of stone it is impossible to tell."[51]

Plath had written a dramatic poem titled "To Ariadne (deserted by Theseus)" at age sixteen, what Aurelia had identified as her daughter's first attraction to the "tragic muse."[52] But as a mother of two young children, Plath may have been particularly moved by the image of a mother abandoned by her children in death in composing "Edge." She had noted feeling susceptible to the melancholy of Mrs. Trask, also a poet, a mood directly addressed in drafts of "Private Ground."

Color and Emotion in the Child's Eye and the Woman's Heart

In "Medallion," "Private Ground," and "Edge" the snakes sustain the focus on the seeing eye and the imaginative "I" that Plath associated with the life and mind of the child. In many of the *Ariel* poems, including those where colors rarely surfaced in the text, the presence of eyes or the act of seeing maintain the reader's focus on the visual. This characteristic of Plath's imagination is beautifully conveyed in "Child," written eight days before "Edge," most likely in reference to her first child Frieda, who has blue eyes. The word "color" is followed by objects that are associated with basic hues—yellow ducks, white snowdrops, green stalks, and blue pools that are set in contrast to the unhappy darkness without being noted by color. The eye, a "pool of images,"

. . . .
Not this troublous
Wringing of hands, this dark
Ceiling without a star.[53]

This last stanza replaces earlier lines written in a draft: "not this / Grubby dishcloth . . . this black paper, without moon or stars,"[54] leaving no direct reference to black or dreary domesticity. This dark and colorless world, with a ceiling that encloses the child, as opposed to that of the open sky, recalls the encaged state Sylvia Plath feared for herself and perhaps now feared for the daughter. Yet the "clear eye" of "Child" may also be likened to the pool of reflecting images and color scheme found in another four-stanza poem Plath wrote at age thirteen about a lake, personified as the untamed child, that served as (mother) earth's mirror to the sky. In this poem, as in many of Plath's works, the beautiful dark-haired daughter can be seen flying, free of responsibility and worry, on the star-path of her imagination:

> The lake is a creature,
> Quiet, yet wild,
> Rough, and yet gentle,—
> An untamed child. . . .
>
> . . . .
>
> The lake is really
> The earth's clear eye
> Where are mirrored the moods
> Of the wind and the sky.[55]

While Plath used the visually rich "intimate wonderland" of the free child as a creative touchstone all her life, it was the act of listening to poetry—her "new way of being happy"[56] she experienced at age eight while listening to her mother read—that formed her approach to the *Ariel* poems. During her last two years of her life, when she was writing reviews of children's literature, listening to BBC radio recordings nearly every day, and reading to her own children, she began composing poetry that was meant to be read out loud. Plath had taken Hughes's advice to write poems for their aural impact, relying less on visual expression. The rhythms, rhymes, and wordplay of children's books in particular, notably in the works of Dr. Seuss (his famous *Green Eggs and Ham* was published in 1960), were developed to great effect in groundbreaking poems such as "Daddy" and "Lady Lazarus." Yet Plath still used emotionally charged visual objects when composing for aural impact, for these are also the poems that critics cite for their visual effects. The red hair of "Lady Lazarus" and the black shoe of "Daddy" are among the more formidable images in the history of modern poetry.

Written the same month as these two famous poems, "Poppies in October" and one of its drafts demonstrate how Plath's highly developed color strategies delivered mood with subtlety and force. The final version only mentions the color red, but this red is not used to describe the late-blooming poppies, but the woman's heart that blooms (while the flowers wear skirts) in the poem's first lines:

> . . . sun-clouds . . . cannot manage such skirts.
> Nor the woman in the ambulance
> Whose red heart blooms through her coat . . .

Set against the cool, assumed black of bowler hats, the frost at dawn, and the blue of cornflowers in the following stanzas is the urgency of a medical emergency. Yet a draft version shows how Plath reduced the event to its simplest form, free of excess adjectives, objects, or exposition. Between the ambulance and the red heart she placed two lines, where white and gray are associated with death of a male and a state of uncertainty:

> The white, decorous hearse,
> . . . will roll him forever
> In to the diminishing grey architectural perspectives
> of limbo.[57]

Their deletion served to return the focus to red, to human life, to the woman whose heart opens.

The full-color, clustered descriptions Plath used in earlier poems were now largely relegated to letters and journal entries, often reserved for use in her fiction. The final poems are loaded with black, white, red, and blue imagery, with some green, gold, or silver. Even in late journal notes gathered for a planned poem dated October 21, the dozens of fleeting word fragments, placed within Dickinson-like dashes—from the heat of a woman's fury to the impersonal forces of nature she confronts—are all white and black, except for one reference to red:

Poem

Wild hot fury—cold snow: Thick white moor—mist—. . .
bunked blackbird: rage—. . . walk in white blank world—
symbol of shutting off from normal clear vision . . . black
stone fences—. . . red coal fires, burning cheeks . . . vast
power of cold, snow, stars & blackness . . . against small violent spark of will.[58]

For the person walking the moors, black and white passions are seen to
obscure the sense of "normal clear vision." Plath's rainbow palette,
after all, belonged to the world of modern art, to children and her
beloved flower gardens, to beginnings and hope, as seen in her "Midsummer Mobile" poem, where the artistic process of the young poet
began with a dip into "clear light" from which all colors emanate. During Sylvia Plath's final years, when she mastered her art and turned her
gaze on the world into powerful poetry, the division between her writing pen and paint brush had blurred.

NOTES

1. *LH*, 39–40. Aurelia Plath's edited version of this diary passage omitted
significant statements between Sylvia Plath's first and second famous quotes.
Acknowledging that she is dictating from the position of judge, along with omni-
science Plath hopes for a spark of "divine insanity," which she feels can reshape the
crippled existence that deforms humanity (4).

2. Plath's eight art poems are "Virgin in a Tree" and "Perseus, or The Triumph
of Wit Over Suffering," based on Klee's etchings of the same name; "Battle-Scene:
From the Comic Operatic Fantasy The Seafarer," after Klee's painting of the same
name; "The Ghost's Leavetaking," based on Klee's painting *The Departure of the
Ghost* (per Plath, *LH*, 336—perhaps also translated as *Fleeing Ghost*); "The Disqui-
eting Muses," based on de Chirico's painting of the same name; "On the Decline of
Oracles," after de Chirico's painting *The Enigma of the Oracle*; "Snakecharmer,"
based on the Rousseau painting *The Snake Charmer*; "Yadwigha, On a Red Couch,
Among Lilies: A Sestina for the Douanier," based on Rousseau's painting *The
Dream*.

3. Ted Hughes inaugurates the tradition of reading "Poem for a Birthday" as the
first sign of her *Ariel* voice in *Collected Poems* ("On Sylvia Plath," *Raritan* 14, no. 2
[1994]: 1–12).

4. The "Eye Rhymes: Visual Art and Manuscripts of Sylvia Plath" exhibition,
featuring 225 works from the Lilly and Smith collections, was held in conjunction
with the Sylvia Plath 70th Year Literary Symposium and Birthday Commemoration
in fall 2002 on the Bloomington campus of Indiana University.

5. E-mail from Karen Kukil of Smith's Mortimer Rare Book Room, December
16, 2004.

6. For a summary of benefits provided by interdisciplinary arts education, see http://communitydisc.westside66.org/HTML/sdm/whyarts.html. For principle publications of Howard Gardner and Eliot Eisner, two leading theorists on arts education and cognitive development, see www.pz.harvard.edu/PIs/HGpubs.htm and www.education.miami.edu/ep/contemporaryed/Eliott_Eisner/eliott_eisner .html. For cross-disciplinary traditions of linking visual learning to the archival histories and stylistic signatures of major twentieth-century writers, see Andrew Brown's *Roland Barthes: The Figures of Writing* (Oxford: Clarendon Press, 1992).

7. Letter and valentine to Otto Plath, February 20, 1940 (Smith: Series II. Correspondence, Otto Emil Plath); illustrated letter to Aurelia Plath, February 19, 1940 (Smith: Series II Correspondence, Aurelia Schober Plath).

8. Although Plath worked with all media at Smith College, she found oils difficult to manipulate and generally avoided using them. The largest portion of Plath's art and juvenilia is housed at Lilly. Along with many pastels, temperas, and ink drawings, works at both archives include numerous graphite sketches and portraits in a variety of formalist styles (mostly at Lilly); illustrated diaries (Lilly); colored pencil and mixed-media works, illustrated articles, gouache and watercolor paintings (both archives); illustrated poems (Lilly); illustrated journals (Smith); cartoons, a few photographs, and stencils (mostly at Lilly); a block print series (Lilly); painted furniture, one oil painting, and one formal collage (Smith). For a detailed analysis of this 1960 collage, the archives' latest artwork, see Robin Peel's *Writing Back: Sylvia Plath and Cold War Politics* (Madison, N.J.: Fairleigh Dickinson University Press; Cranbury, N.J.: Associated University Presses, 2002).

9. Lilly: Plath MSS II, Box 7, Folder 2.

10. Ibid.

11. Lilly: Plath MSS II, Box 8, Folder 15.

12. This twenty-six-page story is about a girl who befriends a fairy named "Stardust" (Lilly: Plath MSS II, Box 7, Folder 17).

13. Lilly: Plath MSS II, Box 7, Folder 3. "My Memory Book" is Plath's first 1947 diary that ended in July.

14. Ibid., February 10.

15. Lilly: Plath MSS II, Box 8, Folder 11.

16. Wanda Hazel Gág's diary is *Growing Pains: Diaries and Drawings for the Years 1908–1917* (New York: Coward-McCann, 1940).

17. Lilly: Plath MSS II, Box 7, Folder 3. This 1947–48 diary covers the second half of 1947 through March 1948 and contains decreasingly few illustrations. Plath kept a notepad dedicated to her summer dates and activities for two months at Star Island in 1949. Plath's formal 1949 diary booklet starts November 13, 1949, and has only a few entries thereafter on mundane events.

18. Smith: Series II, Correspondence, Ann Davidow (undated, 1951).

19. Lilly: Plath MSS II, Box 8, Folder 11.

20. *UJ*, 34–35 (undated, 1951).

21. Lilly: Plath MSS III, Large Format, Temperas, Folder 6 (titled for "Eye Rhymes" 2002 exhibition).

22. *UJ*, 54–56.

23. Ibid., 60.

24. Lilly: Plath MSS II, Box 8, Folder 8.

25. Lilly: Plath MSS II, Box 8, Folder 7.

26. Ibid.

27. Lilly: Plath MSS III, Large Format, Temperas, Folder 6 (titled for "Eye Rhymes" 2002 exhibition).

28. Lilly: Plath MSS II, Box 10, Folder 2.

29. Smith: Series II, Correspondence, Ann Davidow (undated, 1951).

30. Lilly: Plath MSS II, Box 9, Folder 1.

31. *CP*, 324.

32. *LH*, 336–37.

33. *UJ*, 35 (undated, 1950).

34. *JP*, 21.

35. *UJ*, 359.

36. Ibid.

37. Ibid., 510.

38. Ibid., 520–21.

39. Ibid., 520.

40. *CP*, 131.

41. *UJ*, 510.

42. *CP*, 130–31.

43. Ibid., 172–73.

44. Ibid.

45. Ibid., 272–73.

46. *UJ*, 525.

47. Ibid., 516.

48. Ibid., 507.

49. Ibid., 124–25.

50. For more information on Yaddo, see website: www.yaddo.org.

51. *UJ*, 359.

52. *LH*, 36.

53. *CP*, 265.

54. Smith, "Child," draft (holograph).

55. Lilly: Plath MSS II, Box 7, Folder July 16–Dec. 1946. This untitled poem was written in a letter home from camp (on June 25, 1946).

56. *JP*, 21.

57. Smith, "Poppies," draft (holograph).

58. *UJ*, 583 (no year noted).

Sylvia Plath's Voice, Annotated

One snow-lit January afternoon in 1958, Sylvia Plath and Ted Hughes spent their teatime listening to an album of the late Gene Derwood's poems, recorded before her death:

> A cardboard wrapped packet of a record for Ted, compliments of Oscar Williams, whom we have never met. His dead poet-ess-wife's face looms pale, high-cheekboned, with lowered eyes, out of the shiny record-cover with the eulogies on the back. For what reason? To haunt us with her live words, her live voice, her live face, she who lies some-where rotten, unstitching stitch by stitch? . . . So, blown ghost, she comes to our tea, more substantial then [sic] many inarticulate mortals. That is strange: the deadness of a stranger who is somehow never dead—the knife of death unfelt, the immortals hovers in our heads.[1]

Plath's reaction: fascinated, creeped out, studiously defensive, and romanticizing in equal parts. She was, that winter in Northampton, Massachusetts, an ambitious young writer burdened with early success, actively fretting in her journal over the nature of her own poetic voice and self-aggrandizing potential for literary immortality ("What is my voice? Woolfish, alas, but tough. Please, tough"),[2] while simultaneously teaching freshman English for a tortuous year at her alma mater, Smith College. Only Hughes, her husband of less than two years, had by then published his first book—in part thanks to Plath's already honed professionalism. The Sylvia Plath who had returned to Smith was weighed down as much by the urgency of her aspirations as by the external pressure toward traditional avenues of accomplishment that she felt from her family and her former teachers, now her colleagues. And that prodigal Plath is transparent in her simultaneous recoil from and hopeful anxiety toward Gene Derwood's voice: would someone, somewhere, some time be listening to her live words, her live voice when she was "unstitching, stitch by stitch"?

Forty years later, I was. I listened to audiocassettes of Sylvia Plath reading her poems and answering the questions of interviewers while I folded laundry, cooked dinners, sat at my desk, and drove my children to and from school and preschool. I knew the reason: I was writing a book about Plath and her assembly of the manuscript of *Ariel*. After many months of hearing Plath's voice, I was acutely attuned to her breath, her delivery, her nuanced emotions riding the surface of her poems as well as her carefully measured statements—her performance, in other words. Familiarity, in my case, did not breed contempt but overfamiliarity: I was lapsing into the cool mind of the maker, something that can overtake the initial fever of meaning and reduce it to so much imagined archaeology. I was hardly registering the ruthlessly affecting power and presence of a live performance—until the day I reached for the volume control on my car stereo and heard two voices recite in furious tandem,

> Soon, soon the flesh
> The grave cave ate will be
> At home on me
>
> And I a smiling woman.[3]

I looked up into the rearview mirror. I saw in the reflection my two-year-old daughter strapped into her car seat, grinning at me, reciting "Lady Lazarus" along with the poet, repeating words she didn't understand, but that the poet—and I—did.

Voice for Plath was a problem, a metaphor, a theme, a mode of access to a style for which she became famous. Figures of voice and voicelessness furnish a number of well-known motifs in *Ariel*: the theme of silence or being silenced as ominous, menacing, or downright harmful ("Elm" and "Medusa"); the theme of listening to external voices that are frequently unintelligible or parasitic (for example, the stampede of "jungle gutturals" let loose by the weak husband's revelation in "A

Secret");[4] the theme of the speaker's voice as valuable and powerful, but potentially threatening to others—it shrieks, screams, astounds, frightens ("Do not be afraid," the narrator has to reassure the person addressed in "A Birthday Present," "No falling ribbons, no scream at the end. / I do not think you credit me with this discretion").[5] Yet critical studies of Plath have generally neglected the contexts of Plath's voice *recordings,* the performed and recorded word as a dimension of her art and cultural reception.

I am interested in annotating Plath's voice in at least two ways: I want to consider voice as a subject that becomes more complex in the evolution of Plath's voice recordings, and I offer commentary and explanation on contexts of well-known and difficult-to-access (and consequently less well known recordings), noting how these embodiments of voice coalesce in the trajectory of Plath's development as a poet. (The "Oral Archive," an annotated guide to commercially released and unpublished recordings made during Plath's lifetime, some archived at Harvard and Smith, others at the National Sound Archive located in the British Library, is included as an appendix at the end of this volume.)

While the performed word is as old as poetry itself, attention to audiotexts of poets in performance has increasingly become the focus of what Charles Bernstein terms "close listening"—a recognition of the complex, multilayered, multiply coded dimensions of the acoustics of utterance, apprehended in the presence or absence of a text.[6] Such a tuning of the ear involves both public and private orientations. Published tapes offer a "public tuning" of a voice recorded; but listening to the spoken word that performance evokes also involves intersubjective dimensions. As a more intimate record, the spaces of close listening have also been described as a kind of "holding environment" between poems and persons. In sounding—and listening to—language, then, we indeed find what poet-critic Nick Piombino suggests are "analogies to the world that grounds us in sentient relations and transactions."[7]

Plath's Voice, Recorded

What is astounding about the recorded voice of Sylvia Plath, so many years after her self-inflicted death during the frozen London winter of 1963, is that it remains such an *embodied* voice, especially in the poems and interviews and prose audiotaped in the last years of her life, in which the full force of the signifying body is evoked, but also, in a different way, in the recordings made earlier in her career. Susan Stewart reminds us that we can never reproduce the acoustic conditions of a poem's production or performance at a given moment in time—there is always an element of recasting, of assigning qualities to the "play of transformation" in language so that grains of association (of timbre, of articulation, of resonance), are attributed to a single speaking person.[8] But this hasn't stopped many close listeners, myself included, from rendering impressions of Plath's voice, fixing the fluidity of sound, and finding that these soundings signify.

A considerable history of critical impressions of Plath's voice follow a similar route of listening and recasting, often resorting to metaphorical extravagance. "The earnestness and opulence of her earlier work is apparent in the poet's delivery," wrote poet-critic J. D. McClatchy, responding to a recording Plath made in Springfield, Massachusetts, in 1958: "This is a world of forest-shadow and mirror-sheen, of sculpted silences and watery tangles, and Plath's singing style—rich and exact—matches the weave of the work."[9] Those early recordings are almost too revealing of Plath the poet, a magician pulling levers behind a sheer curtain; their diction, as novelist Cynthia Ozick comments, is "burnished, precise, almost inhumanly perfected,"[10] but it isn't until the late recordings that Plath seems to feel, to inhabit, rather than intellectually cogitate upon what she's saying. Plath's reading voice in the early recordings, mimicking her figurative voice in the early poetry, as McClatchy noted, "consistently portrays her prowess as a poet rather than her experience as a woman."[11] For these critics, the dramatic trajectory of her evolution as a poet—and her embrace, however painful, of her life as a woman—is inescapably evident in the voice overheard in recordings made after the breakup of her marriage to Hughes: "In the 1962 recordings she does not exaggerate or melodramatize—she lives the poems, and the intensity is almost unbearable," wrote Wen Stephensen in the April 2000 issue of *Atlantic Monthly*.[12] Uncanny and supple and under exquisite, thrilling control, Plath's voice in the late recordings impresses Ozick as "dark and deep and dangerous . . . its register is surprisingly low and nearly sinister; it surprises and unsettles."[13] The poems and the poet, like the horse Ariel and its rider, have become one, a driving force in the late recordings:

"the stanzas work like pistons," according to McClatchy.[14] And the result is that "you can hear all the colors of her kaleidoscopic voices, unstilled and unblanched by the grave-cave," as Erica Jong commented in the *New York Times Book Review*.[15]

The "true, deep voice" that Plath sought was not a critical invention after the fact, but a conscious goal we find underscored frequently in the *Unabridged Journals*: "What inner decision, what inner murder or prison-break must I commit if I want to speak from my true deep voice in writing . . . and not feel this jam up of feeling behind a glass-dam fancy façade of numb dumb wordage."[16] Nonetheless, Plath's performed voice is as much a plurality as her famously changeable personality. Always attracted to complication, even as a toddler Plath would ask her mother for "a many"; many things of the same size and kind—beads or blocks or bits of whatever, "anything that could be placed in order and design."[17] Later Plath looked for "a many" in the intricate structures and rhyming patterns of her poetry, in her relentlessly industrious domestic life, and in her visual art; Ted Hughes wrote that she was compulsively, almost perversely attracted to making drawings of anything "complicated and chaotic, like a high heap of junk."[18] By the fall of 1962, Plath was no longer primarily a poet of visual rhythms on the page, a poet who counted off syllables on her fingers as Hughes observed her doing in his poem "Portraits," with its memory of her composition of "Medallion" at Yaddo in September 1959:

> . . . your fingers counting
> The touches of your thumb, delicately
> Untangling on your fingers a music
> That only you could hear.[19]

Plath states definitively in her October 1962 interview with Peter Orr that she had recently undergone a technical development in the writing of poetry: she was now composing poems to be read aloud, and she felt the necessity of hearing her own words as they formed; the style that marked her earlier work now bored her.[20] Commenting in a BBC program in September 1963 on the radical shift in Plath's late work, critic A. Alvarez further defines the accomplishment of *Ariel* as a disturbance of sound. Alvarez observes that unexpectedness is no longer by rote—a gesture on the surface of the poem. It is instead part of what she's actually saying. . . . The difference, in short, is between finger count and ear count. One measures the movement by rules, the other catches the rhythm by the disturbance it creates. And she could only write poems out loud when she discovered her own speaking voice, that is, her identity.[21]

Here Alvarez has echoed Plath's comment in her October 1962 interview in which she registers her excitement about the oral life of poetry; increasingly Plath recognizes poetry recordings and readings as a return to the "old role of the poet, which was to speak to a group of people, to come across. . . . To sing to a group of people."[22]

At a November 2004 reading to which I return near the end of this essay, Plath's daughter, Frieda Hughes, told a rapt audience what it was like to read her mother's manuscript of *Ariel* for the first time, in preparation for the long-awaited publication of *Ariel: The Restored Edition.* "I saw how she put her emotions to work," Frieda Hughes said of her mother, "each one a string to her instrument."[23] We can listen closely, then, to each of these strings in Plath's recordings—to the orchestral warm-up, as she rolls her tongue over confected early phrases like "dolt pig ripe for heckling" or "Shrilling her hulk / To halt for a swig"[24] or "the house still hugs in each drab / Stucco socket / The purple egg-stones,"[25] revealing a voice that struggles with ladylike poise to keep vocal pace with the grandiloquent rhythmic schemes she patterned on the page. There is the brittle earnestness of her ambition in the recordings of 1958 and 1959: that clipped, high nasal voice, the cultivated East Coast Smith-girl enunciation, the fastidious way she pronounces "po-eh-trayh" and "Vat-ee-CAN" and "palOOstrul." One can count the repetition of coy mannerisms in which she appears to disguise fiercely believed opinions: "if I may" and "I must say." In the later recordings of 1962, she is snatching flaming arrows bare-handed out of the sky in efficient, needle-sharp phrases (or so it seems to me) such as "Christ! they are panes of ice, / A vice of knives, / A piranha / Religion, drinking / Its first communion out of my live toes."[26] One can marvel at her perfect-pitch dramatic modulations, at poems in which emotions and characterizations evolve one from the other, just as her metaphors transmogrify—"Fever 103°" for example. Or hear her unscripted chuckles of surprise at an interviewer's question or response, and her stage-whispered conspiratorial asides, such as this one to Peter Orr: "*anything* but writers. I think writers are the *most* narcissistic people. Well, I *mustn't* say this, I like *many* of them, a great many of my friends are writers."[27]

Lee Anderson Recording (1958)

"I shall try, later, to record that memorable Friday recording poems in Springfield."[28] Unfortunately, Plath did not complete this journal entry of her experience of reading her poems and being interviewed on April 18, 1958, by Lee Anderson in Springfield, Massachusetts. Plath had been recorded twice before, once in 1955 on the Mt. Holyoke College station, WMHC, when she tied for first place in the Glascock poetry contest, and a second time in November 1957 for the Woodberry Poetry Room at Harvard's Lamont Library; since both of these recordings seem to be lost, the Springfield session is the earliest recording of Plath still available to listeners.[29]

Nine of the thirteen poems Plath read at Springfield were recorded subsequently in another session, again for Harvard's Lamont Library on June 13, 1958. Stephen Tabor's *Sylvia Plath: An Analytical Bibliography* gives details of the idiosyncracies in these and other readings, including isolated word changes and sometimes entire stanzas dropped from the final published version of the poems. Those inside details are often fascinating. Why, for example, did Plath change the word "tits" for "teats" in the published version of "Sow"?[30] Did she decide "tits" was too vulgar, though she used it later in "The Courage of Shutting-Up"? Now that the National Sound Registry has archived online histories of recording sessions with well-known writers, we also know how Plath registered herself in an unusual way in the autograph book Lee Anderson used to document recordings, quoting the first line of the last stanza of "The Lady and the Earthenware Head": "Yet, shrined on her shelf, the grisly visage endured."[31] The earthenware head of this poem is itself an emblem of authorship—did Plath intend herself to be remembered in this way? To what extent are the apparent idiosyncrasies of changes in text from reading to reading the result of her awareness of shifts in settings, from the more collegial contexts of the university recording studio to the more public settings of the BBC?

"Sostenuto" is how Hughes characterized Plath's Chaucer recitation to a herd of cows in his *Birthday Letter* poem, "Chaucer"[32]—a scene captured with precision by actors Gwyneth Paltrow and Daniel Craig in the recent film *Sylvia*—and it's an apt description of Plath's reading style in this earliest example of her lofty, heavily postured reading voice. A musical directive from the Latin *sustinere,* meaning "to sustain," *sostenuto* means to play at a slow but sustained tempo, holding each note for its full value. In response to Anderson's questioning her about the musicality and rhythm in her poetry, Plath says she'd "ideally" like to be "musical" without being "artificial," which I think is sometimes difficult. Indeed, the proof of its difficulty is Plath's "sustaining" of each sound as she forms it, creating almost a dissection of the words and phrases in the resulting slow, stilted formality of her delivery. "But I don't want to baffle anybody," she comments during the interview as she gives her opinion of the importance of readers being able to understand the poem from the start—as opposed to simply "ramping about" in sound, or pursuing musicality and lyricism for its own sake. Addressing the topic of reading poetry aloud, in the same recording, Plath states that the reason poetry is often "ugly to the ear" is that its patterns and rhymes are made for the eye. Although she thinks that poetry should be readable on and off the page, with musical as well as visual qualities, she draws her aesthetic line in the sand when she declares that she likes "ugly" effects. "I mean, one of my favorite sounds is *rock . . . black*—all words that go against that very hard 'k' sound, and yet—which, of course, I suppose, are *ugly,* they're all piled up, but they're not to me."[33]

Although Lee Anderson's questions on even the best-quality copy of this recording are muffled and often not much more than a background muttering, Plath's voice is clear and present, fairly relaxed, but at times betraying a light diffidence as she finishes her response, her final comments sometimes fading out almost apologetically. This is perhaps what is most interesting about this recording. Plath's reading is a demonstration of where she is developmentally: she admits in a comment that she has no idea what reaction readers or listeners have to her work, as so few have seen it. In one subtle but touching moment, Plath addresses Hughes for his opinion, apparently turning toward him, the physical shift suggested by the shifting timbre of her voice, which softens with intimacy as she asks him her question. Earlier in the recording, Hughes makes a humorous quip—incomprehensible on the tape—to which Plath bursts out laughing, unself-conscious and apparently genuinely amused. "*Nothing* else! Doing *nothing* else!" she says with accentuated facetiousness at another point, in answer to whether she allowed any incursion into all-consuming attention toward the writing of a poem.[34]

This recording locates Plath's first public reference to W. B. Yeats as an important prosodic influence, when Plath is asked about the poets she reads, a list that, in addition to Yeats, who she likes "*very, very* much," includes Hughes, T. S. Eliot, John Crowe Ransom, Robert Lowell, Thomas Wyatt, Gerald Manley Hopkins, Shakespeare, and Chaucer. Elaborating on her answer, Plath reveals what it was in Yeats that had influenced her prosody—"I learned my first changing in sound, assonance and consonance, from Yeats—which, I mean, actually it's technical—I was very excited when I discovered this. . . . I'd never worked with anything but rhyme and very rigid rhythm, and so I began developing themes and patterns of sound that were somehow less obvious." Such patterns come "through your ear if not through your eye." And, she adds, this she "just happened" to learn from Yeats.[35]

"Poets in Partnership" (1961)

The joint interview that Sylvia Plath and Ted Hughes recorded in mid-January 1961 for the BBC series *Two of a Kind*—the episode was titled "Poets in Partnership" when it aired on January 31—took place at the culmination of a monumental year in the careers and marriage of the couple, the year in which they took up residence in England. For Hughes, 1960 saw the release of his second acclaimed collection, *Lupercal*, during the same month that his first collection, *The Hawk in the Rain*, won the prestigious Somerset Maugham Award. At the BBC the broadcasting of poetry and plays written for the air offered Hughes what it offered a number of other poets—an environment that favored risk-taking and new forms of intimacy with the listener, a public role in defending the values of literature against those who feared its decline, and an alternative to teaching.[36] Plath wrote to her mother that Hughes's income from the BBC that year had equaled a salary.[37] Nonetheless, Hughes found the "literary life" exhausting and counter to his need for time and privacy to write; late in 1960 he turned down the BBC's offer to appear as "Poet of the Year."[38]

Achievement came more easily to Plath as well. By her twenty-ninth birthday on October 27, her first poetry collection, *The Colossus and Other Poems*, was published in England, and Plath was writing short stories, publishing new poems in notable magazines, and had received a guest editing commission from the respected journal *Critical Quarterly* as well as being featured on the BBC's *Poet's Voice* series. Although *The Colossus* garnered nowhere near the degree of attention that Hughes's poetry had received, Plath had been recognized as a "New Yorker poet in her own right" in the *Observer* by A. Alvarez, who later in the year wrote a significant, insightful, if not wholly laudatory review of her first book.[39] Despite their impressive list of literary accomplishments, the most significant event of 1960 in the lives of both Plath and Hughes was the birth of their first child, Frieda, on April 1.

Although it is arguable whether Plath would have, like Hughes, turned down an invitation to be anyone's "Poet of the Year," the temperamental differences and complementarities highlighted by the *Two of a Kind* interview demonstrate how in sync Plath and Hughes were in their shared ambition of building a life that individually supported their creative goals, and in particular did not assume a sacrifice of Plath's literary career at the altar of motherhood. In the introduction to *Her Husband: Hughes and Plath—A Marriage,* Diane Middlebrook locates the "plot" of the "Poets in Partnership" dialogue.

> The interviewer, Owen Leeming, asked whether theirs was a "marriage of opposites." As if in a movie by Woody Allen, Hughes said they were "very different" at the same moment Plath said they were "quite similar."[40]

Hughes, in explaining his answer, conceded the compatibility of their tempo of living and their sympathetic, even telepathic union in a "single shared mind" while clarifying his belief that their imaginations led "secret lives." Middlebrook concludes that at this time of their lives, the account that Hughes and Plath give of their "creative partnership" suggests "contradictory forces" in their relationship were operating in a "dynamic balance."[41]

That balance extended itself to actively seeking out ways to free each other from the distractions of a child and the responsibilities of public life. In January 1961 Plath was working each afternoon at a temporary copyediting job for *The Bookseller,* a trade magazine, bringing in extra income that permitted Hughes to concentrate on his current play. Hughes shared in caring for the baby, a responsibility split by the couple just as they split the windfall of using neighbor W. S. Merwin's study: Plath wrote in the morning while Hughes took care of Frieda, and they reversed roles at midday.

Implicitly, the *Two of a Kind* recording for the BBC brought Plath closer to a broader audience of "professional writers," with the "professional" and the "private" life juxtaposed. In the 1960 Christmas card in which Plath tells her family, "Ted and I will probably decide to appear on a radio program called *Two of a Kind,* an interview series with husbands and wives who have the same profession," she also states, "I am very excited that children seem to be an impetus to my writing, and it is only the lack of space that stands in my way."[42] Asked by Leeming in the *Two of a Kind* interview how the baby had changed her life, Plath replies in largely pragmatic terms—rather than being devoured by motherhood, she's found that Frieda is an easy baby who is content to play by herself and rarely cries and fusses; she fits in beautifully to the household routine, providing both parents with endless entertainment and inspiration for poems.[43] But Plath was also attuned to the psychological shift in herself since becoming a mother, expressed in a letter after the birth of Nicholas in January 1962:

> I have the queerest feeling of having been reborn with Frieda—It's as if my real, rich, happy life only started just about then. I suppose it's a case of knowing what one wants. I never really knew before. . . . I feel I'm just beginning at writing, too.[44]

Hughes's poem "Remission," in *Birthday Letters,* appears in tune with Plath's self-description on this point: she "flourished only / In becoming fruitful. . . . / That was the you / You loved and wanted to live with."[45] He adopts imagery likening Plath's maturity, through motherhood, as a matter of artifices peeling away when he describes the maternal Plath as being like the innermost, solid doll of a *matroyshka* nesting doll set.

The Plath whose voice is captured by *Two of a Kind* sounds more sure of herself and of her opinions than in earlier recordings. Her voice is unexpectedly placid and paced, although periodically emphatic, as when she recalls first reading a poem by a Ted Hughes at Cambridge: "I was very impressed [and] . . . wanted to meet him."[46] The British inflection has seeped in here. But the most intriguing statement on this recording is by Hughes, an ambiguous comment regarding Frieda's impact on their lives. After Plath states that she and Hughes had each written a number of poems to their daughter, Hughes suggests that the poems are not just to Frieda, but also written through the agency of her inspiration; he figures Frieda as "kind of aerial."[47] Or does he mean "kind of Ariel, who brought such beautiful unearthly music into Shakespeare's The Tempest?" Middlebrook wonders in Her Husband.[48] Both explanations, in the analysis of Hughes's statement, have validity, though Frieda-as-Ariel, for Hughes, may have been less about the musicality of Frieda's sounds echoing through the household than of Ariel as a "daemon of the Goddess's transcendental positive magic"— that is, fertility and flowering and redemption—which Hughes would later write about in Shakespeare and the Goddess of Complete Being.[49] This interpretation is given further credence by Hughes's poem "Isis," in Birthday Letters, which begins with the invocation of the embryonic Frieda as the couple's "lightest / Bit of luggage"[50] at the end of their two-year sojourn in America and culminates, at Frieda's birth, with Hughes's observation that their antiquarian engraving of Magnae Deorum Matris—the many-named great goddess Isis, the muse of poetry, the moon goddess, the great mother of the gods—had become personified in Plath.

Recordings with Marvin Kane (1961–62)

Less than a year after she had settled in England, Plath made additional recordings for the BBC, two of them facilitated in some way by Marvin Kane, an American-born author and actor. The BBC practice of pairing actors with poets (a male voice would be typically paired with a woman poet's) for poetry readings was indicative of the close, cooperative relationships between dramatic and literary performances at the Third Programme; these pairings encouraged theatrical as well as call-and-response effects of a kind similar to those appearing in Plath's and

Hughes's poems around the same time.[51] On June 5, 1961, Plath recorded a twenty-five-minute selection of nine of her poems with commentary for the BBC Third Programme series *The Living Poet*, for broadcast in July 1961. Poems were read alternately by Plath and Kane, although the commentaries were read exclusively by Plath. The circumstances leading to the joint reading are not known, although Plath wrote to her mother that she was paid sixty dollars for the morning of recording, accomplished with "an American boy reader for some of them," and that she would be paid additionally for the poems themselves.[52]

Although not shrill, Plath's performing voice in this reading of her poems is higher pitched than it will be in later recordings—perhaps a tremor of nervous eagerness to do well. After making a general introduction to the poems as being about "the things of this world" (a side compliment to Richard Wilbur), Plath reads "The Disquieting Muses" before Kane continues with "Sleep in the Mohave Desert" and "Suicide off Egg Rock." Somewhat surprisingly, since it is such an early poem, Plath then reads "Spinster" (dated 1956 in *CP*), which she introduces by saying it is a poem about a woman who is "in love with order" and "all that is formal"[53]—true to perfectionistic form, Plath meticulously emphasizes her correct pronunciation of "tumult" as "TOO-mult." Interestingly, Kane reads "You're" and "Magi," poems that emerged out of Plath's recent shift into motherhood, a role that she addresses with discreet indirection in her knowing commentaries to these poems as well as in poems she reads herself on this recording, such as "Parliament Hill Fields," written in elegiac response to a pregnancy lost early in 1961.

Kane reads "Medallion" after "Magi," and the tape seems to have caught the unmistakable sound of stomachs rumbling in the studio. Plath closes with "The Stones," the final segment of her multipart "Poem for a Birthday," written in November 1959 at Yaddo. In an essay on Plath's journals first published in *Grand Street*, Hughes designates "The Stones" as the poem that ushered in Plath's final phase of artistic maturity, calling it the "birth of her real poetic voice."[54] Plath's prissy mispronunciation of "lichens" as "litchens" is less interesting than her commentary on "The Stones," during which she states that the speaker has "utterly lost her sense of identity"; in Hughes's account of the composition of this poem, which captures the essence of what is spoken on tape, her recovery begins as she accepts the renewal of bonds that will lead "the self, shattered," to "suddenly find itself whole."[55]

In letters to her mother, Plath mentions a second interview with Kane—and the subsequent fan letters she received after the BBC broadcast—but the interview itself, entitled "What Made You Stay?" has never been published, and to my knowledge has not been illuminated in any critical writing on Plath. Snippets from it were used in the Public Broadcasting Series *Voices and Visions* video production.[56] Its obscurity is a pity, because Plath is at her most wittily appealing and, for the most part, unguarded in this interview. The historical context of the recording, known through Plath's correspondence and her journal, adds resonance and humor to Plath's comments.

In late March 1962, Marvin Kane had written to Plath about the possibility of interviewing her for a program to be broadcast on the BBC Home Service; the topic was Americans who choose to live in England—"What Made You Stay?"—something Plath and Kane had in common. While delighted at the invitation, Plath responded that it would be virtually impossible for her to come to London for a taping, as her son was only eight weeks old; she suggested that Kane conduct the interview by tape recorder at Court Green. Although Plath was already back at work in her study ("just happy piddling,"[57] she wrote to her mother) and publishing poems that had been submitted to magazines before the baby's birth, she had reason to be pleased at the prospect of the interview as a chance to reassert herself professionally.

Kane and his wife, Kathy, accompanied by an acquaintance and her two young children, came to Court Green on April 10, 1962, on their way to a short holiday in Cornwall. Plath later recorded her indignance at the bad manners of the visiting children in a letter to her mother and in her journal: the children, ages five and six, tracked mud through Court Green, "descended shrieking,"[58] on playthings, disturbed the baby, and ran noisily through the rooms, creating, no doubt, a less than ideal atmosphere in which to expound on her expatriate opinions for the benefit of a radio audience she was keen to cultivate. But in the audiotape, she gives a charming, droll, and tempered interview that outlines her idiosyncratic observations and opinions on British life. Her voice is high and a bit nasal until she laughs, her frequent, deep chuckle betraying how much she was enjoying herself despite the squealing, door-slamming children in her house whose behavior she pointedly addresses when she states why she prefers to raise her children in England. Explaining that she is a bit old-fashioned—a claim she makes frequently in her interview—Plath states that she and her husband find that American children tend to be given too much freedom and social centrality, while in England there was still a trace of the Victorian attitude that children must fit into adult life, rather than adults scrambling to fit their lives around children.[59] Plath intimated to her mother, in her blow-by-blow letter after the event, that the visiting little monsters were Australian, *not* Brits.

Plath's comments on this reel-to-reel tape suggest she was aware of the presence of a larger listening audience for the BBC's Third Programme, a literary audience just out of sight from the English country setting in which the recording was made. After making the expected Anglophile noises regarding remembering one's childhood reading of Dickens and other English literature when walking the streets of London, Plath takes pains to position herself and Hughes as writers who lead a "peculiar" life to which England is more hospitable than America, where they would have difficulty pursuing lives as artists while also maintaining a "normal and rather placid family life" without being pressured. She explains that they live in the country, an ideal situation in which the "voices . . . are really of cows and sheep,"[60] and yet the cultural enticements of London are still accessible.

While commenting that weather affects her mood, Plath misspeaks—the weather "infects" her—and laughs at herself.[61] Plath's letters from this period tell of the lengthy, wet, and cold winter that year, and her knowledge of its morbid effect on her attitude; she had even joked to her mother that if the weather didn't change before the Kanes' arrival, she might not have anything positive to say about why she stayed in England. Perhaps with this thought still lingering, Plath begins to tell about her "joy" in learning that no place in England is more than seventy miles from the seaside, only to have her story sidetracked into a recounting of a depressing trip to a Yorkshire seaside village complete with pouring rain, mucky beach littered with gum wrappers, and soggy people on summer holiday in their woolens. As she continues unself-consciously, her voice is full of mocking astonishment about the awful trip—the sooty ugliness of Yorkshire, the people foolish enough to think they're having a holiday, the trashiness of it all—lingering over how disheartening and bleak she found this introduction to the English seaside to be. Almost imperceptibly, Plath's voice slows when she comes back to her topic, her audience, and herself. Finally, she blurts optimistically that she's hoping for sunshine and the beaches of Cornwall this summer—an insider's wink to her new friends, the Kanes.

Plath's description of English butcher shops on this recording is Plathian in wit and description: she describes, first, shopping for meat in America, with its automatic doors opening of their own accord, "Muzak playing tender melodies" while one stands at the counter, and the behind-the-scenes mystery of beef wrapped bloodlessly in cellophane.[62] By contrast, she expresses shock at first seeing English butcher shops with blood on the floor and whole pigs hanging from the ceiling, large and pink and "turning themselves off and on." Plath says she's become devoted to British butcher shops and the need to understand cuts of meat, a "creative process" for both the shopper and the butcher, whose precision comes from "some marvelous intuition." The interview ends with Plath's appreciation of British eccentricity. She tells of the first English home in which she stayed overnight and of her hostess's industrious work at a charmingly quaint, English hobby, which turned out, on closer inspection, to be a needlepoint pattern for penicillium mold. The footstools had needlepoint covers not of flowers or cherubs but of geometric rattlesnake skin patterns. Marvin Kane can be heard snickering in the background of the tape as Plath concludes, tongue in cheek, by telling that this same hostess, at bedtime, offered her a hot water bottle or a cat. Plath deadpans that she chose the cat.

Recordings with Peter Orr (1962)

Later the same year, in six letters to her mother, brother, and Olive Prouty, there is no mistaking Plath's heady, restless anticipation of her trip to London to be interviewed and record her new poems on October 29 and 30, 1962, with Peter Orr. Plath had more than adequate reasons to take this opportunity so to heart. On the professional side, Plath would be recording "Berck-Plage" for BBC broadcast in November, now her estranged husband's peer in this illustrious professional arena; presenting her new work to *Observer* critic A. Alvarez, who recently told her she was "the first woman poet he'd taken seriously since Emily Dickinson";[63] meeting with the head of the British Council, who had offered her the chance to organize and present the American poetry night of the international Poetry Festival to be held at Royal

Court Theater the following year; and would return to the BBC a second time to be interviewed by Peter Orr and record fifteen of her new poems for the Harvard Lamont Library. Socially, there was reason to be nervous: she had plans to stay with friends and attend a literary party for an anthology to which she had contributed, but more significantly, this was her "coming out" in London's literary circles after her breakup with Hughes. Given the bone-crunching work and loneliness of single parenthood and the dazzling, unexpected outpouring of her new poems, she was, as she had written in "A Birthday Present" that fall, "ready for enormity."[64]

Plath's interview with Orr is marked by an air of self-possession. Conversational, quick-witted, and responsive, Plath shows her eagerness to engage and to be engaged, her intelligence sharp-edged and natural. Answering Orr's questions about what subjects attract her attention, Plath expresses her excitement regarding the recent movement into "taboo" subjects in American poetry, particularly in the work of Robert Lowell and Anne Sexton: "this intense breakthrough" into "serious, very personal emotional experience." And yet she is careful to qualify her interest—in her own work as well as in the work of others—in "sensuous and emotional experiences" that are controlled and artistically manipulated, not untransformed "cries from the heart." Delving further into her own position as an American writer living in England, on occasion feeling the "full weight of English literature on me," Plath identifies the danger of gentility in English poetry: "I must say," she states with emphasis, using one of her favorite recurring expressions, "that I am not very genteel." When Orr suggests that she is a poet and a woman who "straddles the Atlantic," Plath's answer— that hers was an "awkward position, but I'll accept it"—is delivered with the oral equivalent of a smirk.[65]

Transcripts of the Orr interviews, later organized in a collection, *The Poet Speaks* (1964), with a preface by Frank Kermode, offer us something else, too—a way to locate the emergence of Plath's *Ariel* voices in an acoustic environment in which taped recordings of poems are increasingly embedded in conversational formats. In Orr's terms, the interview setting, "produc[ed], as far as possible, the flavor of conversation which might crop up between friends who share a common interest." Orr's introduction to the interview scripts from the *The Poet Speaks* hint at just what was at stake, as he saw it, in a recorded reading and conversation format that might re-create intimacies of listening without, however, appearing to cater to the tastes associated with the less bookish audiences for the "inquisitorial" television talk shows that "seem to have become fashionable of late in interviews on radio and television."[66] While improvisational techniques of conversation may have been foregrounded, lending a recorded "quality of immediacy" to the voice, the issue that worries Frank Kermode, in his reluctant preface, is that the new "force field" of literary spoken word events, the "revived fashion of speaking verse aloud," ran the risk of overtaking the older, modernist ideal of the poet as a learned scholar.[67] Kermode's preface to Orr's collection singles out Plath's recording in particular; he notices that within the new "genre" of interview and recording common to the cultural programming at the BBC, "one cannot avoid being impressed by the manner in which all" poets, presumably including Plath, "embrace the new medium, avoiding 'speaking by the book,'" as he puts it; at the same time, Kermode openly worries about the proximity of the new poetry to the "pseudo-events of television, the half-lies of advertising," fearing that it will "reduce our interest in actuality and truth."[68] There was the new poetry, then, and there was the new, presumably more dangerous, poetry that challenged the authority of impersonality with the flavor of the casual, conversational pseudo-event. Without her knowledge, Plath's voice recording in Peter Orr's studio is drawn into the net of controversy over the gradients between pseudoconfession and the "real thing." This is a controversy that will trouble confessionalism—and Plath's reception—for some decades to come.[69]

But the sound of Plath's reading of her poems—the risks and the extension of her range of voices—is the watershed: it is, simply, a staggeringly affecting reading (one imagines the sound technicians agog in the glassed-in studio). The voice is deeper, more supple, more insistent, more controlled, and, interestingly, it is more easily colloquial in its handling of American vernacular expression. The "terrifically hard" goal she pursued to "speak out, you know, straight out, the way you talk . . . while getting all the allusions and richness in"—spoken of four years before in her Springfield interview—has been achieved.[70] Each of the fifteen poems Plath reads in this session works theatrically to produce a distinct tone, dramatic action, and personae. The personae serve as cues for vocal performance. The result is that the consistent undertone of voice we are often taught to listen for becomes, at another level, a remarkable, and at times startling array of vocal and acoustic possibilities.

If the recording in October 1962 constitutes a kind of early anthologizing of *Ariel* poems, it is an anthologizing in which the order of poems maximizes crescendo effects and insists on overlapping connections between public and private. The implied listener for the late poems is, like the poet herself, someone who is more capable of taking risks in an acoustic environment that foregrounds an expanded and more concentrated range of performance-effects already available in the theatricalized situation of the poem. Plath begins with "The Rabbit Catcher," which is cool and serene, an elegy on low simmer. "Ariel" is next, delivered in a clipped staccato, verging on the imperious in its urgency. "Poppies in October," like "Ariel" written just three days prior to the recording, is delivered in an anguished voice, its power held back, on the verge of unstoppable release with the expressive mime, "Oh my god, what am I. . . ."[71] "The Applicant," however, has an altogether different delivery; Plath's tone here is chilled, emotionless, sneering. "Lady Lazarus" follows, relentless and disdainful, challenging and caustic, Plath's emotions concentrating themselves into episodes, at times welling with near-overflow of emotion ("The sour breath / Will vanish in a day"), at other times sarcastic and full of loathing ("What a trash / To annihilate each decade. / What a million filaments."), and at others rolling into singsong ("I rocked shut / As a sea shell").[72]

In "A Secret," Plath's humor bites through the scorn of her delivery as she stalks almost breathlessly through her taunts, changing masks hand to hand in the imagined exchange, drawing out the pronunciation of lingerie ("laansheray") comically. "Cut," too, has subversive humor and reticulating echoes ("O my / Homunculus, I am ill. / I have taken a pill to kill")[73] refuted by the poem's grisly scenario, which renders tone—almost a caricature of her early reading style—nothing less than harrowing. "Stopped Dead," though, is blatantly funny, Plath's voice derisive and facetious. She delivers the line, "Is that *Spain* down there?"[74] with mocking surprise: perhaps a private swipe at Hughes, who, she had recently learned, had disappeared with Assia Wevill to Spain—where Plath and Hughes had spent their honeymoon. Hughes also appears in "Nick and the Candlestick"; once an ardent panther who hunted Plath down in the first poem written to him in March 1956, now Hughes is the figure of Atlas being clawed and castrated by the panther pelt he wears on his head. She delivers the last line with droll relish: "I leave to *you* the mystery."[75]

Plath is even more bold in the reading of "A Birthday Present," in which she allows her voice to play the scales of her emotions. She cajoles, she questions, she flatters and jeers and shames and manipulates, her voice curdling with nastiness as she underscores "my sheets, the *cold dead* center / Where spilt lives *congeal* and *stiffen* to history," and threatening in its anger in "The world will go up in a shriek, and your head with it." But the coup de grace is the line delivered with withering innuendo: "Do not be ashamed—I do not mind if it is *small*," the word "small" emphasized with an upward inflection.[76] "Purdah," in contrast, is a case study in murderous seduction, an incantatory, undulant, sensuous reading until the terrifyingly ferocious delivery of the phrase "the small jeweled / Doll he guards like a heart"[77]—each word a mortal blow.

The last poem of this set that Plath reads, "Fever 103°," is a showcase of ecstatic delirium as well as the most meticulously shaped combination of sound and letter in its prosodic effects. Plath's dramatic voices as well as images melt into the poem's fevered synaesthesias—"All by myself . . . a huge camellia / Glowing and coming and going, flush on flush"[78]—giving us at once an oracle intoxicated by the smoke of the candle, a grumpy-voiced invalid, or a heroic Camille on the verge of a faint as images evolve from candle smoke to scarves caught in a wheel to radioactive fallout, from baby to orchid to leopard to ash. Plath likely recognizes the triumph not just of this poem but of her commanding reading of it; she chose it in December 1962 to end the script she wrote for the BBC as well.

Douglas Cleverdon Recording (1962)

In a letter dated December 11, 1962, BBC Program Features producer Douglas Cleverdon wrote to Plath to suggest a twenty-minute program of reading and commentary of her new poems.[79] Plath would have had reason to be aware of Cleverdon's status as one of the prime movers behind innovative programming at the Third Programme.[80] Hughes had been working closely—lucratively—for several years with Cleverdon, who had produced Hughes's plays and hired him for broadcast work; in August, Cleverdon had produced Plath's *Three Women,* a play written for radio. Although Plath had not taken part as a reader, it would be a mistake to underestimate the impact that both writing for radio and making spoken word recordings of her own work was having for her development as a writer.

Cleverdon's interest in her poetry and in her return to London supplied Plath with even more of a sense of reconnection and renewed "voice"—that figurative lifeline—than the sums of money Cleverdon's commission represented. In Cleverdon's next note of December 20, he tells Plath that he thinks the script of "New Poems" (which she had sent him after an evening's preparation) is wonderful, and that he is passing it through "the necessary channels"; he also suggests that she use his name as a reference in her attempt to get a telephone installed in her flat on Fitzroy Road, a process that was expected to take months.[81] Plath did not, in fact, ever receive installation of phone service in London; neither did the script of "New Poems" succeed in getting through the "necessary channels" prior to her death.

The text of Plath's script for the hoped-for BBC broadcast is included as an appendix in *Ariel: The Restored Edition* and begins with her introductory note in which she reveals the importance of oral transmission in her new poems: "they are written for the ear, not the eye: they are poems written out loud."[82] "Written out loud," of course, is a step beyond "written for the ear"—it suggests a greater immediacy between the performed word and the aesthetic processes of composing. "Sheep in Fog" is the only poem in Plath's script that was not recorded in October 1962, and the only one of the scripted poems not included in Plath's manuscript of "Ariel and Other Poems." What is notable about the inclusion of this poem in Plath's BBC script from mid-December 1962 is that she so wholly revised the ending of "Sheep in Fog" in late January 1963. That later revision not only changed the mood and meaning of the poem, but withdrew Plath's triumphant *Ariel* voice as well, replacing it with the far more resigned fatalism of her final poetic phase, evident in the final recording of her voice.

On December 2, 1962, when Plath first considered this poem complete—complete enough to type and date and to include in her "New Poems" script eleven days later—"Sheep in Fog" ended with the image of the narrator's heart softening at the sight of benevolently patriarchal sheep wearing "heavenly wools" and the "faces of babies."[83] On December 13, when Plath first read Cleverdon's invitation, she was still buoyed by the optimism lent to her by the writing of the *Ariel* poems; something in the next six weeks profoundly changed her viewpoint and voice. In the final version of "Sheep in Fog," the sheep have disappeared completely, along with their patriarchal blessing, their innocent faces, their heavenly wools. All that is left is the ominous threat of entering "a heaven / Starless and fatherless, a dark water"[84]—a threshold to Plath's last twelve recorded poems.

New Comment *Recording with Philip French* (1963)

On January 10, 1963, a few days before *The Bell Jar* was to be published in England, Plath recorded her live review of Donald Hall's Penguin anthology, *Contemporary American Poetry,* for the BBC Third Programme show *New Comment.* In this last known recording, Plath's "voice" finds a dual focus, speaking from the perspective of an American poet living in England and as a transcriber of what Hall terms the "new direction in American poetry."[85] *New Comment's* arts magazine format reflected its proximity to other spoken-word hybrids, innovative alternatives to the separation of literary and media arts in the late 1950s and early 1960s at the Third Programme. Like "imaginary conversation" and the "radio ballad," *New Comment's* "arts review of the airwave" offered a venue in which writing from a contemporary poetry anthology and the mass listening audience could move toward shared cultural ground.[86]

Domestic situations noticeably shape the voice of Plath's final recording. By mid-January, she was regularly seeing a physician and being visited at home by a nurse he had arranged for her and her children. Snowstorms of historic dimensions had paralyzed London since the day after Christmas, and Plath was forced to cope with frequent power outages as well as her chronic loneliness: her car was snowed in, and she wrote to her mother of feeling "very gloomy" and isolated with her lack of phone and child care.[87] Despite discouragement, Plath's public voice on this occasion—thickened by a head cold—demonstrates critical acumen: she begins by acknowledging the particular inwardness of images, their "plummeting subjectivity," that Hall points to as "genuinely new on the American scene."[88] Hall's printed introduction indeed offers a compendium of references to the way that the "new American poetry" sounds, but it does not contextualize that "sound" of the "new American poetry" in a cultural field. Plath's presentation and selection, however, recognizes a number of specific cultural influences—notably psychiatry and the cinema, at one point using the metaphor of the shifting focus of a telescopic lens to describe the effects that disturb vision, oscillating between "stillness and motion, near and far." She also notes the tendency in poetry that identifies animate and inanimate, rendering a sense of a world in which all is "listening, trembling, sentient," without "sure objective ground."[89] Plath chooses to read excerpts from recent works of poets such as W. D. Snodgrass, Louis Simpson, Robert Bly, James Merrill, James Wright, and Galway Kinnell that invariably highlight their implicit similarity to her own recent work—she is creating a canon of contemporaries and positioning herself within it. The images from these poems are of personal pain, alienation, hearses and hell and death, graves, loneliness and uninvited guests, homelessness, terrible accidents, dragging for bodies, and crying. Referring to a Louis Simpson poem, Plath notes, "The word 'eros' falls away with the hiss of some disease."[90] We can hear the closing excerpt selected from Galway Kinnell's "Flower Herding Pictures on Mount Monadnock" with a shudder at the future anterior enacted in its lines, especially considering Hughes's unclarified allusion to the flower sprite and its inspirations for the couple, through parenthood, in the earlier *Two of a Kind* interview:

> The appeal to heaven breaks off.
> The petals begin to fall, in self-forgiveness.
> It is a flower. On this mountainside it is dying.[91]

"And now you try / Your handful of notes"[92]

On November 20, 2004, at the Proshansky auditorium of CUNY's Graduate Center, a historic recording was made, yet one very much in the tradition of Plath's recorded past: the public reading, for the first time, of *Ariel* as she had arranged the manuscript prior to her death. The occasion marked the publication of *Ariel: The Restored Edition,* a facsimile of the manuscript that included Plath's original typescript and an introduction by her daughter, Frieda Hughes. Hughes and six American poets and critics—Frank Bidart, Jorie Graham, Kimiko Hahn, Richard Howard, Katha Pollit, and Helen Vendler—read Plath's forty *Ariel* poems in their original order, with the book's centerpiece, "Ariel," read by Plath herself, from the voice recording of October 1962. ("The Swarm," which seemed to have been eliminated from Plath's manuscript at some point prior to her death, was not included in this reading.)

During their welcoming comments, Alice Quinn of the Poetry Society of America and Tree Swenson of the Academy of American Poets reminded their audience that *Ariel: The Restored Edition* had an "order with a significantly different arc than the *Ariel* published previously."[93] The *Ariel* arrangement of poems that her mother intended, Frieda Hughes's introduction proposes, was not only undertaken "to cover the ground from just before the breakup of the marriage to the resolution of a new life, with all the agonies and furies in between,"[94] but also to inscribe the arc of Plath's quest for and discovery of a voice through a vehicle that made hers accessible: her refigurations of motherhood.

"A museum mammoth" is how Plath pictured herself, after having been forsaken through the birth of a younger sibling, in the autobiographical essay "Ocean 1212-W."[95] But in the first poem of *Ariel*, "Morning Song"—a poem that is on an essential level about the voicing of an achieved and separate self—the relationship between museum and statue has been inverted. Rather than being superfluous, a relic of some earlier time, here the "new statue" is the baby itself, a recent acquisition to take note of, something to be observed and understood, a piece of living memory; everything else is "drafty museum."[96] The stanza in the poem that begins, "I'm no more your mother,"[97] too easily read as a sign of Plath's hostility toward motherhood, is a metaphoric re-creation of this idea of maternal connection and separation: Plath is equating the process of a cloud "distilling" itself into a rain puddle that reflects its dissolution as similar to the mother's evaporating role in its child's life as it eventually becomes separate. It is in the poem's culminating lines that Plath's narrator becomes completely and willingly "effaced," allowing her child full ownership of its separateness while at the same time standing back to admire the child's expression:

> And now you try
> Your handful of notes;
> The clear vowels rise like balloons.[98]

It is not hard to see why Plath would have chosen such an exquisitely realized, complex poem to begin *Ariel,* but her customary patterning of theme, image, and narrative trajectory becomes more obvious when one considers "Morning Song" and "Wintering" as the poems that begin and end a story told. At first glance these poems have very little outward relationship but for the common images of motherhood, expression, and the mouth as a means of nurturance and expression. In "Wintering," the woman still attends a child "At the cradle of Spanish walnut," but she is "too dumb to think." Her body is a "bulb in the cold": on the surface a negative image, except that many bulbous plants require such cold in order to activate cyclical flowering. If one reads "Wintering" as the extension of a narrative arc begun with "Morning Song," one sees that the image of fertility has become internalized, just as her expressiveness ("Too dumb to think") is not intellectualized but felt and integrated, unlike the gestures on the surface of Plath's early work. "This is the easy time, there is nothing doing,"[99] Plath states in the opening lines of "Wintering," but her industry is no longer outward; she has progressed from "bald cry"[100] in "Morning Song" to knowing a voice, arrived, from within.

The last lines of both poems work in tandem. Through the imagery of flying bees and balloons, there is a figurative flight of fruition, or of life itself, even of the creation of an archive-image of memory-trace (that papery, many-celled beehive) achieved by way of mouth. Just as the baby in "Morning Song" has tasted the mother's milk, eventually nourished to the point of self-expression and self-sufficiency, the bees in "Wintering" taste of the flowering that will keep them alive: "The bees are flying. They taste the spring."[101]

Nothing could have made a more fitting tribute to Plath's aim in structuring the narrative of Plath's *Ariel* than Frieda Hughes's 2004 public reading—a living demonstration of "Morning Song" and of the declarative optimism of "Wintering." It was on another level a courageous expression for Plath's daughter, who in reading these two poems made the symbolic gesture of uniting herself with the mother whose poetic wish was that her child be separate enough to develop her own voice, "A clean slate, with your own face on," as Plath wrote to her unborn child in the January 1960 poem "You're."[102] Perhaps that is why, at the close of the very long evening reading, Frieda Hughes teased the patient audience before reading "Wintering": "After this one we're all free, like the bees."[103] How ironic, or merely appropriate, that seventy years after Plath's impossibly "beautiful fusion with the things of this world"[104] was lost, a performance of the "restored" voicings of *Ariel* resounded Plath's opening impulse for *Ariel,* making room for a daughter's voice.

NOTES

1. *UJ,* 314–15.

2. Ibid., 315.

3. *CP,* 244. Unless otherwise noted, all lines of recorded poetry are cited from *The Collected Poems* in order to prevent inaccuracies or distortions. Italics mine.

4. Ibid., 220.

5. Ibid., 207.

6. Charles Bernstein, ed., *Close Listening: Poetry and the Performed Word* (New York: Oxford University Press), 4.

7. Nick Piombino, "The Aural Ellipses and Nature of Listening in Contemporary Poetry," in Bernstein, *Close Listening,* 55.

8. Susan Stewart, "Letter on Sound," in *Close Listening,* 29.

9. J. D. McClatchy, "Sylvia Plath," *The Voice of the Poet: Sylvia Plath* (New York: Random House Audio Books, 1999), 12–13.

10. Cynthia Ozick, "Smoke and Fire," *Yale Review* 89 (2001): 99.

11. McClatchy, "Sylvia Plath," 8.

12. Wen Stephenson, "High-performance Poets," *Atlantic Monthly,* April 2000, 64.

13. Ozick, "Smoke and Fire," 99.

14. McClatchy, "Sylvia Plath," 13.

15. Erica Jong, "An Art Like Everything Else," *New York Times Book Review,* December 12, 2004, 4.

16. *UJ,* 469.

17. Aurelia Plath, unpublished notes for the introduction of *LH* (Smith).

18. Ted Hughes, *Winter Pollen,* ed. William Scammel (New York: Picador, 1995), 161.

19. *BL,* 105.

20. "Sylvia Plath," transcript of recording, in Peter Orr, *The Poet Speaks—Interviews with Contemporary Poets Conducted by Hilary Morrish, Peter Orr, John Press, and Ian Scott-Kilvert* (London: Routledge and Kegan Paul, 1966), 171.

21. A. Alvarez, "The Poetry of Sylvia Plath: A. Alvarez Discusses the Work of the American Poet who Died in London Earlier This Year," BBC Third Programme, London, September 23, 1963 broadcast, British Library (SA).

22. Orr, *Poet Speaks,* 171.

23. Author's notes, Frieda Hughes, poetry reading, City University of New York, New York, November 30, 2004; *AR,* 12.

24. *CP,* 60 and 61.

25. Ibid., 110.

26. Ibid., 241.

27. Orr, *Poet Speaks,* 171.

28. *UJ*, 376.

29. Stephen Tabor, *Sylvia Plath: An Analytical Bibliography* (London: Mansell, 1987).

30. Ibid., 139.

31. "Autograph Book," Series VI, Box 39, Lee Anderson Papers, Washington University of St. Louis, http://library.wust.edu/units/spec/manuscripts/mlc/anderson (accessed June 2, 2006); the same lines from "The Lady and the Earthenware Head" appear in *CP*, 70.

32. *BL*, 52.

33. All quotes from the 1958 Lee Anderson Springfield material are from Archive of Recorded Poetry and Literature, Library of Congress, and the Washington University of St. Louis Libraries with kind permission of John Hodge and the Estate of Lee Anderson.

34. Ibid.

35. Ibid.

36. On the social history of poetry at the BBC, see Lilias Fraser, "'The Appreciation of Real Worth': Poetry, Radio, and the Valued Reader," in *Poetry and Contemporary Culture: The Question of Value,* ed. Andrew Michael Roberts and Jonathan Allison (Edinburgh: Edinburgh University Press, 2002), 69–84. Lilias traces a long-running commentary on the rhetoric of intimacy in broadcasting and listening to poems on the air in the 1950s.

37. *LH*, 398.

38. Elaine Feinstein, *Ted Hughes: The Life of the Poet* (New York: Norton, 2001), 104; and *LH*, 403.

39. A. Alvarez, *The Savage God: A Study of Suicide* (New York: Norton, 1990), 26.

40. Diane Middlebrook, *Her Husband: Hughes and Plath—A Marriage* (New York: Viking, 2003), xv.

41. Ibid., xv–xvi and 273–74.

42. *LH*, 402.

43. *Two of a Kind,* sound recording of January 31, 1961, broadcast, British Library (SA).

44. *LH*, 450.

45. *BL*, 109.

46. *Two of a Kind,* British Broadcasting Corporation; Middlebrook, *Her Husband,* captures the reciprocal flavor: xv, 157.

47. Middlebrook, *Her Husband,* 142.

48. Ibid.

49. Ted Hughes, *Shakespeare and the Goddess of Complete Being* (New York: Farrar, Straus and Giroux, 1992), 440.

50. *BL*, 111.

51. For a history of the Third Programme in this period, see *The Envy of the World: Fifty Years of the BBC Third Programme and Radio 3: 1946,* ed. Humphrey Carpenter (London: Weidenfeld and Nicholson, 1996), 288.

52. Sylvia Plath, unpublished letter to Aurelia Schober Plath, June 6, 1961. Plath mss. II, Box 6a (Lilly).

53. Sylvia Plath, voice recording, *The Living Poet,* British Library (SA).

54. The *Grand Street* essay appears in Hughes, *Winter Pollen*, 184.

55. *The Living Poet*; Hughes, "Notes on the Chronological Order of Sylvia Plath's Poems," *The Art of Sylvia Plath*, ed. Charles Newman (Indiana University Press, 1970), 188.

56. *Voices and Visions*, Public Broadcasting Corporation (Winstar Corporation: PBS), 1999; see also *LH*, 451.

57. *LH*, 448.

58. Ibid., 452.

59. *The Living Poet*; emphasis added.

60. Ibid.

61. All quotes in this paragraph are from *The Living Poet*.

62. Ibid.

63. Alvarez's praise is mentioned in *LH*, 448.

64. *CP*, 207.

65. All quotes in this paragraph from the sound recording, *The Poet Speaks*, British Broadcasting Corporation, with permission of the British Library (SA). The text of the program is quoted in Orr, *The Poet Speaks*, 167–72. For commentary and quotation on Plath's mid-atlanticism see Tracy Brain, *The Other Sylvia Plath*, 45.

66. Orr, *The Poet Speaks*, vii.

67. Frank Kermode, preface to Orr, *The Poet Speaks*, xi. See also the broader debate in Max Horkheimer and Theodor Adorno's seminal essay, "The Culture Industry as Mass Deception," in *Dialectic of Englightenment* (New York: Herder and Herder, 1972).

68. Kermode, preface, ix.

69. See also Janet Badia, "The 'Priestess' and Her 'Cult,'" this volume.

70. Lee Anderson, interview recorded in Springfield, Mass., April 18, 1958, Archive of Recorded Poetry and Literature, Library of Congress, Washington, D.C.

71. *CP*, 240.

72. Ibid., 244–45.

73. Ibid., 235.

74. Ibid., 230.

75. The line "I leave to *you* the mystery" is not included in *CP*.

76. *CP*, 240.

77. Ibid., 244–45.

78. Ibid., 235.

79. Letter from Douglas Cleverdon, unpublished, December 10, 1962, Smith: Correspondence.

80. Kate Whitehead, *The Third Programme: A Literary History* (Oxford: Clarendon Press, 1989), 45–53.

81. Letter from Douglas Cleverdon, unpublished, December 20, 1962, Smith: Correspondence.

82. *AR*, 195.

83. "Sylvia Plath: The Evolution of 'Sheep in Fog,'" in Hughes, *Winter Pollen*, 191–211.

84. *CP*, 262

85. *New Comment*, January 10, 1963, British Broadcasting Corp. recording (live), British Library (SA).

86. Whitehead, *Third Programme*, 45–53.

87. *LH*, 495.

88. *New Comment.*

89. Ibid.

90. Ibid.

91. Ibid. Galway Kinnell, "Flower Herding on Mt. Monadnock," transcribed from *New Comment.*

92. *CP*, 157.

93. Author's notes, *AR* reading, City University of New York, November 30, 2004.

94. *AR*, xiv.

95. *JP*, 23.

96. *CP*, 157.

97. Ibid.

98. Ibid. Diane Middlebrook gives a reading of "Morning Song" from an incisive perspective, although somewhat different from mine, in *Her Husband*, 154–55.

99. *CP*, 217–19.

100. Ibid., 157.

101. Ibid., 219.

102. Ibid., 141.

103. Author's notes, *AR* reading.

104. "Beautiful fusion" is Plath's reference to the presymbolic in her autobiographical essay, "Ocean 1212-W," *JP*, 21.

PART TWO

■■
■■

Culture and the Politics of Memory

SANDRA GILBERT

On the Beach with Sylvia Plath

⊞

September 24, 2002. Hot equinoctial sun, a chill relentless wind from the north, and a cloudless sky over Picardy, where we sit in a nearly empty café on the seafront, at Berck-Plage. My partner, David, and I have come here to see what Sylvia Plath might have been seeing when she began the poem she named after this place, for increasingly it seems to me that the ambitious, seven-part sequence she entitled "Berck-Plage"[1] offers crucial, if disquieting, insights not just into its author's life and her often death-drenched work, but more generally into our contemporary poetry of mourning.

Berck-Plage is a desultory, rather worn-looking little town set on the edge of La Manche, the channel that divides England from the continent. Our old Michelin for the Nord de la France, Champagne, Ardennes, describes it coolly as *"une station à la fois balnéaire, familiale et médicale climatique"*—a place that's at one and the same time a bathing resort, a family vacation spot, and a medical haven.[2] But right now, though the sun's so fierce on this out-of-season Tuesday, the seaside seems deserted and a bit desolate, as if bathers, families, patients, had all fled inland for the French *rentrée,* a kind of communal back-to-school week in which the whole nation participates.

Sylvia Plath and Ted Hughes came to this town at a very different time of year. In June 1961, the young parents of one child with another on the way, they were taking a fortnight's holiday in France while Sylvia's mother, Aurelia, babysat little Frieda back in London. After what was by all accounts an ill-starred five-night stay with their friends Bill and Dido Merwin in the Dordogne, they must have traveled north by northwest as they made their way back to England.[3] Berck-Plage may have been their last stopover before they got on the ferry at Calais, and they probably chose the spot because it was a lot cheaper than the ritzier resort of Le Touquet-Paris-Plage a few kilometers up the coast. By the early sixties, Hughes and Plath were already literary luminaries, recording for the BBC and publishing widely; indeed, as the poet Peter Porter put it not so long ago, they then "appeared in poetic assemblies with almost Charles and Di radiance, the youthful princelings of romantic promise."[4] But nonetheless, they had to scrimp like any other not-very-well-off young couple.

The sea that David and I gaze at today from our perch on the sun-struck concrete beachfront promenade is flat and vast in all directions, for, as Plath notes in her poem, the beach is huge—"*se prolonge durant une douzaine de kilomètres,*" according to Michelin—so that a "sandy damper" does indeed stretch "for miles." Right now, though, despite steady sun, the wind's so strong that hardly anyone has ventured out onto the enormous glaring plain of that "sandy damper." Only a middle-aged couple in heavy sweaters walk, or try to walk, a tiny dog who looks as though the powerful blasts might blow him away any minute, while a younger couple, struggling to shield a small baby, huddle next to the boarded-up bathhouses, and—rather bizarrely—a man in swim trunks seems to be sun (and wind) bathing in the dubious shelter of a few buildings Plath described as "concrete bunkers," which now (as they very likely did then) house a cluster of hot dog and ice cream stands, all closed down because the season's over.

And even along the seaside Esplanade Parmentier, a number of cafés and souvenir shops are shut and locked, though a few lingering tourists—ourselves among them—sip coffee, collars raised against the wind, among the folded umbrellas on the terraces, and one or two of the many wheelchairs betokening the town's status as a *station médicale* proceed along the front at a steady pace.

Of course, much has no doubt changed in Berck-Plage since Plath and Hughes strolled here in 1961. But much is surely still the same; not just the damper, the concrete bunkers, the hospitals, and the tubular steel wheelchairs glittering in the sun but, in particular, what I suspect must be another distinction of the place: the rickety little wooden *cabines* in a rainbow of pastels that serve as private bathhouses, tilting crazily as they sink into—or are gradually buried in—the drifting sand, which right now hisses in the wind as layers and layers of fine gritty

BERCK-PLAGE - L'Hôpital Vincent

L'Hôpital Vincent in Berck-Plage, France, a town known in Michelin guides as a "medical station," a motif in Plath's poem, "Berck-Plage." Postcard ca. 1920.

grains are driven, low to the ground, along the shore. As images of mortal frailty teetering in the sands of time, these peculiar structures seem singularly appropriate in such a medicalized setting. Plath's "Berck-Plage" is too strange and original to mention them, but maybe they haunted her and her text anyway, as they seem to haunt the beach.

It was probably hot and calm when the couple visited this multipurpose resort. Certainly Plath's poem tells us that the sun was shining and it was warm enough for ice cream (some people eating "colored sherbets"), bright enough for sunburn (the sherbet-eaters have "scorched hands"), a good day for swimming and loafing (there are women in the dunes wearing bikinis), either a holiday or weekend (children are playing on the beach), and relatively windless (the air is "still").[5] Yet here, on a sunny beach, among frolicking vacationers, she was prompted to begin a poem whose ultimate configuration suggests to me that she is perhaps *the* poet of modern death.

To begin with, what might have been a carefree vacation spot was from the start blighted for Plath by the ubiquitous medicalization of the place, which, as Hughes later remembered, "was one of her nightmares stepped into the real world."[6] Thus, with extraordinary power she represented even the most innocent aspects of a holiday by the sea as either sick or sickening. In the passages below from the first two sections of the poem, the sea is an "abeyance," the heat of the sun is a "poultice," the colors of the sherbets are "electrifying" (never a cheery qualifier for a onetime sufferer from shock treatment), sunburned hands are "scorched," voices are "shrunk" and "crutchless," a priest has a "dead foot," and a pool is "sick with what it has swallowed":

(1)

This is the sea, then, this great abeyance.
How the sun's poultice draws on my inflammation.

Electrifyingly-colored sherbets, scooped from the freeze
By pale girls travel the air in scorched hands.
. . . .
A sandy damper kills the vibrations;
It stretches for miles, the shrunk voices

Waving and crutchless, half their old size . . .

. . . .

(2)

This black boot has no mercy for anybody.
. . . it is the hearse of a dead foot,
. . . .
Obscene bikinis hide in the dunes. . . .

While a green pool opens its eye,
Sick with what it has swallowed—[7]

Given this brilliant portrayal of a pervasively diseased geography, I guess it isn't surprising that I still remember the curiously chilling combination of bafflement and envy with which I read "Berck-Plage" when it first came out in a magazine. My bafflement was partly generated by my envy or maybe the other way around. I was puzzled and piqued by what I understood was far beyond my writerly (and even readerly) grasp: a presiding tension that gave shape, depth, and mystery to the poem, a tension between coolly controlled formal precision, on the one hand, and, on the other, enigmatically, almost mystically daring metaphorical leaps. But I was also unnerved. Nor was my reaction all that unusual. The critic Alfred Alvarez, a friend to whom Plath read "Berck-Plage" aloud in September 1962, "sitting cross-legged on the uncomfortable floor" of his studio, reported later that he'd "had a vague impression of something injurious and faintly obscene."[8] And a more recent student of the work, Jack Folsom, goes so far as to declare that it "contains 126 lines of seemingly unmitigated malaise and funereal gloom."[9]

Although such words as *injurious, obscene, malaise,* and *gloom* are somewhat hyperbolic, they're understandable attempts to get at what is certainly disconcerting in this poem. Plath's "shrunk voices / Waving and crutchless" are succeeded by a first glimpse of the black-booted priest who seems so ominous that a group of fishermen—"mackerel-gatherers"—"wall up their backs against him" in section 1.[10] And the mackerel gatherers themselves are so subtly sinister, "handling the black and green lozenges like the parts of a body," that they, too, troubled me when I first read the piece, especially because I didn't understand why and how they mattered in this gravely elegiac work.[11] I was inexplicably sickened, too, by the riddle of the passing priest in section 2, with his "high, dead, toeless foot," and in the same section by the "obscene bikinis" and the furtive lovers who weirdly "unstick themselves" behind "concrete bunkers," by the plight of the "onlooker, trembling," who is drawn "like a long material // Through a still virulence" and by the "weed, hairy as privates" that this cryptic observer confronts.[12]

As for the old man who is dying in section 3 of the sequence, then dead in section 4, those prophetic anxieties that, like most aspiring poets, I carefully cultivated made his meaning all too clear to me.

(4)

A wedding-cake face in a paper frill.

How superior he is now.

. . . .

They propped his jaw with a book until it stiffened.[13]

The poet's observations—of, say, the partly shrouded dead man's "wedding-cake face in a paper frill," of his surreal, lost "eye-stones, yellow and valuable," and of his useless "tongue, sapphire of ash," along with his grimly propped jaw—were frighteningly ruthless.[14]

I came across "Berck-Plage" in the early sixties—maybe after Plath's death, maybe not—but I'd been following her career with fascination for nearly a decade, ever since I was transfixed by a disturbing story she published in the girls' magazine *Seventeen,* when she must have been little more than that age herself and I was still in myth. Later, as I journeyed into my twenties, I was a barely published poet, a part-time graduate student, and a full-time mother of two—soon to be three—babies. Plath was just enough ahead of me—four or five years older, I gathered—so that I could be secretly competitive without being as overwhelmingly daunted by her achievements as I would be by those of an exact contemporary.[15]

When I first read "Berck-Plage," however, I'd been disappointed by Plath's poems (which is to say, in all honesty, I'd been rather relieved by their apparent docility, their "good girl" decorum). Though I sensed I myself might seem just the kind of dutiful young "wife 'n' mother" produced like vanilla wafers by the cookie-cutter of mid-century America, I didn't want to be a "good girl" in poetry, even though I had no very clear idea how to stop being one. Of course, most of the Plath verses I'd been reading had been the relatively careful texts of *The Colossus,* rather than the great *Ariel* poems, which I was just beginning to discover when I stumbled on "Berck-Plage." Looking back now on those baffled, envious, really quite astonishing reading experiences, I realize how lucky it was for me that I *could* stumble on the *Ariel* poems.

In the early sixties, Plath's vehement last words swam randomly, haphazardly into my ken, and even when, later, I began seeking them out, knowing she had lost her life (although not quite how or why) and eager to see what she had left behind, I remained for quite a while an innocent, if no longer a random, reader. None of her poems had yet been privileged over any other: she was not yet the figure of melodrama who became notorious as the "poetess" of "Daddy." Rather, she was someone from a college cohort just a little ahead of my own who had suddenly written a number of unfathomably compelling poems that kept emerging along with odd, unverifiable rumors about the circumstances of her death.

Compelling, compulsive, almost *compulsory* reading. That was the point about the poems themselves. Whatever their author's story—and no one I knew could explain it to me, at least for a while—there were the poems. Scorching the page with a kind of fatality. Hissing through the page. Burning the paper. Weird. I had never seen anything like them, nor have I since.

"Berck-Plage" wasn't, to be sure, the most searing of Plath's late works. (Even all those years ago I'd have reserved that adjective for the notorious "Daddy" and "Lady Lazarus," as well as "Fever 103°," "Getting There," "Stings," and a few others.) But its metaphoric leaps had a disciplined dazzle that I sensed was rooted in something hectic, something that in lesser hands would be out of control. At the same time, control was clearly manifest in the poem's surprisingly dispassionate as well as somber tone, despite the speaker's sometimes almost paranoid edginess.[16] Indeed, studying the piece today, I begin to suspect that what I'm calling "control" or "discipline" is the flip side of a kind of madness, a narrative estrangement that makes it possible for Plath the artist to fashion such material into superb elegy that is both deeply moving and deeply skeptical.

For "Berck-Plage" is, of course, an elegy, perhaps the finest one this often indefatigable mourner ever produced, though the gravity of its lamentation has been overlooked in favor of the more conventionally confessional "family elegies" the writer addressed to her father.[17] Its comparative neglect is particularly odd in view of its ambition: with the exception of "Poem for a Birthday" (more a suite than a sequence) and the radio play, *Three Women,* "Berck-Plage" is the longest and most complex of the texts included in Plath's *Collected Poems.* Its seven sections—each arranged with elaborate formality in nine fluid couplets—are as technically accomplished as they are meticulously, austerely, observant. And in its eloquent articulation of a nihilistic vision that dominated much verse in English after, say, Eliot's *Four Quartets* and Robert Lowell's "The Quaker Graveyard in Nantucket," this restrained and elliptical seaside poem offers an extraordinarily useful model of the poetry of lamentation that was produced in the second half of the twentieth century.

Like so many strong elegies, "Berck-Plage" juxtaposes the world of the desirous flesh—what Yeats, in "Sailing to Byzantium," called "those dying generations at their song"[18]—with the *timor mortis* that the very processes of generation inevitably beget. Carnal appetites flourish on Plath's beach, bordered by the sea, that "great abeyance" of the solid and the known, but so does fear, in the person of the deathly Father, a priest who no doubt "plumbs the well of his book" to uncover the awful truth of ashes to ashes, dust to dust. For on this "sandy damper" that stretches for miles, the earth is depicted as (what at least part of the *plage* quite literally still is) the ground of a hospital where the "onlooker, trembling," observes the hosts of material *things,* the quotidian objects in which we put our trust when we put our trust in human life, just as bathers, dressing themselves for the sea, put their trust in those fragile little changing *cabines.*

"On the balconies of the hotel," Plath writes in section 3, "things are glittering. / Things, things." "Tubular steel wheelchairs," aluminum crutches, even a surgeon with a clinical "mirrory eye"—all have been assembled to stave off death, but nonetheless a representative old man is inexorably "vanishing" on a "striped mattress in one room."[19] This old man's death nearly halfway through the seven-part poem sets off the work's remaining (and its major) action: in section 4, the laying out of the body, the problematic condolences of mourners as they confront the long coffin of soap-colored oak; in sections 5 and 6, the rituals of wake and funeral; and in section 7, the final resolution of burial, attended by the poem's speaker, "dark-suited, and still, a member of the party."[20]

"A member of the party": that Plath, as it turned out, was literally one of the mourners who followed the coffin of her octogenarian neighbor Percy Key to its "stopping place" in Devonshire powerfully testifies to the conscious craft with which she fashioned this apparently seamless work. For the old man who is said to "vanish" at the center of "Berck-Plage" (and presumably therefore at or near the "real" Berck-Plage) did not actually expire anywhere near the beach in northern France where the poem's protagonist moves "smilingly" though she knows she is "not a smile" and fears her heart is "too small to bandage" the "terrible faults" of the children who are "after something, with hooks and cries."[21]

When I first read "Berck-Plage," I understood as little about someone in Devon named Percy Key as I did about the town of Berck, on the shore of Picardy—which is to say I understood nothing of either. Instead, I assumed that the episode the poem purports to represent was a single coherent event that took place at a seaside hospital in France or Belgium. Nor did I learn the work's sources until decades later, when one of Ted Hughes's endnotes in Plath's *Collected Poems* explained that Berck-Plage is a beach "which Sylvia Plath visited in June 1961" and where "there was a large hospital for mutilated war veterans and accident victims—who took their exercise along the sands." Added Hughes, the "funeral in the poem is that of Percy Key . . . who died in June 1962, exactly a year after her visit to Berck-Plage."[22] Later still, I discovered in our old Green Michelin what might explain the importunate children with "hooks and cries": that Berck, with its *"immense plage de sable fin, très sûre"*—its huge firm sandy beach—is world famous for treating childhood maladies that include tuberculosis of the bone, though the diseases of its young patients aren't contagious, so they're free to romp on the shore.

According to one scholar who's worked with the manuscripts of "Berck-Plage," a "fragmentary rough draft" begins with an image of the sun, "silent and violent," laying "its bright poultices on the promenade"; this may well have been a jotting on or near the beach at Berck. Eventually, these sketches of the local scene mingled observations *balnéaire* ("Electrifyingly-colored sherbets" floating above the long "sandy damper"), *familiale* (bikinis, children, sea crockery), and *médicale* (the sun's "poultice," wheelchairs, crutches, the "green pool . . . Sick with what it has swallowed," and the priest whose black boot is the hearse of a dead foot).[23] But the work's genius is evident in the skill with which Plath brought such notations to bear on the elegiac tradition in which she undertook to compose a work memorializing the death of Percy Key. For as in T. S. Eliot's "East Coker," where the "whole earth is our hospital / Endowed by [a] ruined millionaire,"[24] the sanitoria at Berck-Plage become monitory establishments, with each crutch and wheelchair a memento mori meant to warn all alike—sick or well, consumers of sherbets or wearers of obscene bikinis, mackerel gatherers or trembling onlookers—that priestly death comes always and inexorably closer with this "black boot [that] has no mercy for anybody."[25] Unlike Eliot, however, Plath imagined no Christlike, "wounded surgeon," capable of plying the redemptive "steel"[26] that might cure the disease of mortality.

Inevitably, as Hughes understood, Berck-Plage constituted one of Plath's "nightmares stepped into the real world" because hospitals and the illnesses they signified had long had especially terrifying meta-physical as well as physical resonance for her. Her own unpriestly father's "dead foot"—destroyed by gangrene that developed from long-untreated diabetes—killed him when she was only eight, and she herself was (notoriously) institutionalized with multiple physical injuries as well as a mental breakdown at the time of the suicide attempt she fictionalized in *The Bell Jar*.[27] Thus the turn in "Berck-Plage" from beach scene to death scene is unobtrusively and apparently effortlessly accomplished in section 3, through the poet's intense focus on "night-mare" associations with medical images. First her gaze is fixed on pros-thetic "Things, things—// Tubular steel wheelchairs, aluminum crutches"; then she moves to thoughts of her own inadequacy in the "face of mutilated children" with "hooks and cries"—her "heart too small to bandage their terrible faults"—and then, with apparent inevitability, she swivels to examine "the side of a man: his red ribs" and the surgeon, "One mirrory eye," who's tending—also inade-quately—the opened body.[28] That opened body (once the object of surgery, now in the last stages of an illness surgery couldn't cure) belongs, at least implicitly, to the old man "vanishing" on "a striped mattress" in one room. He seems to be dying in a chamber of the hotel where the speaker is staying or perhaps in one of the nearby hospitals, but in fact his death is based on an event that actually took place in the parlor of a cottage in Devon.

Plath had met Percy Key and his wife, Rose, in August 1961, on the day she and Hughes moved to Court Green, the old manor house in North Tawton, Devonshire, that they bought soon after returning from their vacation in France. A retired London pubkeeper who seemed to her "about 20 years older" than his wife, Percy Key was "very tall, spare, almost cadaverous," and it quickly became clear that he was suf-fering from some sort of chest ailment.[29] By the following February he was in the hospital for a series of lung surgeries, and in "Among the Narcissi" Plath portrayed him recovering from one of these on a breezy early-spring hillside where the flowers are "vivid as bandages" and the "octogenarian . . . is quite blue" because the "terrible wind tries his breathing."[30]

Then, on April 17, 1962, Percy suffered multiple strokes in one day. At this point, he became a subject of Plath's continued clinical (though not unsympathetic) surveillance.[31] Her journal entry for that date records [emphasis added]:

A terrible thumping on our door about 2 o'clock. . . . Rose's hysterical voice "Ted, Ted come quick, I think Percy's had a stroke." . . . she cried, turning to rush back to her cottage, Ted after her. I thought I would stay and wait, and then something in me said *now, you must see this, you have never seen a stroke or a dead person.* So I went. Percy was in his chair in front of the television set, twitching in a fearsome way, utterly gone off.[32]

By early June, Plath noted that "Percy Key is dying. That is the verdict."[33] And on July 2 she told her journal that "Percy Key is dead" and "I have written a long poem 'Berck-Plage' about it. Very moved. Several terrible glimpses."[34]

Those "glimpses"—still unflinchingly clinical yet sorrowful and shocked—came as the result of another deliberate, no doubt writerly choice: *"I decided to see him, I must see him."*[35] And they're worth quoting here at some length because they include a great deal that she incorporated into her poem, seamlessly merging them with the details of her holiday visit to France the previous summer. (And Plath's comments on what she "glimpsed" are obviously also illuminating.)

The living room was full, still, hot with some awful translation taking place. *Percy lay back on a heap of white pillows in his striped pajamas,* his face already passed from humanity. . . . *His eyes showed through partly open lids like dissolved soaps or a clotted pus.* . . . The end, even of so marginal man, a horror.

Went down after his death, the next day, the 17th. Ted had been down in the morning, said Percy was still on the bed . . . *his jaw bound and a book . . . propping it till it stiffened properly.* . . . He lay . . . in a long *coffin of orangey soap-colored oak with silver handles, the lid propped against the wall at his head with a silver scroll: Percy Key: Died June 25, 1962.* The raw date a shock. . . . A sheet covered the coffin. Rose lifted it. *A pale white beaked face, as of paper, rose under the veil that covered the hole cut in the glued white cloth cover.* . . . They have no hearse, they have only a cart.

Friday, the day of the funeral . . . Ted & I, dressed in hot blacks, passed the church, saw the bowler-hatted men coming out of the gate *with a high, spider-wheeled black cart.* . . . We strolled round the church in the bright heat, *the pollarded green limes like green balls, the fat hills red, just ploughed.* . . . *We went in. Heard priest meeting corpse at gate, incantating,* coming close. *Hair-raising.* We stood. *The flowery casket, nodding and flirting its petals, led up the aisle.* . . . I hardly heard a word of the service, Mr. Lane [the rector] for once *quenched by the grandeur of ceremony, a vessel,* as it should be.

Then we followed the funeral party . . . up the hill to the cemetery. . . . Ted motioned me to look *at the slow uplifted faces of children in the primary school yard* . . . utterly without grief, only bland curiosity, turning after us. We got out at the cemetery gate, the day blazing. . . . *Six bowler hats of the bearers left at the first yew bushes in the grass.* The coffin on boards, words said, ashes to ashes—that is what remained, not glory, not heaven. *The amazingly narrow coffin lowered into the narrow red earth opening, left* . . . an unfinished feeling. Is he to be left up there uncovered, all alone?[36]

That Plath is forcing herself to attend to every detail of Percy's death and burial ("something in me said, *now you must see this*") despite being so horrified by what she's seeing that at one point she's "seized by dry retching"[37] no doubt gives "Berck-Plage" some of its unnerving quality, even perhaps the disturbing tone that Alvarez rather theatrically defined as "injurious and faintly obscene." At the same time, even before the introduction of a terminally ill patient, the sheer *strangeness* of the beach at Berck—both its foreignness and its uncanny juxtaposition of jovial holiday making and sorrowful curetaking—fosters the tone of solemn estrangement that governs the sequence from the start. Certainly such distancing is apropos, like muffled drum, in the presence of death, but this beautifully crafted elegy has, throughout, a firmness of defamiliarization that seems singularly suited to the "*immense plage de sable fin, très sûre*" on which it is so dramatically set.

The aesthetic processes that shape such defamiliarization are, moreover, as nightmarish as Plath's worst medical dreams might have foretold. One the one hand, as priestly death stalks the living, people are disassembled into surreal fragments of themselves, with the "toe-less foot" of doom drawing ever nearer to the "shrunk voices" of the bathers and to the "confectioner's sugar" of breasts and hips hidden in the dunes, while the "green pool" sick from swallowing "limbs, images, shrieks" and the "mirrory" surgical eye, along with the tongue of the dead man, the pallid hands and visages of mourners, and the crusted "blood of limb stumps" evoked by the red earth graveyard. On the other hand, as the living disintegrate into body parts, inhuman objects ("Things, things") take on a bizarrely autonomous existence. Finally, indeed, the thoughts of his widow are "Blunt practical boats // Full of dresses and hats and china and married daughters," as if there were no distinction between people and possessions, and the "actions" of the dead man have solidified "like living room furniture, like a décor," while the trees with serene composure "march to church."[38]

Such processes of distancing and estrangement set the scene with extraordinary effectiveness for the climactic funeral and burial passages of "Berck-Plage," two episodes (6 and 7) set inland in Devon, far from the medicalized beaches in Picardy, which nonetheless appear to have evolved as astonishingly out of the poet's encounter with the "great abeyance" of the sea on a foreign shore as out of the journal entries I just quoted.

It's hard now to ignore every aspect of the moment when the "naked mouth" of earth opens, "red and awkward," to swallow the coffin of the dead man who turns out to have been Percy Key but obviously signifies Everyman. I don't think I noticed, though, when I was first seized by the austere ferocity of this elegy, how carefully—how theologically!—Plath prepares for such a denouement, from the very beginning of the work dressing death in the black cassock of a priest and juxtaposing his affectation of piety with the cryptic (and perhaps desperate) ritual of the mackerel gatherers who "wall up their backs against him" to handle "the black and green lozenges [of fish] like the parts of a body."[39] But if only unconsciously I must have been gripped by the fatality with which the sacramental "lozenges" of dead mackerel dissolved into the distanced and defamiliarized "lozenge of wood" in which the body parts of the dead man have been secreted. And I must have at least intuited, too, the bitter skepticism that shaped the transformation of priestly death (from the poem's beginning) into (at the end) a hopeless human cleric who is merely a "tarred fabric, sorry"—in several senses—and "dull," though he presides dutifully over the ceremonial futility with which the "coffin on its flowery cart like a beautiful woman, / A crest of breasts, eyelids and lips" (echoing the obscenely titillating breasts and hips of section 2) storms the hilltop graveyard.[40]

I'm sure, though, that I didn't quite appreciate the brilliance with which Plath assigns the poem's final vision to a group of children in an enclosed yard—children who in their representation of mortal innocence and fleshly entrapment surely share with the children in section 3 the faults the speaker cannot "bandage." From their (ironically) naive perspective, the last communion in which the earth must swallow a eucharistic "lozenge of wood" is a "wonderful thing."[41] But the speaker—and I believe I trusted her when I was a "twenty-something" baffled and envious would-be competitor—knows better. Though the "sky pours into the hole" in the graveyard as plasma might be desperately poured into a fatal wound, she concludes, "there is no hope, it is given up."[42]

Here "it" of course has multivalent references. Most obviously "it" is the lozenge/coffin that must be "given up" to the voracious earth mouth. But too, "it" is hope for some ritual of redemption from the "sorry and dull" human priest. And "it" is even the sky, which only pours *like* plasma but can neither resuscitate the dead one nor offer him and his mourners the promise of a heavenly home. To the question Plath had posed in her journal, as she recorded her "unfinished feeling" after the graveside ceremony for Percy Key—"Is he to be left up there, uncovered, all alone?"—the answer this passage offers is *yes, he is.* Oh, of course he'll be covered with earth, but no ceremony else will clothe his termination with anything resembling celestial radiance.

Whether sacrifice or surrender, says this classic mid-century elegy, giving up is what one does in the face of death. In *Four Quartets*, Eliot assuages his terror of going "into the dark" of "the silent funeral" by telling his soul to "be still, and let the dark come upon you / Which shall be the darkness of God,"[43] and in "The Quaker Graveyard at Nantucket," Lowell comforts himself with the assurance that "The Lord survives the rainbow of His will."[44] But like so many of her contemporaries and descendants, Plath merely concludes that the circumstances of defeat must be scrupulously recorded and set against the oncoming priest of the grave: the living must "wall up their backs against" his "black cassock" as the mackerel gatherers do, even if the details out of which they build their defenses are as nauseating as the "Limbs, images, shrieks" that have sickened the eye of the innocent green pool among the dunes. In this respect, I think even my earliest readings of "Berck-Plage" prepared me for much of what I've come to believe about late-twentieth-century public as well as private procedures for mourning and perhaps, more generally, laid the foundations for my thoughts about the theological "damper" on which our aesthetic locates itself. Certainly these readings have prepared me to regard Plath herself as our most highly sensitized and representative poet not, as is often asserted, of suicidal extremism but rather of later-twentieth-century mourning.

To be sure, the skeptical resignation with which Plath gives "it" (the coffin, hope, the sky) up at the end of her desolate elegy wasn't without precedent, even before the twentieth century dawned with the "growing gloom" that Thomas Hardy depicted in "The Darkling Thrush,"[45] his bleak greeting to New Year's Day 1900. In 1851, for instance—over a century before Plath and Hughes visited Berck-Plage—Matthew Arnold had recorded the "melancholy, long, with-drawing roar" of the "Sea of Faith" in "Dover Beach." But the channel dividing Berck-Plage from Dover Beach is obviously even more histor-ical than geographical. On the "French coast the light / Gleams and is gone," mourned Arnold, but he insisted that "the cliffs of England stand, / Glimmering and vast, out in the tranquil bay" and imagined that there might still after all be something substantive to fight about, even if the battle was joined by "ignorant armies" who "clash by night."[46] For Plath, though, the sea that primordially crystallized body parts, limbs, images, shrieks, simply "Creeps away, many-snaked, with a long hiss of distress."[47] I suspect it was that devastating and devas-tated "hiss of distress" I found so eerily compelling in "Berck-Plage" almost four decades ago.

Now, certainly, the long hiss of distress, permeating so much of Plath's work, means to me that among the countless modern poets who have found themselves willingly or unwillingly stationed beside death's door, this nearly legendary young woman has a special status. For per-haps more than anyone else, she really did articulate not just a post-modernist vision of death itself but also the kind of "mythology of modern death"[48] that Wallace Stevens, a precursor whose art she much admired, once tentatively proposed. And as the sinister liminal zone of "Berck-Plage" suggests, hers was a mythology whose fathomless points of origin and destination were in what Matthew Arnold calls "the unplumbed, salt, estranging sea."[49]

NOTES

1. *CP*, 196–201.

2. *Michelin*, 57.

3. For the couple's vacation with the Merwins at their farmhouse in the Dordogne, see Anne Stevenson, *Bitter Fame: A Life of Sylvia Plath* (Boston: Houghton Mifflin, 1989), 215–17, 336–42.

4. Peter Porter, "Poetic Justice" (July 30, 2001) at http://www.theage.com/au/entertainment/2001/07/30FFX3ZSW4.RPC.html.

5. Ibid.

6. Hughes, note to "Berck-Plage," *CP*, 293; he offered the same explanation in "Notes on the Chronological Order of Sylvia Plath's Poems," in *The Art of Sylvia Plath*, ed. Charles Newman (Bloomington: Indiana University Press, 1970), 187.

7. *CP*, 196–97.

8. A. Alvarez, *The Savage God: A Study of Suicide* (1971; New York: Norton, 1990), 31.

9. Jack Folsom, "Death and Rebirth in Sylvia Plath's 'Berck-Plage'" (Temple University, 1994), http://sylviaplath.de/plath/jfolsom.html. Folsom goes on to argue that the "poison" of Plath's "festering memory" of her father's death "distorts her vision of the scene" and "must be drawn out by the poultice of the poem's making and be replaced by healthy tissue" (3).

10. *CP*, 196.

11. Ibid.

12. Ibid., 197.

13. Ibid., 198.

14. Ibid.

15. That I, too, had been guest managing editor of *Mademoiselle* (albeit four years after she was) during the triumphant "prize" month she later so devastatingly portrayed in *The Bell Jar*—that I'd indeed worked closely with Cyrilly Abels, the very "Jay Cee" of that novel—cemented what I considered an obscure bond between my own quotidian domesticity and the more glamorous life of this author strolling a European beach of which I'd never heard. See also my "A Fine White Flying Myth: The Life/Work of Sylvia Plath," in *Shakespeare's Sisters*, ed. Gilbert and Susan Gubar (Bloomington: Indiana University Press, 1978), 245–60.

16. *CP*, 198.

17. For a fine and influential discussion of the "American family elegy," see Jahan Ramazani, *The Poetry of Mourning: The Modern Elegy from Hardy to Heaney* (Chicago: University of Chicago Press, 1994).

18. W. B. Yeats, "Sailing to Byzantium," *The Collected Poems of W.B. Yeats*, 2nd ed., ed. Richard J. Finneran (New York: Macmillan, 1989), 204.

19. *CP*, 198.

20. Ibid., 200.

21. Ibid., 198.

22. Hughes, note to "Berck-Plage," 293.

23. See Folsom, "Death and Rebirth," who discusses variant drafts of the poem, but doesn't indicate whether the Berck-Plage passages were begun earlier than (or separately from) the Percy Key material.

24. T. S. Eliot, "East Coker," *Four Quartets* (New York: Harcourt Brace, 1943), 27.

25. *CP*, 197

26. Eliot, "East Coker," 127.

27. Among Plath's hospital poems, see "Morning in the Hospital Solarium," "Tulips," "In Plaster," "The Surgeon at 2 A.M.," and "Paralytic." She also fictionalized medical scenes in such prose writings as "Johnny Panic and the Bible of Dreams" and "The Daughters of Blossom Street."

28. *CP*, 198.

29. *UJ*, 64.

30. *CP*, 190.

31. In his fine *Sylvia Plath: A Critical Study* (London: Faber and Faber, 2001), Tim Kendall notes that Plath had been "charting the gradual decline of her neighbor, Percy Key, for several months," and adds that "Percy's fate colored—or corrupted—Plath's imaginative life during these months; not only her notebooks, but also 'Among the Narcissi' and 'Berck Plage' are heavily preoccupied with his deteriorating health and approaching death. This ever-present intimation of mortality also inspires 'Apprehensions,' a meditation on dying and the fear of death, in which the speaker confesses to 'a terror / Of being wheeled off under crosses and a rain of piètas.' 'The Rabbit Catcher' and 'Event' . . . [works whose] concerns inspire and become part of a more general malaise: as Plath reports, 'Everybody, it seems, is going or dying in this cold mean spring'" (97).

32. *UJ*, 667–68; italics added.

33. Ibid., 670.

34. Ibid., 672.

35. Ibid., 671–72; italics added.

36. Ibid., 673; italics added.

37. Ibid., 668.

38. *CP*, 199.

39. Ibid., 196.

40. Ibid., 200.

41. Ibid., 201.

42. Ibid.

43. Eliot, "East Coker," 27.

44. Robert Lowell, "The Quaker Graveyard in Nantucket," *The Collected Poems of Robert Lowell*, ed. Frank Bidart and David Gewanter (New York: Farrar, Straus and Giroux, 2003), 18.

45. Thomas Hardy, "The Darkling Thrush," *The Complete Poems*, ed. James Gibson (New York: Macmillan, 1976), 150.

46. Matthew Arnold, "Dover Beach," *The Portable Matthew Arnold*, ed. Lionel Trilling (New York: Viking Press, 1949), 165–67.

47. *CP*, 196.

48. Wallace Stevens, "The Owl and the Sarcophagus," *The Collected Poems of Wallace Stevens* (New York: Knopf, 1955), 435.

49. Matthew Arnold, "To Marguerite–Continued," *Portable Matthew Arnold*, 111–12.

ANN KENISTON

The Holocaust Again

SYLVIA PLATH, BELATEDNESS, AND
THE LIMITS OF LYRIC FIGURE

⊞

All lyric poetry is stuck between thing and word: although the lyric impulse may be triggered by experience, sensation, or memory, poems are made of language. The poem itself is in some ways an artifact of the struggle between the impulse to transparency and the compulsion to acknowledge and even exploit its impossibility. Sylvia Plath's late poems enact this struggle with particular ferocity. They meld apparently forthright autobiographical statement and allusions to the events of Plath's time with disembodied, vatic utterance in ways that often raise questions about their accuracy. Indeed, many of the most contentious debates about Plath's poems have focused on such questions. Even the 2004 "restored" edition of Plath's *Ariel*, which draws on archival evidence from Plath's manuscript of her final volume, is touched by such debates: the published volume includes, in its foreword, a biographically inflected analysis by Plath's daughter, Frieda Hughes.[1] The persistence of these critical and textual controversies forty years after *Ariel*'s first publication reveals the difficulty of determining how exactly Plath's poems draw on and represent the world. To what extent, that is, is Plath a documentarian, concerned primarily with getting down what Robert Lowell has called "what really happened,"[2] and to what extent are her poems concerned primarily with the fact and circumstances of their utterance?

Plath's so-called Holocaust poems offer dense and suggestive material through which to consider this question.[3] In this essay, I will reexamine these notorious but (perhaps surprisingly) critically neglected poems, arguing that they reveal Plath to be concerned not so much with capturing the essence of the Holocaust as with the ways the Holocaust resists representation.[4] The belated, physically removed speakers of these poems insist that the Holocaust is available only in fragmentary and corrupted form, and Plath's emphasis on the materiality of her poems themselves, on their often awkward or obtrusive mechanics, intensifies this sense of distance. The poems in this way connect historical with textual violence, making the Holocaust's corruption visible through the corruption of the poems themselves. More exactly, Plath reveals the failures of chronology and intimacy engendered by the Holocaust through similar failures in the poems themselves.

The Holocaust, Jacqueline Rose has argued in relation to Plath's "Daddy," is "the event which puts under greatest pressure—or is most readily available to put under such pressure—the concept of linguistic figuration."[5] The implication of Rose's assertion—which draws on and echoes the conclusions of many theorists of the Holocaust—is that the Holocaust cannot be represented in straightforward or direct form. Rather, the event is revealed only through the "pressure[s]" it exerts on conventional modes of representation. Poems reveal the strains of the Holocaust not only by describing but by enacting these strains, by permitting the poems' rhetorical, figurative underpinnings to strain. In what follows, I will amplify the implications of Rose's claim by systematically examining the relation between the Holocaust and the tropes and figures (in particular metaphor, metonymy, and apostrophe) manipulated by Plath in "Daddy" and "Lady Lazarus," her most explicit Holocaust poems. While Rose focuses on the psychoanalytic basis of Plath's Holocaust imagery, I will emphasize this imagery's relation both to the actual events of the Holocaust and, more significantly, to Plath's notion of the function and limits of lyric itself.[6]

Plath wrote about the Holocaust after it had ended; as a non-Jewish American, she was geographically and culturally as well as chronologically excluded from firsthand experience of its events. Plath's position as a nonwitness has led to many of the most vehement condemnations of her Holocaust imagery. Yet Plath's speakers do not in fact pretend to be witnesses or survivors of the Holocaust. Rather than revealing proximity and immediacy, they occupy a position of distance and belatedness. This position resembles what Marianne Hirsch has characterized as the experience of "postmemory" distinctive to nonsurvivors, in which "identification" with what trauma victims have suffered combines with a sense of "unbridgeable distance" from this suffering.[7] A similar sense of distance, though, characterizes the experience of actual trauma victims for whom, in Cathy Caruth's terms, trauma "is not assimilated or experienced fully at the time, but only belatedly, in its repeated *possession* of the one who experiences it."[8] Peter Nicholls similarly argues that trauma can be assimilated only when "a second event release[s the] traumatic force"[9] of the original trauma in such a way that "the second event is presented now as the 'cause' of the first." As a result, the survivor remains estranged from the original trauma, feeling that it "has never been *present* and hence that it exists only as a repetition."[10] The distance and belatedness that separate Plath from the Holocaust thus recall the similar sense of belatedness that characterizes the experience of the survivor. The crucial difference is that Plath was not helpless before her belatedness; her poems not only express but exploit this position of belatedness. Plath's poems, that is, convert the survivor's unwilled psychological response into an aesthetic strategy.

The chronological disruptions experienced by the trauma survivor also characterize Plath's chosen genre. As Sharon Cameron has argued, lyric is fundamentally preoccupied with "the anxieties of the temporal sequence";[11] lyric acknowledges narrative, chronology, and history even as it attempts to exclude them from the space of the poem. Lyric often bears the marks of this struggle. It tends, that is, to include violent disruptions of its present moment in the form both of flashbacks and, more often, the representation as if present of what has not yet occurred; it exposes the infelicities involved in the process of remembering. Plath's allusions to the Holocaust in this way draw attention to even as they exaggerate tensions already present in lyric.

Both "Daddy" and "Lady Lazarus" begin in and explore the ramifications of ruptured and impossible time frames, emphasizing what Nicholls calls disruptions of "traditional notions of causality";[12] their position in the *Ariel Restored* if anything links them more directly than does the 1966 published version.[13] What is most fundamentally disrupted in both poems is the notion that death is final. In "Daddy," the speaker struggles to kill a father who is already dead; "Lady Lazarus" asserts a roughly corresponding (although also inverse) ability repeatedly to revive its dead speaker. Both poems emphasize repetition ("I have done it again," begins "Lady Lazarus"), but both are also evasive: the scene, for example, of the father's death in "Daddy" is never "*present*," in Nicholls's term, but rather conveyed through a series of displaced scenes, both in terms of time—the speaker describes his subsequent murder—and of character—she focuses on her husband and on her own suicide attempts.

The speaker's belated position in "Daddy" is partly that of any bereaved survivor who cannot unmake the other's death but is condemned to live on in his absence. Plath's manipulations of the poem's time frame, though, are more extreme than those in much elegy. The poem's temporally impossible narrative—in which the speaker attempts to kill her already-dead father—leads to a fundamental irony in the poem: any success the speaker achieves (that is, in killing him) is, according to the poem's central premise, superfluous.[14] Several contradictory narratives thus coexist: while most of the poem chronicles in fairly straightforward terms the speaker's struggle to kill Daddy, the speaker also alludes to two distinct accounts of Daddy's previous death, one in which the daughter is responsible for Daddy's death and another in which Daddy has long since died, apparently before the daughter could intervene. The speaker thus experiences Daddy's death both as a past and a future event, one both within and exceeding her control; she is simultaneously an adult and a child, a situation that helps account for the poem's inconsistencies of tone, its juxtaposition, for example, of "Luftwaffe" with "gobbledygoo."

The temporal disruptions in "Lady Lazarus" are if anything more extreme. Despite its chronologically untenable premise, "Daddy" is structured narratively: the speaker repeatedly attempts to gain access to and kill Daddy while he becomes, paradoxically, imbued by her with more and more power, as expressed through the changing terms through which she describes him. Although the Holocaust is, if anything, more central to the poem than to "Daddy," "Lady Lazarus," written about two weeks later, excises much of this narrative framework. Lady Lazarus is, catlike, capable of multiple deaths: she is impelled to keep repeating the death-rebirth dynamic whose third iteration the poem recounts. Moreover, the poem insists on the simultaneity of several distinct time frames, including the biblical era of Lazarus, the time of the Holocaust, and an apparently more recent scene of a carnival sideshow. The poem in these ways intensifies the anachronism and sense of removal of "Daddy," as two similar passages reveal. In "Daddy," the speaker describes in narrative terms the relation between Daddy's death and her subsequent suicide attempt: when she was ten,

Daddy died, and when she was twenty, she attempted suicide. But "Lady Lazarus" recalls the same two events in a way that unmakes the distinction between them. Lady Lazarus recalls her own death: her suicide has been successful (in contrast with the *attempted* suicide in "Daddy"), not impelled by a particular external event (in contrast with Daddy's burial), and repeated: it has occurred twice so far.

In addition to such straightforward manipulation of time frame, Plath's treatment of familiar poetic tropes and figures intensifies what I have been calling the poems' belatedness by emphasizing the disruption of conventional lyric notions of equivalence and intimacy. Plath's poems disrupt and distort both trope—the mechanism of equivalence or analogy—and apostrophe—conventionally a strategy through which intimacy or proximity is gained between the speaker and the addressee. In the process, Plath reinforces her speakers' removal from the Holocaust in several ways: Plath's speakers represent the Holocaust as corrupted, and the corruption of the figures themselves reveals the failure of conventional poetic mechanisms of representation in relation to the Holocaust.

Many readers, though, have seen Plath's Holocaust imagery very differently, as an enactment of what several have called an "identification" or "metaphoric" equivalence between the characters in the poem (the daughter, the father) and characters from the Holocaust (the Jew, the Nazi).[15] Such a model of identification has often led these readers to condemn the poems; Plath's analogy between private suffering and the calamity of the Holocaust is in the words of the influential critic Irving Howe "monstrous, utterly disproportionate."[16] Although several recent critics have, in pointing out the limits of models such as Howe's, helped redefine the terms in which Plath's Holocaust imagery has been theorized, they have not challenged the notion that the poems are essentially metaphoric, that they represent one realm in terms of another. Rather, even recent critics tend only to invert the relation between what Howe calls "private suffering" and the Holocaust. That is, while earlier readers saw the political or public content of the poems as their metaphoric vehicle or the visible manifestation of their underlying personal content, more recent readers have tended to read the personal as a vehicle for an underlying political tenor.[17]

Such readings assume that metaphor involves a static and fixed equivalence between two unlike entities. Yet as Paul Ricoeur has argued, metaphor is more complex. It points not only to the likeness of two entities but to the limits of that likeness: "instead of giving the name of the species to the genus, of the genus to the species, or of the species to another species, metaphor . . . blurs the conceptual boundaries of the terms considered" and thus "confus[es] . . . established logical boundaries."[18] Holocaust literature may tend particularly to such blurrings or breakdowns of equivalence because, as James Young has suggested, the Nazis "literaliz[ed] metaphor"—for example the notion of exterminating the Jewish vermin—and thus removed metaphor from "innocen[ce]."[19]

That Plath herself resisted straightforwardly metaphoric interpretations of her Holocaust imagery is suggested by two quite different comments she made about what she metonymically calls "Hiroshima." Both these assertions refuse the possibility that images of Hiroshima and related public atrocities in her poems clearly or directly represent the personal or any other realm. In an essay published in October 1962, the month she wrote "Daddy" and "Lady Lazarus," Plath directly refuses the idea that "Hiroshima" stands for the personal realm, for example, of maternity. Emphasizing her reliance on "deflection," Plath distinguishes these realms: "My poems *do not* turn out to be about Hiroshima, *but about* a child forming itself finger by finger in the dark."[20] In an interview the same month, she suggests a more direct connection between the personal and the public realms: "personal experience . . . should be *relevant,* and relevant to the larger things, the bigger things such as Hiroshima and Dachau and so on."[21] Yet here too she stops short of suggesting that these realms are equivalent.

Plath's treatment of the Holocaust in "Daddy" and "Lady Lazarus" suggests a similar resistance to fixed equivalences and in the process reveals her preoccupation with interrogating the assumptions on which poetic meaning often relies. Plath draws on a range of references in "Daddy"; Daddy is identified not only with a German and a swastika but also with a shoe, statue, devil, and a vampire. The shifts in these metaphors suggest not a fixed or stable resemblance between Daddy and some other entity but rather the randomness and fluidity of metaphoric identification itself: each metaphor, found to be inadequate or perhaps too mild, is abandoned for another. The poem's repeated references to the difficulty of speech—"The tongue stuck in my jaw," "I could hardly speak"—partly express this struggle: the string of metaphors reveals Daddy's evasion of the speaker's attempts to locate and pin him down.

The tropological position of the Holocaust in the poem is also unstable, as several similes make clear.[22] At times the speaker presents the Holocaust as an actual, physical event:

> In the German tongue, *in the Polish town*
> Scraped flat by the roller
> Of wars . . .

At others, references to the Holocaust—here the Fascist, the boot, and the heart—are the tenor of the simile; they describe in physically immediate terms the brute that Daddy resembles:

> Every woman adores *a Fascist,*
> The boot in the face, the brute
> Brute heart of *a brute like you.*[23]

But Plath also uses the Holocaust as a metaphoric vehicle, a concept that describes or defines something else:

> And the *language* obscene
>
> An engine, an engine
> Chuffing me off *like a Jew*
> . . . .
> I made a *model of you,*
> A man in black with a Meinkampf look.[24]

In the first part of this passage, the language is the tenor; the Jew, identified by "like," is the vehicle. Similarly, in the second image, the Hitler-like man in black is a copy or model of "you."

The inconsistent and incomplete quality of many of the poem's metaphors is intensified by the fact that, as Rose and others have noted, many of the analogies in "Daddy" are not metaphoric at all.[25] The poem relies on simile, as in the examples above, as well as on metonymy, an analogy of contiguity rather than resemblance that is generally seen as more provisional and arbitrary than metaphor. Metonymy, as Rose notes, emphasizes the "partial, hesitant, and speculative" quality of identification and thus the "instability [of] any identity thereby produced,"[26] although metonymy also gestures, albeit by revealing a series of fragments, at wholeness. The metonymy of "Daddy" is for the most part synecdochic: Plath tends to allude to concepts and entities by means of one or several of their constituent parts. Daddy is not described as a Nazi; the term never appears in the final poem, although, significantly, "Hitler" and "Nazi" appeared in and were excised by Plath from the poem's early drafts.[27] In the final version, Nazis and the Holocaust are represented by their attributes, including mustache, eye, and swastika; in the case, at least, of "swastika," Plath was aware of the term's multiple meanings, which further remove it from fixed metaphoric significance.[28] The fragmentary quality of these analogies marks not only the speaker's state of mind—which Rose describes psychoanalytically in terms of "displacement"[29]—but the fragmentation of the Holocaust itself, which Plath's speaker makes clear is available to her only in pieces and clichés.

In this context, it is worth elaborating on Rose's observation that the poem's association of speaker with Jew is not metaphoric but instead relies on simile and metonymy. The analogy between speaker and Jew is repeated, yet it becomes more provisional with each iteration (my italics):

> I *thought* every German was you.
> And the language obscene
>
> An engine, an engine
> Chuffing me off *like a Jew*.
>
> . . . .
>
> I began *to talk like a Jew*
> I think I *may well be a Jew*.
>
> . . . .
>
> With my gipsy ancestress and my weird luck
>
> . . . .
>
> I *may be a bit of a Jew*.[30]

The passage as a whole resists the logic of metaphoric equivalence suggested by the initial, already somewhat tentative, analogy of "German" with "you." Daddy remains separate from the engine (itself a metonym for the infliction of Nazi suffering); rather, it is the German language that forces the speaker into the train, which itself seems created by that language, as the proto-German sound of the neologism "chuffing"—a word not identified as a verb in Plath's often-consulted dictionary—suggests.[31] Thus, while Daddy may resemble a German, the speaker distances herself from this already indirect relation: she is not Daddy's victim but the victim of language itself. The shift to a more direct equivalence between self and Jew is similarly qualified. Insofar as the speaker is a Jew, the resemblance is limited to particular attributes (she talks like one) or it is multiply qualified (*"I think I may* well be a Jew"). The association of self with Jew leads to a shift into a more purely metonymic mode, one in which a series of objects possessed by and synecdochically associated not with Jews but with Gypsies, another class of Nazi victims, undermines the speaker's analogy with Jew just at the moment that it is most directly stated. These disruptions of metaphoric equivalence by metonymy help explain why the speaker's final statement on the matter is not only tentative ("I may be") but partial: she is not a Jew but "a bit of a Jew."

"Lady Lazarus" explores far more directly the question of possession, and more exactly of the significance of material possessions, to which "Daddy" alludes, and in the process it more radically undermines fixed equivalence and analogy. Holocaust imagery begins, ends, and recurs throughout nearly the entire poem. But the Holocaust in "Lady Lazarus" does not appear as a conflict or even as a historical event. Absent are the references to objective, public images—the barbed wire, swastika, and train of "Daddy"—along with the sense of conflict in "Daddy" between Jews and Nazis and between the speaker and Daddy. What persists in "Lady Lazarus" is the body of the victim, nearly distinct from that of the enemy or doktor she only a few times addresses. (The appositive "Daddy," by contrast, recurs five times in the earlier poem and the pronoun "you" in reference to Daddy sixteen times.) Moreover, in "Lady Lazarus," the speaker is less cohesive than the speaker of "Daddy." In "Daddy," the speaker is "a bit of a Jew"; she renders unstable a concept (Jewishness) that is generally seen as coherent. But in "Lady Lazarus," the speaker is herself broken into bits, as the phrase "a bit of blood" suggests; she is described not as a person but as a series of body parts. This bodily fracturing makes physical the mechanics and logic of synecdoche. The poem asserts that the corpse can be revived, the broken bits reassembled. Yet the intensity with which the speaker describes her dismemberment belies the possibility of reconstitution in ways that question the logic of synecdoche: can the severed, dissociated part (of the body, of the Holocaust itself) stand for something whole?

At times Lady Lazarus directly insists that the fragments of her body represent a consistent and whole self, most clearly when she claims, "I may be skin and bone, // Nevertheless, I am *the same, identical* woman" (my italics). Yet this notion of wholeness is also undermined, especially toward the end of the poem:

> Ash, ash—
> You poke and stir.
> Flesh, bone, *there is nothing there*—
>
> A cake of soap,
> A wedding ring,
> A gold filling.[32]

The dash after "there" elides a series of conflicting ways that flesh and bone—already synecdoches for the speaker's body—might be linked to the images of soap, ring, and filling. Flesh and bone have vanished completely ("there is nothing there"), yet the phrases after the dash undermine this claim. Insofar as the Nazi soap persists, deriving like the ash from human flesh and bone, the relation seems partly one of physical transformation: these artifacts are what her body has become. The ring and filling, though, suggest something else. They are former possessions of the speaker that now seem metonymically to represent her.

The passage thus compactly proposes and allows to coexist a series of inconsistent connections between intact body and what remains after it has burned. The effect is that the poem's narrative logic of reconstitution and resurrection is complicated by a kind of overload of options. Yet this overload, as another passage makes more explicit, does not so much multiply the significance of the speaker's body as convert it into a commodity, something to be manipulated and exploited:

> There is a charge
>
> For the eyeing of my scars, there is a charge
> For the hearing of my heart—

. . . .

And there is a charge, a very large charge,
For a word or a touch
Or a bit of blood

Or a piece of my hair or my clothes.[33]

Here the bits of blood, hair, and clothes, like the Catholic relics wor-
shipped as a representation of the intact saint, evoke an archetypal version of synecdoche: they seem to stand for and become valuable
through their evocation of the lost, whole body. Yet the image is inconsistent. The word and touch suggest that the speaker persists in intact
form even as she has been broken into fragments. More significantly,
the metonymy is complicated by the pun on "charge," which stands
not only for the speaker's thrill of self-revelation but also the admission
fee charged the crowd eager to witness this spectacle. As with the
description of the ring and filling, the image suggests an economic as
well as a synecdochic model: the speaker in her willingness to reveal
her scars and bestow her blood for a price seems to adopt the Nazi val-
uation of gold filling over living person; the gold pieces are valuable
not only because they allude to or represent the now-burned body but
more obviously for their monetary value. Plath's preoccupation with
the multiple significance of gold is clarified by her dictionary annotations, the text on the verso of her draft, and, perhaps most crucially,
the poem's late image of the golden baby, which "melts to a shriek,"
the apparently permanent residue of gold dissolving into a temporary,
intangible cry of pain or rage.[34]

By replacing the synecdochic logic on which the poem seems to
rely—the notion that the parts allude to the whole—with an economic
one—in which the speaker's body is a commodity, an item to be
bought or sold, which does not stand for anything else—"Lady
Lazarus" undermines the notion of figuration itself. The implication of
this dissolution is scandalous, not only with respect to the supposed
sanctity of human life and the integrity of the human body, but to the
memory of the Holocaust. Commodification, the image suggests, has
infected what might otherwise be a more benign tropological mode in
the poem: as the body parts are valuable for their concealed gold, the
speaker here flaunts her conversion of horror not only into a spectacle
but a moneymaking venture. The poem suggests that the Holocaust

itself—available to the belated onlooker only in pieces or through catch phrases—cannot function otherwise.

The "charge" in "Lady Lazarus" simultaneously refers, as Plath's dictionary annotations make clear, to an emotional thrill, a moral obligation, and a financial transaction.[35] In referring to something experienced both by the speaker herself and by those who witness her, the poem sets forth an unstable power balance that is arguably central to much lyric: is the speaker in control, or are the spectators? Even as it turns away from its reader, lyric tends to rely on apostrophe, the figure of address to an inanimate, dead, or absent other. Indeed, apostrophe has been called the preeminent figure of lyric.[36] In Plath's *Ariel* poems, a particularly negative apostrophe predominates. This apostrophe raises questions about the autonomy and authority of the speaker: apostrophe tends to vest the absent other with power, yet it is highly artificial, even stagey, and so it ultimately (in that the other is by definition absent) recalls the speaker's isolation.[37] I have been arguing that Plath's use of trope challenges both the fixity of metaphoric equivalence and the logic of synecdoche in the specific context of the Holocaust, linking the Holocaust itself to the failure of conventional means of lyric equivalence and representation. Plath's apostrophe similarly represents the failures of proximity and communication associated by trauma theorists with the Holocaust. As Plath's challenges to trope exaggerate instabilities that Ricoeur and others have found to inhere in all trope, her apostrophe similarly exaggerates the uncertainties about the power of the other implicit in all apostrophic utterance.

The intersections between lyric models of address and trauma theory's notions of testimony are striking. Lyric address, I have been claiming, involves duplicity, a fiction of presence that both undermines and intensifies the underlying assertion of absence. Uncertainties about the position of the other are also central to trauma theory, which both insists that the Holocaust dismantled the possibility of address and also, paradoxically, celebrates the restorative possibilities of subsequent or belated testimony. In Dori Laub's terms, the Holocaust "produced no witnesses"[38] and rendered "the very imagination of the *other* . . . no longer possible."[39] Yet the subsequent, belated act of testimony before an actual other allows "something like a repossession of the act of witnessing."[40] As Caruth claims, such testimony confirms the belatedness of the trauma: "The history of a trauma, *in its inherent belatedness,* can only take place through the listening of another."[41] While

Plath is not a survivor, her manipulations of address intensify this sense of distance, isolation, and failed witness.

In "Lady Lazarus," Plath manipulates the ambiguity inherent in the figure of apostrophe in ways that reveal the difficulty of representing the Holocaust itself. The claim I am making about Plath methodologically resembles Shoshana Felman's reading of the insistent and shifting apostrophe of Paul Celan's emblematic Holocaust poem "Death Fugue." For Felman, Celan's poem is "not simply about violence but about the relation between violence and language."[42] Its apostrophe, or more exactly its "radical disruption of address," expresses "the very essence of the violence, and the very essence of the Holocaust"[43] in ways more powerful than those allowed by straightforward thematization of that violence—for example, a discussion of "killing."[44]

"Lady Lazarus" is very different from Celan's "Death Fugue," but its apostrophe and its preoccupation with performance and spectatorship articulate something similar to what Felman claims about Celan. "Lady Lazarus" does not simply describe the Holocaust; it formally enacts its violence and in the process does violence to its own apostrophe. The address of "Lady Lazarus" formally recalls the possibility of intimacy and reciprocity often marked by apostrophe. But it refuses even the curtailed version of proximity, the sympathetic "repossession of . . . witnessing"[45] associated by Laub with Holocaust testimony. "Lady Lazarus" thus structurally recalls the therapeutic model of testimony suggested by Laub: the speaker can only gain mastery or possession of her suffering at the hands of the Nazi "Herr Doktor" belatedly, through the subsequent enactment of her suffering before the group of spectators. Yet Lady Lazarus's reenactment of injury remains parodic rather than restorative and reveals the unbridgeable gap, thematized as mutual contempt, between the speaker and her witnesses.

The address of "Daddy" is relatively straightforward: the poem apostrophizes Daddy, while the reader is not represented in the poem. "Lady Lazarus," though, sets up a more complex situation. The speaker at the poem's beginning addresses the singular "my enemy" using the elevated and artificial "O" of apostrophe. Toward the end, she addresses him again; this addressee is in the last stanzas equivalent or perhaps transformed to Herr Doktor, Herr God, Herr Lucifer. (The "O" here, though, becomes the less formal, less archaic, more evaluative "So".) But midway through, as the speaker abandons the imagery of the

Holocaust for the very different scene of a circus sideshow or "strip tease," the address shifts briefly to a group whose members are first described, then addressed:[46]

> The peanut-crunching crowd
> Shoves in to see
> . . . .
> *Gentlemen, ladies*
>
> These are my hands
> My knees.[47]

While Plath's shift from description to address is rhetorically dramatic, hinting at immediacy, it intensifies without substantially altering the contempt expressed all along by the speaker for her reincarnation. Thus the tone of the address to the enemy in the poem's fourth Holocaust-situated stanza is not substantially different from the address to the gentlemen and ladies in the eleventh. And rather than redeeming or rendering into "history" the earlier, already temporally doubled scene of Lazarus / the Holocaust, as Caruth claims the subsequent recounting of trauma can, the striptease scene permits Lady Lazarus to articulate directly her separation from her spectators. For Caruth, the trauma survivor belatedly struggles to repossess a trauma that has taken possession of her. Plath's speaker similarly struggles. She is unwrapped by an unidentified "them" but retains control of her body, identifying her revealed parts as "*my* hands / *My* knees"; her ambiguously impersonal insistence, "There is a charge," suggests more clearly an attempt to wrest mastery from the others in the poem (my italics). Yet this struggle exposes only the speaker's compulsion to perform or enact her victimization. Rather than affirming the integrity of either victim or witness, this passage insists, as several readers have noted, that it is all an act.[48]

The address to the gentlemen and ladies intensifies this sense of artificiality. Inserted between an acknowledgment of vulnerability (the speaker is "only thirty") and a relatively straightforward chronological personal history, this passage undermines the pathos and verisimilitude of those moments. Interrupting the poem's Holocaust setting, the scene reveals that the Holocaust, even when abandoned, recurs, not as an authentic much less intimate act, but rather as a way of revealing the absence of any authentic essence. Just as the poem's tropological manipulations reduce the Holocaust to a commodity, Plath's address repudiates reciprocity. To address someone in this post-Holocaust situation—one that here literally follows the poem's Holocaust references—the poem implies, forces the addressee into a position of contemptuous consumption.

The address of "Lady Lazarus" is not reader address. But in that it stages the speaker's self-exposure before a crowd of greedy viewers, it can plausibly be read as an articulation of Plath's relation to the actual readers of her self-exposing or "confessional" poems.[49] The scene in this way invites a kind of negative identification, one in which the drama within the poem evokes the drama of the poem's reception, a connection that resembles what Caruth calls the "'contagion' . . . the traumatization of the ones who listen."[50] It is significant that this identification itself occurs only belatedly and outside the scene described within the poem. That is, Plath seems to have anticipated her readers' subsequent response to her poems, and insofar as these readers have responded both ravenously and contemptuously to her self-revelations, they have fulfilled a role Plath already scripted for them. In this way, any implication that the poem's apostrophe stands in for reader address creates a space into which the poem's actual, belated, contemptuous readers can enter. But entering it, they end up trapped: their negative evaluations are evidence of their inability to recognize the poem's fiction. The more vociferously they condemn the poem, the more they reveal its success as a credible performance.

Plath's Holocaust poems recall and extend the notion of belatedness in ways, I have been suggesting, that evoke what is distinctive about lyric even as they interrogate lyric figure itself, especially its representational, mimetic, and communicative qualities. In this way, Plath's poems do something nearly directly opposed to much writing about the Holocaust: rather than seeking to keep it alive or to bring it back to life, they confirm the Holocaust's as well as the speaker's deanimation.[51] Lyric for Plath occupies a similarly extreme position. Yet just as death does not in these poems exist without the animation of the dead, Plath's poems do not kill lyric off or even repudiate lyric trope and figure. Rather, they reveal lyric to be flexible enough to survive such violence.

The violence to which Plath subjects her own lyric in this way helps explain her unstable position in the poetic canon: her poems reveal not so much her mastery of lyric conventions as her interrogation and defiance of them. Any dazzlement the poems produce is partial and occluded, a result of their ability to employ lyric trope and figure to represent at once the unrepresentability of the Holocaust and of the near-dissolution of those tropes and figures themselves. At the same time, Plath's insistence on dismantling what might more easily have remained intact helps reframe, if not answer, the questions about representation with which I began. The reading I have been offering has attempted to connect Plath's formal practices to the actual events she describes. Yet "Daddy" and "Lady Lazarus" reveal the difficulty of doing so: in these poems, Plath looks at the Holocaust from the estranged position of the nonsurvivor; her speakers are impelled back to a Holocaust they insist cannot be represented.

If these poems suggest Plath herself to be inaccessible, her different personae or incarnations never fully reconcilable, this, in the end, is how the Holocaust also seems in these poems. It exists, for the physically removed, temporally belated poet, as a specter, poised between the living and the dead. Plath's *Ariel* poems make clear that if the Holocaust cannot be possessed, it also cannot be vanquished. Its images— of smoke, corpses, burning, and rituals in which the body is rendered unnecessary—infect even poems that contain no direct allusions to the Holocaust. Perhaps more crucially, the Holocaust impels the one who comes after always to inhabit an aftermath, even if it is not precisely the Holocaust's aftermath, to be defined by the state of looking back from some impossible position, as many of the speakers of Plath's late poems recall their own death.[52] This pattern confirms the Holocaust's evasive power: not the Holocaust itself but the experience of belatedness impels Plath's speakers, awkwardly, illogically, yet with an authority that marks Plath's particularly negative lyric mastery, to speak.

NOTES

I am grateful to Aaron Santesso, Jen Hill, and E. Jane Hedley for their comments on various versions of this essay. Thanks also to Karen Kukil of the Sylvia Plath Collection at Smith College for her generosity and hospitality.

1. Frieda Hughes's foreword argues that Plath's version of *Ariel* is neither definitive nor particularly authentic; rather, it is, she claims, marred by its bond to Plath's life in that the volume reveals its author "caught" in a particular "moment" (xxi), that of "revenge" (xx) against Ted Hughes.

2. Robert Lowell, *Day by Day* (New York: Farrar, 1977), 127.

3. I am using *Holocaust* to refer to the acts perpetrated by the Nazis because it is the most commonly used term, although I am aware of the problems and controversies surrounding the term. Plath's "Holocaust poems" include "Mary's Song" (published in Hughes's U.S. edition of *Ariel* but omitted from Plath's ordering of the manuscript), "Lady Lazarus," "Daddy," and "Getting There."

4. These poems have been mostly excluded from the large-scale recent reevaluation of Plath's work prompted in part by the 1998 publication of Hughes's *Birthday Letters,* his poetic chronicle of his relationship with Plath. Among the few recent critics who have addressed Plath's Holocaust imagery are Strangeways, who attempts to defend her "motives" in writing about the Holocaust and to connect her "historical" references with her "mythic" ones, and Parmet, who reads Plath's Holocaust imagery as an essentially confessional utterance affected by the "widespread diffusion of . . . Holocaust images" in Plath's culture (75). Several other critics have noted that Adolph Eichmann's trial took place in 1961, when Plath was writing the *Ariel* poems. For summaries of earlier readings of Plath's Holocaust imagery, see Young (129–31) and Hungerford (24–27). Al Strangeways, "'The Boot in the Face': The Problem of the Holocaust in the Poetry of Sylvia Plath," in *Contemporary Literature* 37, no. 3 (1996): 370–90; Harriet Parmet, *The Terror of Our Days: Four American Poets Respond to the Holocaust* (Bethlehem, Pa.: Lehigh University Press, 2001); James Young, *Writing and Rewriting the Holocaust: Narrative and the Consequences of Interpretation* (Bloomington: Indiana University Press, 1988); Amy Hungerford, *The Holocaust of Texts: Genocide, Literature, and Personification* (Chicago: University of Chicago Press, 2003).

5. Jacqueline Rose, *The Haunting of Sylvia Plath* (Cambridge: Harvard University Press, 1991), 207.

6. Ibid. Rose's claim is that "Daddy" represents Plath's relation to what she calls "the fantasies underpinning metaphor" (214); the poem draws attention to a "crisis of representation in the place of the father" (227). She argues more generally that Plath occupied a position of abjection or exclusion from the dominant and particularly patriarchal culture of which she was a part.

7. Marianne Hirsch, "Marked by Memory: Feminist Reflections on Trauma and Transmission," in *Extremities: Trauma, Testimony, and Community,* ed. Nancy K. Miller and Jason Tougaw (Urbana: University of Illinois Press, 2002), 76.

8. Cathy Caruth, ed., *Trauma: Explorations in Memory* (Baltimore: Johns Hopkins University Press, 1995), 4. Italics in the original.

9. Peter Nicholls, "The Belated Postmodern: History, Phantoms, and Toni Morrison," in *A Practical Reader in Contemporary Literary Theory,* ed. Peter Brooker and Peter Widdowson (New York: Prentice Hall, 1996), 444.

10. Ibid., 445. Italics in the original.

11. Sharon Cameron, *Lyric Time: Dickinson and the Limits of Genre* (Baltimore: Johns Hopkins University Press, 1979), 24–25.

12. Nicholls, "The Belated Postmodern," 445.

13. Plath set the poems in symmetrical positions in *Ariel* so that they bracket the central poems and clarify their less specific imagery of violence; "Lady Lazarus" is the seventh poem in the volume (*AR,* 14–17), while "Daddy" is the seventh poem from the end (*AR,* 74–76).

14. It is worth noting that this narrative reading is complicated by the poem's

syntax. In particular, the copy of Daddy, which the speaker marries, rather than Daddy himself, may be the one whose death the last stanza recounts.

15. Irving Howe asserts that in "Daddy" "Sylvia Plath *identifies* the father (we recall [Plath's father's] German birth) with the Nazis" (my italics). George Steiner claims that Plath's "last, greatest poems culminate in an act of *identification,* of total communion with those tortured and massacred. . . . Sylvia Plath **became** [boldface in the original] *a woman being transported to Auschwitz* [my italics] on the death trains." Plath for Steiner "commit[ted] the whole of her poetic and formal authority to the metaphor, to the mask of language." Many subsequent readers have also seen Plath's Holocaust poems as essentially metaphoric. Irving Howe, "The Plath Celebration: A Partial Dissent," in *Sylvia Plath: Modern Critical Views,* ed. Harold Bloom (New York: Chelsea House, 1989), 11; George Steiner, *Language and Silence: Essays on Language, Literature, and the Inhuman* (New York: Atheneum, 1967), 300–301.

16. Howe, "The Plath Celebration," 12.

17. Mary Kinzie, *A Poet's Guide to Poetry* (Chicago: University of Chicago Press, 1999), defines the tenor as the metaphor's "originating scene, situation, object, or state" (436) and its vehicle as its "figurative idea" (479). Robin Peel, one of several recent critics to read Plath in what Claire Brennan calls "broadly cultural materialist" terms (Brennan, ed., *The Poetry of Sylvia Plath* [New York: Columbia University Press, 1999], 64), emphasizes Plath's "writing in its relation to the *public,* often *political* discourses from which it emerged" (*Writing Back: Sylvia Plath and Cold War Politics* [Madison, N.J.: Fairleigh Dickinson University Press, 2002], 18; my italics). His reading is implicitly metaphorical, suggesting that "Plath's poetry and prose" should be read "as reconstructed *barometers of their time* rather than diverse expressions of *autobiography*" (19; my italics). Another recent critic who makes this metaphoric way of reading particularly clear is Susan Gubar, whose recent revisionary study of Plath's Holocaust poems attempts to transform what others have viewed as the "mere figure" of her poems into their vehicle. Gubar's claim is that the poems are "'really' about the psychological repercussions of Auschwitz on literature and Jewish identity" ("Prosopopoeia and Holocaust Poetry in English: The Case of Sylvia Plath," *Yale Journal of Criticism* 14, no. 1 [2001]: 194).

18. Paul Ricoeur, "Word, Polysemy, Metaphor: Creativity in Language," in *A Ricoeur Reader: Reflection and Imagination,* ed. Mario J. Valdes (Buffalo: University of Toronto Press, 1991), 81.

19. Young, *Writing and Rewriting,* 93.

20. *JP,* 64 (my italics).

21. Peter Orr, ed., *The Poet Speaks: Interviews with Contemporary Poets* (London: Routledge, 1966), 169–70 (my italics).

22. Simile, with its insertion of the intermediate *like* or *as* between the two objects compared, is less stable than metaphor, whose insistence of similarity is less contingent and more permanent. Kinzie suggests that simile tends to be "more explanatory (even didactic[)]" than metaphor (*Poet's Guide to Poetry,* 460–61).

23. *AR,* 75 (my italics).

24. Ibid., 76 (my italics).

25. Rose explores the simile and metonymy of "Daddy" in terms similar to my own, although she does not discuss the function of this trope in other poems.

Young sees in Plath's metonymy a more literal inscription of the "part-whole" relationship between "the massive suffering of the Jews" and "the poet's pain" (Rose, *Haunting of Sylvia Plath,* 227–29; Young, *Writing and Rewriting,* 126–27).

26. Rose, *Haunting of Sylvia Plath,* 228.

27. The first, holograph draft of the poem described Daddy as possessing a "Hitler moustache" and included the phrase "my Nazi" and, a few lines later, "with a . . . Nazi look"; both phrases were crossed out by Plath (Smith).

28. Plath underlined the etymology of *swastika* in her dictionary: "*svastika,* fr. *svasti* <u>welfare</u>, *fr. su* <u>well + asti being</u>, <u>prop.</u>, is" (Smith).

29. Rose, *Haunting of Sylvia Plath,* 228.

30. *AR,* 75 (my italics).

31. *Chuff,* which Plath did not mark as she did terms she had studied, is defined as "a rustic; boor; churl"; the adjective "chuffy" is defined as "chubby" (Smith).

32. *AR,* 16 (my italics).

33. Ibid.

34. Gold, Plath highlights in her dictionary, is "very heavy"; it is marked by "yellow color" and signifies "riches." It is thus notable both for its inherent qualities and also as a means of exchange. The notion that gold itself is deceptive is clarified in a passage from a draft of Plath's *The Bell Jar* on the verso of the holograph. Here, while the narrator is greedily eating expensive caviar, her friend Betsy explains a demonstration of "how to make an all-purpose neckerchief out of mink tails and a gold chain, the sort of chain you can get an exact copy of Woolworth's for a dollar twenty-five" (Smith).

35. Plath underlined the following definitions of *charge* in her dictionary: "5. An <u>accusation of a wrong</u> or offence; allegation . . . 7. <u>A person or thing entrusted to</u> the care of another. 8. <u>Pecuniary burden; expense.</u>" Other pertinent definitions in the dictionary include "3. A duty or task laid upon a person; responsibility; obligation. 4. An order; a command. . . . 9. The price demanded for a thing or service" (Smith).

36. Jonathan Culler identifies apostrophe with "all that is most radical, embarrassing, pretentious and mystificatory in the lyric." Culler, "Apostrophe," in *The Pursuit of Signs* (Ithaca: Cornell University Press, 1981), 137.

37. More than half the poems in *Ariel* address a "you," an other who is, according to the definition of apostrophe, absent, inanimate, or dead. For a more detailed discussion of apostrophe and lyric isolation, see Ann Keniston, "'The fluidity of damaged Form': Apostrophe and Desire in Nineties Poetry," in *Contemporary Literature* 42 (2001): 294–324.

38. Dori Laub, "An Event Without a Witness: Truth, Testimony and Survival," in *Testimony: Crises of Witnessing in Literature, Psychoanalysis, and History,* ed. Shoshana Felman and Dori Laub (New York: Routledge, 1992), 80.

39. Ibid., 81. Italics in the original.

40. Ibid., 85.

41. Caruth, *Trauma,* 11 (my italics).

42. Shoshana Felman, "Education and Crisis, or the Vicissitudes of Teaching," in Felman and Laub, *Testimony,* 30.

43. Ibid., 33.

44. Ibid., 29.

45. Laub, "An Event," 85.

46. Plath's first draft contains still more shifts in address; the holograph of the poem includes an address to a particular "lady" along with "yessir, yessir."

47. *AR*, 15 (my italics).

48. Van Dyne was among the first readers to view "Lady Lazarus" as "highly theatricalized performance[s] of the feminine victim." Susan Van Dyne, *Revising Life: Sylvia Plath's Ariel Poems* (Chapel Hill: University of North Carolina Press, 1993), 5.

49. Critics disagree about the extent to which "Lady Lazarus" is confessional. Buell argues that the striptease scene "allow[s] *the reader* less room to distance himself from identification with *the mob, those who search confessional poetry* for the 'word or a touch / Or a bit of blood'" (italics in the original); Howe more forthrightly claims that here the "writer speaks *to* the reader" (emphasis in original). Frederick Buell, "Plath's Traditionalism," in *Critical Essays on Sylvia Plath*, ed. Linda W. Wagner (Boston: G. K. Hall, 1984), 150–51; Howe, "The Plath Celebration," 12.

50. Caruth, *Trauma*, 10.

51. Two recent studies make related if ultimately different points about Plath's personification. Hungerford includes Plath in a study of the ways that post-traumatic literature tends to personify and then chronicle the murder of texts. Closer to the parameters of my own study is Susan Gubar's discussion of Plath's prosopopeia, a figure closely allied with apostrophe, as at least partly an attempt to "reanimate[e] . . . the dead." Hungerford, *The Holocaust of Texts*; Gubar, "Prosopopoeia," 192.

52. Other poems chronicling the speaker's death/rebirth include "Ariel," "Fever 103°," and "The Rabbit Catcher."

JANET BADIA

The "Priestess" and Her "Cult"

PLATH'S CONFESSIONAL POETICS AND
THE MYTHOLOGY OF WOMEN READERS

⊞

Loosely based on Shakespeare's *The Taming of the Shrew*, the film *10 Things I Hate About You* tells the story of Kat Stratford, a darkly cynical and socially outcast teenager who has renounced dating after losing her virginity to the untrustworthy boy now pursuing her younger sister Bianca. Having completely and contemptuously rejected the conventional high school scene, Kat is despised by her peers at Padua High and frequently referred to as that "heinous bitch."[1] While it is certainly true that Kat occasionally behaves badly—on one occasion purposely smashing her own car into her former boyfriend's new convertible— she is hardly the Midol-deprived, "muling, rampallian wretch"[2] her peers and teachers make her out to be. Quite to the contrary, Kat sees herself more as a nonconformist who simply locates her self-worth in her rejection of both conventional high school life and the patriarchal order that surrounds her. Emphasizing this aspect of Kat's character, the film portrays Padua High's student body as a collection of absurd cliques (for example, a student can be a "cowboy," "a future MBA," or a "coffee kid") and the patriarchal order as an oppressive apparatus effectively symbolized by both Kat's father, whose initial "house rule" forbids the two sisters to date, and Mr. Morgan, the English teacher who routinely sends Kat to the principal's office for "terrorizing" his class, including once after she challenges the omission of important women writers in his lectures. But even as Kat regards herself as a nonconformist above the rigid boundaries that shape her peers and her family, the film typecasts her in another way: seething with sarcasm, grungily dressed, and a fan of riot-girl music, she is a millennial version of the angry feminist intellectual, or at least one in the making.

The reason for my portrait of Kat Stratford at the opening of this essay is clear if one also considers another important fact about Kat: she is a Plath reader.[3] Indeed, it is Sylvia Plath, among other (supposed) feminist writers, whom Kat wishes to see added to Mr. Morgan's syllabus. Underscoring this initial allusion to the poet, the film also offers a revealing look at Kat as she sits in a family-room chair reading Plath's best-selling novel, *The Bell Jar*. To ensure viewers do not overlook the importance of the scene of Kat reading, the camera carefully pans through the front window of the Stratford home, resting directly on Kat and centering deliberately in its frame the open cover of *The Bell Jar*. To those viewers who recognize the novel Kat holds in her hands, the implication of the scene is unmistakable: all that we need to know about Kat to prepare us for her current behavior in school and at home can be encapsulated by a single scene that, in Hollywood shorthand, figures her as the quintessential Plath reader.

As a scholar who once devoured Plath's writings in daily doses, I am intrigued by this figure of the Plath reader. How did she come about? How exactly did a young woman reading one of the most important best-sellers of the second half of the twentieth century come to signify so much in a Hollywood movie? Furthermore, what cultural attitudes does her presence express about Sylvia Plath, her work, and her readers? Admittedly, this last question assumes that there is a connection between Sylvia Plath, the author, and this figure of a woman reader, and that it is worth our attention as literary and cultural critics. In fact, one of the aims of my examination of Kat Stratford is to call attention to how our assumptions about Plath and our assumptions about her readers have been mutually reinforcing, and almost always in ways that have been detrimental to both. More specifically, as my starting point for this chapter, I want to argue that a close examination of Kat—particularly the ways she and her reading are pathologized in the film—reveals the larger cultural anxieties that are often embedded in both literary and popular representations of Plath, anxieties about the nature of Plath's writing, how it has been read, and the effects of such reading on young women. In shedding light on these anxieties, I seek to explain why discussions about Plath's work have so often placed women readers at the center of their debates about the poet.

Of course, this figure of the young Plath reader is hardly new, even in Hollywood. In many ways, Kat Stratford is merely an updated version of the image Woody Allen evokes in his 1977 film *Annie Hall,* when Allen's character describes Plath, *Ariel* in hand, as an "interesting poetess whose tragic suicide was misinterpreted as romantic by the college-girl mentality."[4] Concretizing this college-girl mentality, Meg Wolitzer's 1982 novel *Sleepwalking* chronicles the interactions of three Plath- and Sexton-obsessed Swarthmore students who, the narrator explains, "had banded together, apparently drawn to each other by the lure of some secret signal as unintelligible to everyone else as the pitch of a dog whistle is to human beings," a lure that earns them a reputation on campus as "the death girls."[5] As the narrator's analogy suggests, the image of a band of death-girls devoted to Plath's and Sexton's poetry is meant not simply to draw laughs but to elicit a particular response from readers, a nod of recognition, a "Yes, I know the type." In other words, if the image is funny, it gathers its humor from the cultural iconicity of the particular woman reader evoked, for just as "the death girls" are instantly recognizable to the students on the Swarthmore campus, the Plath reader is instantly recognizable to us today, even without props like *The Bell Jar.*

And if she is recognizable, it is not entirely because of her cinematic or fictional legend, for the Plath reader owes her existence at least partially to those notorious "real" readers who at one time became virtually synonymous with the poet's name, including the fans who have persistently chiseled off the name "Hughes" from Plath's gravestone in England; the young women who wrote editorials to the London *Guardian* protesting Ted Hughes's alleged abuses as executor of Plath's literary estate, as well as his neglect of her grave; and the poet who wrote about Plath's "murder" at the hands of Hughes.[6] All of which is to say, the Plath reader's presence is palpable and historical, even as she is circumscribed by stereotype and cliché. That she appears to exist simultaneously as both actual reader and mere stereotype makes her all the more intriguing. Whatever the nature of her existence, two points about her are clear: first, she is nearly as big a cultural icon as Plath herself; and second, the defining features of her iconicity are her own apparent depression and obsession with death, just as the defining features of Plath's own iconicity have been her apparent depression and obsession with death. One might even argue that Plath owes her status as cultural icon to the recognizability of her readers. At the very least it is true that the figure of the Plath reader emerged almost simultaneously with Plath's commercial success as a writer, success that culminates with the U.S. publication of *The Bell Jar* and *Crossing the Water* in 1971 and *Winter Trees* in 1972.

In short, then, Sylvia Plath is a writer as remarkable for the kind of reader she attracts as for the writing she produced. But this is hardly a novel observation. Many critics since her work's earliest reception have used the same observation as their entry point into an evaluation of her writing. My own examination of the reception of Plath's work suggests, moreover, that her writing is and will likely continue to be overdetermined by perceptions of who reads it, as well as how and why they read it. In this essay, I am interested in the consequences of these perceptions, particularly the ways they have served to stigmatize Plath and her work. At the same time, I want to be clear that my goal is not to transfer the stigma to her readers by making them responsible for Plath's problematic reputation as a writer and her sometimes precarious status within the literary canon, as so many others have tried to do. Instead, I would insist that Plath's status is inextricably linked to the cultural and literary value of the women who read her. In arguing this point, I hope to uncover not only value in Plath's writing but, just as importantly, the value of her women readers.

The commercial success of her writing throughout the late sixties marked Plath as one of the most notable authors of her time and signaled the beginning of what at least two critics have referred to as her reign as the "priestess" of contemporary poetry.[7] Indeed, by 1971, Plath had arrived full force on the literary scene. According to Plath biographer Paul Alexander, *Ariel* sold in unprecedented numbers, totaling more than a half-million copies its first two decades in print and making it one of the all-time best-selling volumes of poetry from the twentieth century.[8] When *The Bell Jar* was finally released in the United States by Harper and Row in 1971, it too attracted a large audience, making its way immediately onto the *New York Times* best-seller list, where it stayed for twenty-four weeks.[9] Even the eight-year delay in the novel's U.S. publication could not suppress readers' demand for Plath's only published novel. As Frances McCullough explains in her foreword to the twenty-fifth-anniversary edition of *The Bell Jar*, "at least two bookstores in New York carried [bootlegged copies of] the book and sold it briskly."[10] This commercial success, and the devoted reading public it signified, almost simultaneously gave way to perceptions of Plath as "cult poet," a title meant to suggest an obsessive devotion by readers that ostensibly fed the book sales. As Marjorie Perloff wrote in 1973, "During the past year or so, Sylvia Plath has become a true cult figure. At this writing, the Savile Book Shop in Georgetown, D.C., has a huge window display in which copies of *The Colossus, The Bell Jar, Ariel,* and *Crossing the Water* encircle a large photograph of Sylvia Plath, which rests against a copy of A. Alvarez's *The Savage God: A Study of Suicide,* that ultimate tribute to Sylvia Plath as our Extremist Poet par excellence."[11] As Perloff's ironic tone makes clear, the cult poet is one who has been falsely idealized and elaborately mythologized by her readers. For Perloff, who felt the accolades bestowed on Plath's work were well earned, the identification of Plath as a cult figure was one to be overcome, for only then could her work receive the serious treatment it deserved. But for many critics who did not share Perloff's final assessment of the work, the designation of Plath as a cult poet fit all too well. As evidence, they only needed to point to the general "hysteria" that had spread among Plath's readers, a phenomenon that culminates perhaps with the publication in 1972 of Robin Morgan's "Arraignment," a poem that can only be described as a scathing indictment of Ted Hughes for the "murder of Sylvia Plath" and for subsequent abuses of her literary estate. As Paul Alexander explains, the poem became a rallying cry for Plath's most devoted readers, who, already accustomed to harassing Hughes at his poetry readings, now recited "Arraignment" as part of their diatribes against him.[12]

That Plath became an icon for the feminist movement of the seventies only fueled the controversy surrounding her work. It also fueled the public's perception of her readers as fanatics or, to use Frances McCullough's label from her foreword to *The Bell Jar*, as "Plath groupies."[13] Given this perception, it is perhaps not surprising to find that in the literary reviews from this same time, as well as in those that would be written after the publication of Plath's *Collected Poems* in 1981, Plath's readers were often regarded as either an obstacle to a serious consideration of her poetry or as evidence of its inferiority. In either case, a clear portrait of the poet's readership had emerged by the

1970s, if not earlier: Plath's readers were perceived to be young (implicitly white) women who—in overprivileging the disturbed pathology ostensibly feeding the poetry—had "misinterpreted" not only the tragedy of the situation but the work itself. Put more simply, the reception and critical history of Plath's work genders the Plath reader, diagnoses her as depressed and sick, and assesses her as an uncritical consumer of "bad" literature.

Such a construction of Plath's readers leads us directly and unmistakably back to the character of Kat Stratford. When we see her curled up in a chair holding her anniversary edition of *The Bell Jar,* it is difficult not to impose an aura of depression and darkness around her, especially since she is so effectively foiled by a sister appropriately named Bianca. Often dressed in white, Bianca is, at bottom, everything Kat is not: she is perky, popular, and, for the most part, superficial. Contrasted so sharply against Kat, Bianca foregrounds the darkness, one might say melancholy, that lingers over Kat from the film's opening scene when the blare of her Joan Jett music drowns out the pop song coming from the car of a group of popular, Bianca-like girls. Scenes like this one not only prepare us for the moment of Kat reading, but they also prepare us *to respond* to her as a woman reader by inviting us to see her as dark and depressed. The film, in fact, counts on us to impose this aura of darkness and depression upon her. It hopes we do, I would argue, because only then can we accept the transformation of Kat from boy hater to love-driven teen that is central to the film's closure as a romantic comedy. To insure this response, then, the film constructs Kat as a Plath reader who not only reads the author's work but actually mirrors the much-accepted public image of the poet herself: the abandoned daughter, the woman scorned by male betrayal, and the intellectual who haughtily desires to be above it all. As significant as these similarities are, the most revealing image of Kat as a reflection of Plath comes toward the film's end when, in a gesture toward the film's title, Kat recites a poem she has written for her literature class. The poem, written for her new boyfriend, Patrick, after she discovers he has been paid to date her, catalogs all the things she hates about him, reveals the betrayal she feels, and all the while discloses her desire to be with him still. It is a confessional poem modeled as much after Plath's poetry as it is the Shakespearean sonnet Kat was assigned to imitate, and it appears to owe its existence not to Kat's innate creativity but to a boy who inspires the very emotions the poem catalogs.

In other words, it would seem that Patrick plays Ted Hughes to Kat's Sylvia Plath.

As I hope this portrait of the Plath reader shows, Kat Stratford serves as a particularly revealing example of a pathologized woman reader: a woman whose reading practices are defined symptomatically, which is to say, either as a sign of her illness or as a potential cause of it. Her construction, then, grows out of cultural anxieties concerning what she reads, how she reads, and what effects her reading might produce. Throughout literary history, such anxieties have often rendered women "bad readers" in dire need of protection from the corrupting influence of certain kinds of literature.[14] For the most part, Kat is no exception to this image. Toward the climax of the film, for example, Kat is asked to the prom by Patrick and is thus placed in a situation in which she must "read" his motives for dating her. The moment is especially important because it marks for the first time Kat's doubts about Patrick's motives: oblivious to the fact that Patrick is being paid to date her by the two boys scheming for Bianca's attention, Kat simply cannot understand why he wants to go to the prom, a symbol for her of the very high school scene she and Patrick have rejected.[15] But she does decide finally to accompany him to the dance, and when his financial motives are exposed at the prom, Kat leaves in tears, a victim not only of the plot hatched by the young men but of her own "misreading" of Patrick. Reinforcing this image of Kat as a "bad reader," her misjudgment of Patrick echoes a series of previous misjudgments on her part, including her peer-pressured decision to lose her virginity to the arrogant, self-absorbed Joey Donner. The film suggests, in other words, that Kat not only misreads situations but that her misreading has left her in an unhappy, if not altogether depressed, state.

As I indicated earlier, such correlations between what women read and the apparent pathologies they embody pervade literary history. While such correlations have always had their dangers—resulting in prescriptive reading practices for women and even the censorship of their reading materials—their expression in the case of the Plath reader strikes me as especially pernicious. To demonstrate the level of danger embedded in such pathologized constructions, I would like to examine another image of a Plath reader, one many readers will probably be shocked to discover. Mallory (Wilson) Knox, the violent murderer and companion to Mickey Knox in the 1994 film *Natural Born Killers*, is also depicted as a Plath reader, as we learn in one of the early scenes of the film.[16] Just moments before the violence erupts in the Wilson family home, the film offers us a glimpse of Mallory sleeping while an open copy of *The Bell Jar* rests face down beside her on the bed. A close look at the scene reveals that the book's appearance is unusual insofar as its front cover and back cover both prominently feature the title, suggesting the possibility that a particular edition was selected to ensure the book's identification or even that the image of the book had been manipulated altogether. Just as calculated is the scene's placement within the film. As if to prepare us for Mallory's participation in the violent murder of her parents and the subsequent killing spree she embarks upon, Mallory's reading precipitates her plunge into violence and thus works to signal her pathology, just as Kat's reading prepares us for her subsequent behavior toward boys and her overall depressed state. In this case, however, the pathology is far more insidious, pointing not toward rebellious teenage behavior but to severe psychosis: Mallory, the film makes clear, is not a natural born killer but a young woman psychically corrupted—and turned into a murderer—by an abusive father, a neglectful mother, and a culture that glorifies violence and degrades women, to say nothing of the various media she consumes, including, one might speculate, the books she reads.

The film further underscores this disturbed nature of her pathology during Mickey and Mallory's encounter with a Native American elder and his young grandson. In the scene, the four characters sit around a fire in a hogan while the grandfather and grandson exchange thoughts about Mickey and Mallory in their native tongue. During the conversation, the grandson inquires about Mallory, asking the grandfather pointedly, "Is she crazy?" to which the elder replies: "She has sad sickness . . . [she is] lost in the world of ghosts." Literally highlighting this exchange, the words "she crazy?" are projected across Mallory's chest as the grandfather speaks, à la the film's convention of interpolating extratextual images and words into the visual field of the screen. Of course, the question projected is a rhetorical one, as the truncating of the word "is" conveys. Mallory is indeed crazy, at least as crazy as the culture that produced her. Given the preponderance of evidence toward such a diagnosis, one might wonder, then, why it matters that Mallory is framed with *The Bell Jar*.

I would insist that it matters a great deal, for while the presence of *The Bell Jar* on Mallory's bed may tell us little about her violence, it speaks volumes about the iconicity of Plath and her women readers. In particular, I want to posit a correlation between the film's depiction of the public and its depiction of Mallory as reader. As those who have seen the film know, central to *Natural Born Killers* is a critique of mass culture's romanticization of Mickey and Mallory as celebrity murderers: they may be sick people, but they are no less revered by adoring fans who appear at various points throughout the film sporting "I love Mickey and Mallory" T-shirts and holding signs that read "Murder Me Mickey!" The film argues, in other words, that Mickey and Mallory are the products of a culture of uncritical consumers who recklessly transform murderers into pop culture icons.

Given the film's emphasis on uncritical consumption, the depiction of Mallory reading *The Bell Jar* begins to appear far less gratuitous. Like Mickey and the public that adores him for his violence, Mallory cannot critically separate herself from the violence that has surrounded her throughout her life and is thus presented as a "bad" reader. One could even argue that the film depicts Mallory with *The Bell Jar* in order to turn her into another example of an uncritical consumer whose bad tastes and judgments are reflected not only in her reading material but in the poetry she periodically composes for Mickey's ears. Following this line of thinking, *The Bell Jar* comes to stand in for Plath, who, like Mickey and Mallory, serves the film as yet another example of a pop phenomenon who has been propelled into iconicity by a public that, in her particular case, apparently cannot distinguish between sensational autobiography and legitimate literature and therefore wrongly romanticizes Plath's suicide and her work.

While far removed from one another on the spectrum of bad behavior, Mallory and Kat emerge from similar anxieties: in one brief scene (void, interestingly enough, of any speech on their part), each woman asks to be diagnosed as sick and assessed as an uncritical consumer of bad literature. That the diagnosis and assessment are elicited through *The Bell Jar*, of all of Plath's publications, makes the anxieties present especially interesting. Certainly one reason for the novel's selection is its recognizability; it is after all Plath's most commercially successful publication. At the same time, the fact that *The Bell Jar* is also widely regarded as adolescent literature that appeals to young girls rather than grown women also helps explain its selection. In this way, the presence of *The Bell Jar* in the films underscores the supposed immaturity of both women, establishing them as young readers who presumably suffer from inexperience and naïveté. It serves, in other words, to infantilize them, a process made especially clear in *Natural Born Killers* as subsequent scenes in the film depict Mallory bouncing on the front seat of Mickey's car and tossing a doll off a bridge before marrying Mickey.

To demonstrate this process of infantilization more fully, one additional example of a Plath reader is worth mentioning here: Carol Anshaw's novel *Seven Moves* pathologizes the idea of a grown woman reading *The Bell Jar* by depicting her in a fashion that underscores the book's association with juvenilia.[17] The scene occurs early in the novel after Taylor Heyes mysteriously disappears and Chris Snow, the novel's central character and Taylor's lover, goes looking for a photo of her to give to investigators on the case. The photo Chris takes from the refrigerator door captures Taylor in a chair reading a book during what Chris always thought to be a happy period in Taylor's life. Chris's memory of the moment is altered, however, when she realizes upon looking at the photo again that the book in Taylor's hands is *The Bell Jar*. As the narrator explains, "Now, Chris notices that in the photo Taylor is holding a copy of *The Bell Jar,* and she thinks, who over the age of nineteen would be reading Sylvia Plath? Everywhere now she is looking for some dark cast to Taylor's soul which she might have missed, or not wanted to see."[18] Of course, the moment establishes Taylor as the quintessential Plath reader, one whose previously unnoticed propensity for darkness and depression becomes evident through her reading of *The Bell Jar* and whose previously inexplicable behaviors—in Taylor's case her desire to have "codes only [she and Chris would] understand," to get "matching tattoos," to participate in a "blood ritual," and to write "terrible poems" about the lover she "lost her mind over"[19]—begin to make sense in light of her reading material.

A sign of uncritical consumption, disturbed pathologies, inexperience, and naïveté: Has the cover of a book—or a scene of a young woman's reading—ever conveyed such a loaded and complicated story? Can a cover alone even convey all that? Indeed, the image of *The Bell Jar* in both *Natural Born Killers* and *10 Things I Hate About You,* as well as in the novels mentioned above, conveys only a small part of the larger portrait of Kat Stratford and Mallory Knox I have been trying to reconstruct. As I believe my reading of the two films suggests, what makes Kat and Mallory such compelling examples of the Plath reader is the way our understanding of both women depends on—and even invites us to apply to it—a preexisting discourse about women readers in general and about the Plath reader in particular. While it pervades popular culture today, this discourse originates, I would argue, in the reception of Plath's work within the literary establishment of the 1960s and 1970s. If we want to understand Kat and Mallory, then, it is necessary to situate their images within the literary conversations that have taken place over the years about Plath's work. In fact, I would like to propose that what makes Kat and Mallory so interesting and germane to discussions about Sylvia Plath is the way their cultural images reflect literary constructions of Plath's readership that were first posited in the initial reception of her work.

In his 1972 review of Sylvia Plath's *Winter Trees,* a review significantly entitled "The Cult of Plath," Webster Schott describes Plath as the "high priestess of the confessional poem, master of the poem as intimate weapon, snake lady of misery in the literature of ultimate control."[20] If Schott's casting of Plath as "snake lady" seems hyperbolic and Schott too consumed by his own cleverness to be taken seriously as a critic, consider this statement from a *Time* magazine review of *Ariel* in 1966: "*Daddy* was merely the first jet of flame from a literary dragon who in the last months of her life breathed a burning river of bale across the literary landscape."[21] Or this one from a *Newsweek* review of *Ariel* the same year: "The general effect of the book is that of a symphony of death and dissolution, scored in language so full of blood and brain that it seems to burst and spatter the reader with the plasma of life."[22]

For those of us who have encountered one of Plath's detractors firsthand, comments like these may be shocking, but they are not surprising. There is something about Sylvia Plath that seems to compel strong and dramatic reactions, frequently from her detractors but also from her admirers. As a professor I have seen my own students react in just this way as they resort, often simultaneously, to hyperbole—"Plath was a feminazi"—and extreme reductionism—"she was an over-privileged white woman who had no reason to be depressed." When students react in this way, I try to resist the temptation to correct their views of Plath and urge them instead to consider why they are so invested in seeing her in a particular way. I think critical responses to Plath can be approached in a similar vein. For example, in most cases the critics who resort to such extreme metaphorizations of Plath as a "snake lady" or a "literary dragon" are out to debunk what they see as readers' mythic distortions of her poetry. Even in those cases in which the actual metaphors may allow for some measure of ambiguity (e.g., is it bad to be a "literary dragon?"), the critic's final judgment of the work is most often unequivocally negative. Take, for example, Webster Schott's review, quoted at the opening of this section, and the conclusion he reaches about the "high priestess" and her poetry:

> Sylvia Plath was a sick woman who made art of her sickness. One or two of her poems will be read a long time but absent from her work are joy, glory, strong love, any sense of the interdependence of human relationships and the infinite alternatives of life. Some young people, having limited experience, need literature to help them feel bad, and they will celebrate Plath for a while.[23]

The ironic shortsightedness of Schott's judgment is not nearly as problematic as his obvious neglect of many of the poems that appear in *Winter Trees,* poems like "For a Fatherless Son," written about the comfort Plath takes in her son's smiles, or "Three Women" and "Child," both of which demonstrate the poet's acute recognition of the interdependence of mother and child. While my own judgment of Webster Schott will undoubtedly sound harsh, I think it is warranted given the stakes involved in 1972 when the review appeared: namely, Plath's reputation as poet and the status of her work.

In fact, following the release of *Ariel* in the United States in 1966 and throughout the next decade, literary critics reviewing Plath's work were almost singularly preoccupied with her status within the canon. The questions on the minds of most critics: Was Plath's work deserving of the accolades it was receiving? And was Plath, as a poet, deserving of what one critic referred to as the artistic "martyrdom" her readers had bestowed upon her?[24]

Dan Jaffe, in his review of *Ariel* for the *Saturday Review* in 1966, formulates the issue this way: "All of us, I hope, mourn the despair and early immolation of so gifted a writer; but we need to ask whether the poems justify the accolades. I don't believe they do."[25] Two years later, in his 1968 review of *Ariel* for the *Sewanee Review,* Robert Stilwell offers a somewhat less sensitive assessment of the poetry: "I should guess that *Ariel* will linger as a very specialized and rather subterranean book of poems, that A. M. theses will be written on it (doubtless several are already underway), and that it will not, finally, add a major dimension to the poetry of the 1960s."[26] And in 1972, in his essay "Sylvia Plath: A Partial Disagreement," Irving Howe offers a strikingly similar prediction: "After the noise abates and judgment returns, Sylvia Plath will be regarded as an interesting minor poet whose personal story was deeply poignant. A few of her poems will find a place in anthologies—and when you consider the common fate of talent, that, after all, will not be a small acknowledgment."[27] But it is Paul West who, in his review of Crossing the Water, finally encapsulates the debate: "Had Sylvia Plath been ugly, and not died in so deliberate a manner, I wonder if she would have the standing she does."[28]

What I hope this collection of excerpts makes clear is that Webster Schott is more than simply a single critic with a strong dislike for Plath's poetry and a rather idiosyncratic way of expressing it. Taken together, these excerpts suggest that Schott's review exemplifies the modus operandi of many male critics at the time.[29] When one looks closely at how Plath's work has been received by literary critics, the harsh voice of the male critic as the arbiter of the literary world clearly stands out. From even the most cursory review of the criticism, one quickly realizes that to many of the critics writing at the time, especially to those schooled in either New Criticism or the high canonical modernist tradition of T. S. Eliot that sought to create a small, elite audience, Plath's work threatened to disrupt the very reputableness of the literary project and thus had to be contained.

While questions about the value of an author's work are, of course, the concern of literary reviews, the preoccupation among critics with the possibility that Plath may have sneaked in the backdoor of the literary canon is suspicious at best. Such anxieties mark the history of confessional poetry's reception and continue to shape how readers and critics regard those authors who, like Plath, have been and continue to be seen as confessional poets. An examination of this larger history shows that while the anxieties and tensions that characterize the poetry's reception are complex—involving a triangulation of more specific anxieties about genre, the subject matter of poetry, and the perceived reader—they are often masked behind what appear to be purely aesthetic concerns. That it is predominately male critics making the charges against Plath suggests, moreover, that comments like Webster Schott's veil complex anxieties generated not simply by the aesthetic quality of the work under consideration but by the gender of the author, by the so-called feminine subject matter she often chose to write about, and by its appeal to women readers.

Of particular interest to me in this discussion, then, is the way the anxieties present in the reception of Plath's work are shaped by clear gender biases that emerge most fully at the location of the reader. To demonstrate how they do so, I want to return to a seminal essay in the reception and history of Plath's work, Irving Howe's "Sylvia Plath," focusing closely on the implicit link between Howe's assessment of the poetry's aesthetic value and his perception of Plath's readers. Careful scrutiny of this link and the way it emerges out of the essay's rather nuanced argument provides us with a rich context for understanding the figure of the Plath reader I have outlined thus far.

Regarding the aesthetics of Plath's work, Howe is unquestionably clear, describing *Ariel*'s aesthetic shortcomings as "a kind of badness that seems a constant temptation in confessional poetry, the temptation to reveal all while one eye measures the effect of the revelation."[30] Contributing to the "badness," Howe explains, is the "willed hysteric tone, the forcing of language to make up for an inability to develop the matter."[31] At the same time as he faults Plath for not developing the theme and subject matter of the poems, however, he also suggests that the subject matter, insofar as it is "merely clinical," cannot be the basis of a "satisfying poem."[32] Such tensions between his statements lead one to question just what it is about Plath that really bothers Howe.

For starters, Howe is troubled by what he describes, in a (mis)appropriation of Elizabeth Hardwick's words, as the "deeply rooted" and "little resisted" "elements of pathology" central to her work.[33] As my quotation of Howe ventriloquizing Hardwick makes clear, Howe simply cannot abide what he identifies as Plath's vision for her poetry. This vision, to summarize Howe, is predicated on "the personal-confessional element" that seemingly dooms the poetry to being no more than "local act."[34] His choice of the phrase "local act" is critically important to the question I have been exploring here. For Howe, good confessional writing by nature begins as "local act" but arrives at larger meaning through "sustained moral complication" and "the full design of social and historical setting."[35] Insofar as the lyric form does not allow for either, the confessional poem, it follows, cannot but fail to transform confession from local act to larger meaning. Certainly for a social-minded critic like Howe, this relegation of poetry to the status of mere "local act" undermines the raison d'être of the literary project.

By his or her very nature, then, the confessional poet, from Howe's perspective, fails to reflect society sufficiently and thus fails to transform it through his or her writing.

But to understand Howe's relegation of Plath to "local act" as a mere reflection of his preoccupations as a social critic would be to overlook a second tension that pervades the review: Howe's own discussion of Plath makes clear that she is unquestionably more than a local act, if I may play with his use of the term. Howe's own words—especially his description of "the noise" that surrounds this "darling of our culture"—suggest that Plath has reached far more readers than Howe would care to admit.[36] His discussion of these readers and his correlative casting of Plath as a cultural "darling" reveals, moreover, that Howe, while bothered by Plath's confessional tendencies, is equally troubled by her ability to attract a large reading public. To be sure, the very project of Howe's essay—"A Partial Disagreement," he calls it—is to take issue not only with Plath but with those readers who have elevated her above the status she truly deserves as "an interesting minor poet."[37]

Howe begins to define these readers as early as the opening paragraph of the essay when he explains: "A glamour of fatality hangs over the name of Sylvia Plath. . . . It is a legend that solicits our desires for a heroism of sickness that can serve as emblem of the age, and many young readers take in Sylvia Plath's vibrations of despair as if they were the soul's own oxygen."[38] The issues that emerge out of Howe's rhetoric here are myriad. Most interesting perhaps is the rhetoric of consumption so central to his characterization of Plath's readers, for just as Howe transforms Plath from serious poet into glamour girl and "priestess,"[39] he also transforms her young readers from serious readers into cult followers: Plath, no longer perceived as a poet, puts out life-sustaining "vibrations" that are taken in, not read, by those who admire her. In other words, for Howe, the very act of reading and the critical faculty it involves have been supplanted by a mystical process of consumption that leaves the young intellectually and emotionally crippled, one presumes, by the lack of real oxygen.

It is with this suggestion of mystical consumption that we begin to see the two parallel concerns that run throughout Howe's essay: his concern with Plath's exaggerated status as a poet and with the corruption of legitimate reading practices responsible for the exaggeration. This link between his two concerns is crystallized when later in the essay he dismisses Plath's admirers altogether, arguing vis-à-vis the poem "Daddy" that "one must be infatuated with the Plath legend to ignore the poet's need for enlarging the magnitude of her act through illegitimate comparisons with the Jewish-Nazi holocaust."[40] Issues of Plath's Holocaust imagery aside, Howe's characterization of the reader here reveals, I would argue, a kind of rhetorical desperation on his part. Aware that his position as a dissenter leaves him vulnerable—indeed, in his own words, at the risk of "plunging into a harsh *kulturkampf*"— Howe establishes a defensive stance from the essay's outset.[41] His weapon, as his description of the Plath reader makes clear, is circular logic disguised in simple aesthetic concerns: Those who find "Daddy" an aesthetically worthy poem, one not rendered undeserving of the merit bestowed upon it because of its imagery, must be too preoccupied with the glamour of Plath as icon to be good readers of her poetry.

Given the importance Howe places on the poet's "need for enlarging the magnitude of her act" (remember, it is in this respect, he insists, that Plath's poetry fails), the implications of Howe's statement about the reader are in no way small. On close examination, in fact, what emerges from Howe's essay is the sense that he might be inclined to agree with a positive assessment of Plath's work if it were not for the way she has been celebrated as an "authentic priestess" and thus transformed into an icon by her readers. At the very least, it is clear that Howe, despite his own admission at the essay's opening that to do so would be unjust, allows his own "irritation with her devotees to spill over into [his] response to her work."[42]

In highlighting Howe's preoccupation with Plath's "devotees," I have tried to show the intricacies of an argument about Plath that is driven first by deep anxieties about who reads Plath and how and why they read her and second by a desire to contain Plath as poet—to put her back in her place as a "minor" woman poet. The possibility that Plath could be both icon and serious poet never appears to enter Howe's mind, or if it does, it is not a possibility he wishes to entertain. His understanding of confessional poetry, in fact, precludes the possibility insofar as he sees the confessional poem as an unfortunate emblem of a culture preoccupied with "self-exposure, self-assault, self-revelation," the very qualities a good poem shuns.[43] For Howe, moreover, these are the same qualities that in readers' minds lend Plath her authenticity as priestess and icon. In this way, Howe's argument reflects the common assumption that pervades Plath criticism, and this includes criticism written both in her favor and against it: Sylvia Plath, the poet, has to be extricated from the romanticized, one might say Hollywoodized, icon she has been transformed into by an adoring readership, for only then can the actual merit of her poetry be determined. While one would think that this limited perspective would be obviously troublesome from our contemporary vantage point, it nevertheless persists in Plath criticism today. In fact, the most common strategy among contemporary critics who wish to recuperate Plath's reputation is one Howe himself employs in his own critique: expose the typical Plath reader as an uncritical consumer of her work.

In *The Other Sylvia Plath*, one of the most recent critical studies about Plath, Tracy Brain, for example, describes her project as one that seeks "to reveal [Plath's] poems as often being about subjects much larger than one woman's autobiography."[44] Explaining the motives behind this goal, Brain continues:

> There is much unkindness, not to mention little value and reliability, in using poetry and fiction as evidence for Plath's supposed anger towards her husband or parents or female rivals; or, at the opposite extreme, as proof of her presumed victimhood. To treat Plath's writing in this is way is to belittle her work, for the implication of such an exercise is that Sylvia Plath was too unimaginative to make anything up, or too self-obsessed to consider anything of larger historical or cultural importance. . . . Many [readers] do not know that they are being cheated, for the fascination with the personal too often interferes with any serious attentiveness to the writing, thereby limiting the ways of responding to and appreciating it.[45]

As this passage makes clear, Brain critiques autobiographical reading practices as "misread[ings]" that interfere with "any serious attentiveness to the writing" and argues instead for readings that attend to the "technical proficiency of her poetry."[46] Just as important, she constructs Plath's audience as misguided readers who are so intent on applying biographical details to the poetry—so possessed of a "fascination with the personal"—that "many do not know that they are being cheated."[47]

A similar construction of Plath's readers is evident in an essay by

Amy Rea in the *Readerville Journal*. Appearing in February 2003, in an issue intended to commemorate the fortieth anniversary of Plath's death, the essay "Reclaiming Plath" pays homage to the poet and attempts to debunk the myths surrounding her readers. In fact, the stated aim of the essay is to challenge the stereotypical image of the Plath reader as a woman "hung up on death,"[48] to make it "OK to like Plath minus an obsession with death."[49] While Rea seeks to show that Plath's fans are "many and various" and thus do not conform to a stereotype, a goal one can certainly respect, she does so in a way that effectively undermines her purported objective. For Rea, certain ways of reading Plath's writing—and therefore certain kinds of readers—are inherently less valuable than others. As she argues, "labeling the work as strictly confessional strips it of its mythic qualities and detracts from the very disciplined intellectual approach Plath brought to her work."[50] In arguing this point, Rea clearly echoes Brain's rhetoric of "technical proficiency." She also echoes Brain's worries that autobiographical readings "belittle" the work by denying the imagination and effort that go into good poetry. In the end, then, Rea's "reclaiming" of Plath serves only to replicate—and, I would add, reinforce—the paternalistic anxieties about women readers that pervade Plath criticism, anxieties that emerge most fully at the close of Rea's essay when she explains: "With each new generation of young readers who find themselves fascinated with her death, there will be a revival of Plath as suicide icon. But those readers will also age and gain perspective from their own life experiences, and they'll inevitably come to see a more complex Plath—the accomplished and talented poet."[51]

When reading such statements about the naïveté of Plath's young readers, one cannot help but be reminded of Webster Schott's complaints in his review of *Winter Trees*. As he put it in 1972, "Some young people, having limited experience, need literature to help them feel bad, and they will celebrate Plath for a while." Perhaps such anxieties about readers are inescapable within the literary establishment; and perhaps they are sometimes inconsequential within the larger assessment of the literary work. Their pervasiveness within Plath criticism, however, requires us to pay special attention to the connections between critics' rhetoric of uncritical consumption and their biases against women readers. Indeed, that these anxieties are present in criticism that seeks to recuperate Plath's reputation, rather than dismantle it, shows perhaps just how ingrained the rhetoric and its gender biases

have become. That these anxieties are also present in the film characters Kat Stratford and Mallory Knox shows the full force of the terms as
well. As I proposed earlier, Kat and Mallory bring to the forefront a culture's anxieties about Sylvia Plath and women readers. Because both
characters are so thoroughly grounded in these anxieties, it is not at all
surprising to find that by the ends of both films, Kat and Mallory
appear to have been put back in their proper places: Kat, an avid reader
of women's writing, eventually relinquishes her books for a prom
gown, while Mallory, some years after her vengeful murder spree ends,
hits the road in a Winnebago with Mickey and their children. I say
appears, because I think the films leave the slightest room for a second,
albeit perhaps counterintuitive, reading. Most notably, while Kat dons
the normalizing garb of the prom gown for a night, she eventually
abandons it too and returns by the film's end to her dark but artistically
and intellectually expressive self (one who plays guitar, draws, and
plans to attend Sarah Lawrence College in the fall), a return that is easily overshadowed by the final coupling of her and her paid date in the
final scene of the film. Similarly, while Mallory winds up occupying the
conventional position of wife and mother at the film's close, she does
so only after escaping the perversely dysfunctional domestic scene of
her childhood, a scene complete with abusive and neglectful parents
who parodically expose the myth of the idealized nuclear family. Perhaps, then, the characters of Kat Stratford and Mallory Knox open the
door, if only slightly, for a recuperation of the figure of the woman
reader I have been discussing here. I like to think so, and I believe
other recent constructions of the Plath reader work toward a similar
recuperation.

Take, for example, the recent works by cultural critic Elizabeth
Wurtzel. Apparently intent on casting herself as the consummate
autopathographer, Wurtzel constructs herself as the quintessential
Plath reader in her 1994 memoir *Prozac Nation* and again in 1998's
Bitch. In the prologue to the first of the two, the then twenty-some-
thing-year-old Wurtzel previews her struggles with depression and her
ambivalent attitude toward the drugs that keep her from "constant-
level hysteria": "I've been off lithium less than a month and I'm already
perfectly batty. And I'm starting to wonder if I might not be one of
those people like Anne Sexton or Sylvia Plath who are just better off
dead, who may live in that bare, minimal sort of way for a certain number of years, may even marry, have kids, create an artistic legacy of

sorts, may even be beautiful and enchanting at moments, as both of them supposedly were."[52] That Wurtzel should compare herself to Plath and Sexton—and in the process implicitly construct herself as someone who has read their work—is perhaps not all that surprising. Evoking the poster women of what Wurtzel herself calls "aching, enduring suicidal pain"[53] underscores the extent of Wurtzel's illness and drives home the point of the prologue, which is after all entitled "I Hate Myself and I Want to Die." At the same time, the comparison allows Wurtzel to accomplish a less-obvious goal, one interwoven with her own identity as a writer. Indeed, if Wurtzel is like Plath and Sexton because she too may be better off dead, she is also like them because she shares their desire to "create an artistic legacy of sorts."[54] As her qualification of the legacy indicates, Wurtzel is well aware of the constructedness of Plath's and Sexton's authorial identities, of the way they "supposedly were."[55] Such hedging on her part also suggests she is just as aware of the constructedness of the Plath reader, especially of the way she too can construct herself as one and thus capitalize on the image of the poet herself. Her evocation of Plath and Sexton, therefore, serves as a kind of masterful incantation that establishes her authority not only as a reader but as a writer with an astute awareness of her subject matter.

Kat Stratford and Mallory Knox, I would argue in closing, resemble Wurtzel in more ways than one. Most obviously, they show signs of Wurtzel's depression. But they also display a similar empowerment that comes in part at least from their reading of Plath's writings. That is, while it is true that the scenes of the two women reading *The Bell Jar* signal their pathologies, they also signal their sense of entitlement and their willingness to act from such a position. In *10 Things I Hate About You*, for example, the women writers whom Kat reads serve as the only strong female role models she has, and it is through them that she is able to assert her own voice and self-worth. Similarly, in *Natural Born Killers*, the scene of Mallory's reading marks not only her plunge into violence but her stand against her abusive father. Kat and Mallory, in fact, could well serve as additional examples of the difficult and unruly women Wurtzel celebrates in *Bitch*, women who deserve to be revered because they have learned to be difficult and unruly in a society that tells them to just behave. Even in the presence of such promise, however, one cannot overlook the fact that Kat is based on the figure of the shrew in Shakespeare's play and, like her Shakespearean namesake, is destined to be tamed by a boy precisely because she is unruly and empowered. Nor can one overlook Mallory's own dependency on Mickey, the man who makes her escape from the Wilson home possible in the first place. Such endings serve to contain what is threatening and powerful about the Plath reader, strengthening the patronizing and misogynist cultural attitudes that shape her construction. Casting both women as Plath readers, then, appears to be simply another way for the films' writers to put them and their reading back in their place. Certainly the presence of such attitudes today, more than forty years after the poet's death, expresses an entrenched unease about Sylvia Plath and her work—an unease that is only exacerbated by attempts to deny or devalue the women readers who have become synonymous with Plath's name.

NOTES

1. *10 Things I Hate About You*, dir. Gil Junger (Touchstone Pictures, 1999).
2. Ibid.
3. By referring to Kat as a Plath reader, I mean, of course, that she is portrayed as someone who reads Sylvia Plath's writings. At the same time, I want the phrase to convey the image underlying the reality of her reading material. That is to say, Kat is a Plath reader not simply because she reads *The Bell Jar* but because she embodies an image that in many ways reflects the stereotype of women readers of Plath's writing.
4. *Annie Hall*, dir. Woody Allen (MGM Pictures, 1977).
5. Meg Wolitzer, *Sleepwalking* (New York: Random House, 1982), 3.
6. See Jacqueline Rose's *The Haunting of Sylvia Plath* (Cambridge: Harvard University Press, 1991), 65–71, for further discussion of these historical readers.
7. Irving Howe, "Sylvia Plath: A Partial Disagreement," *Harper's*, January 1972, 88–91. Howe refers to Plath ironically as the "authentic priestess" (88), while Webster Schott calls her "the high priestess of the confessional poem" in his review, "The Cult of Plath" in *Critical Essays on Sylvia Plath*, ed. Linda W. Wagner (New York: G. K. Hall, 1984), 3 (originally published in *Sewanee Review*, July–September 1968, 520–35).
8. Paul Alexander, *Rough Magic: A Biography of Sylvia Plath* (Cambridge, Mass.: Da Capo Press, 1999), 343–44.
9. Ibid., 348. According to Alexander, "*The Bell Jar* became so popular that, when Bantam Books brought out an initial paperback edition in April 1972—a run of 375,000 copies—it sold out that printing, plus a second and a third, in one month. In the mid-eighties, more than a decade and a half later, *The Bell Jar* paperback edition was selling some fifty thousand copies a year."
10. *BJ*, xiii.
11. Majorie Perloff, "On the Road to *Ariel*: The Transitional Poetry of Sylvia Plath," *Iowa Review*, Spring 1973, 94.

12. Alexander, *Rough Magic*, 358.

13. *BJ*, xiv.

14. For further discussion of cultural fears regarding women readers, see Kate Flint's study *The Woman Reader 1837–1914* (Oxford: Clarendon Press, 1993).

15. Because the girls' father has previously forbidden Bianca to date until Kat does (a new house rule he imposes because he thinks it will prevent both girls from dating, since Kat has renounced boys altogether), one of Bianca's devotees, Cameron James, develops a scheme to get Kat to date so he can then take out Bianca.

16. *Natural Born Killers*, dir. Oliver Stone (Warner Bros., 1994).

17. Carol Anshaw, *Seven Moves* (New York: Houghton Mifflin, 1996). I am indebted to Susan Van Dyne for directing me to Anshaw's depiction of a Plath reader.

18. Ibid., 69.

19. Ibid., 132.

20. Webster Schott, "The Cult of Plath," *Washington Post Book World*, October 1, 1972, 3.

21. "The Blood Jet Is Poetry," *Time*, June 10, 1966, 118.

22. "Russian Roulette," *Newsweek*, June 20, 1966, 110.

23. Schott, "The Cult of Plath," 3.

24. Jan B. Gordon, "Saint Sylvia," *Modern Poetry Studies* 2 (1972): 286.

25. Dan Jaffe, "An All-American Muse," *Saturday Review*, October 15, 1966, 29–31.

26. Robert L. Stilwell, "The Multiplying of Identities: D. H. Lawrence and Five Other Poets," *Sewanee Review*, July–September 1968, 520–35, reprinted in Wagner, *Critical Essays on Sylvia Plath*, 44–45.

27. Howe, "Sylvia Plath," 91.

28. Paul West, "Crossing the Water," *Book World (Chicago Tribune)*, January 9, 1972, 8.

29. This is not to say that women critics did not often chime in to offer their own objections to Plath's work. Certainly they did, but my review of the early criticism and reception found that they were seldom as harsh or as dramatic in their evaluations as male critics tended to be; at least this is true about criticism written during the 1960s and 1970s.

30. Howe, "Sylvia Plath," 90.

31. Ibid.

32. Ibid.

33. Ibid.; and Elizabeth Hardwick, "On Sylvia Plath," in *Ariel Ascending: Writings About Sylvia Plath*, ed. Paul Alexander (New York: Harper and Row, 1985), 100–115. The uncontextualized quotation of Hardwick in Howe's essay is rather disturbing when Hardwick's words are placed back in their original context. In her work on Plath entitled "On Sylvia Plath," she writes, "In Sylvia Plath's work and in her life the elements of pathology are deeply rooted and so little resisted that one is disinclined to hope for general principles, sure origins, applications, or lessons" (100). Howe's quotation of only those words I have requoted in my discussion leads the reader to think Hardwick would agree with Howe's reading, when in fact her reading of Plath's poetry is much more positive than Howe's own.

34. Howe, "Sylvia Plath," 89.

35. Ibid.

36. Ibid., 88.

37. Ibid., 91.

38. Ibid., 88.

39. Ibid.

40. Ibid., 90.

41. Ibid., 88.

42. Ibid.

43. Ibid., 89.

44. For a more in-depth discussion of the relationship between autobiography and Plath's writing, see my essay "Poems as 'Bloodstains': Sylvia Plath's Confessional Poetics and the Autobiographical Reader," in a/b: (Winter 2002): 180–203.

45. Tracy Brain, The Other Sylvia Plath (Harlow, England: Longman, 2001), 15.

46. Ibid., 15, 3.

47. Ibid., 15.

48. Amy Rea, "Reclaiming Plath," Readerville Journal, January–February 2003, 39.

49. Ibid., 40.

50. Ibid.

51. Ibid., 43.

52. Elizabeth Wurtzel, Prozac Nation: Young and Depressed in America (New York: Riverhead Books, 1994), 8. See also Wurtzel's Bitch: In Praise of Difficult Women (New York: Doubleday, 1998).

53. Wurtzel, Prozac Nation, 8.

54. Ibid.

55. Ibid.

ANITA HELLE

Reading Plath Photographs

IN AND OUT OF THE MUSEUM

⊞

Acetic acid in a sealed tin?
Do not accept it. It is not genuine.
    —SYLVIA PLATH, "THE COURIERS"

Let me first unpack some issues that constitute . . . the heart of the
cultural analysis of photography. That heart involves the photograph's
simultaneous investment in the preciously private and vulgarly public
domains; hence, the way it deconstructs the flawed, illusionary oppo-
sition, or even distinction, between those two. Here lies the photo-
graph's power, and here lies its power to lie, deceive, seduce, and
manipulate: its political, militant, even military agency.
    —MIEKE BAL, "*LIGHT WRITING*: PORTRAITURE IN A POST-TRAUMATIC AGE"

Mieke Bal's inscription of a scene in which the "telling objects" of photography are simultaneously invested in public and private domains
sets an agenda for critical reconsideration of Plath's multifaceted photographic legacy.[1] That legacy consists of photographs of Plath as
objects and images, their multiple forms of creation and distribution,
and the narratives that spring up around them.[2]

Public fascination with Plath's photographic image has been analyzed in relation to her "colossal celebrity,"and as a symptom of the
objectifying gaze.[3] Yet questions remain about how to situate photographic images of Plath culturally and aesthetically so that the mili-
tancy of the photograph—that is, its active power—can be located in
relation to her writing. My larger point here will be to suggest some

ways that reading Plath photographs routinely unpacks and disturbs such distinctions as the separation of the "vulgarly public" and "preciously private" upon which modernism's repudiation of sentimental culture depends, facilitating a more flexible definition of such familiar binaries. I consider how images of Plath pass across porous borders and acquire "public private" meanings in two contexts—the display of photographs and manuscripts in an exhibition and the discovery of a photo album in which eastern Massachusetts places serve as a rhetorical referent for poems written during 1957–59, as Plath assembled her first book of poems.[4] Thus I assume a dual perspective—on photographs as material texts in themselves, and on the possibility of writing triggered by photographs.

Plath has been discussed as a writer who understood fame and self-image in terms of gendered spectacle.[5] This much reverberates in the rough cuts Plath makes in a studio photo, pasted in a page of her Smith diary, a "dead mask here." Plath's double move—reinserting, and reinscribing, writing "across" the photo in her autobiographical prose—marks the photograph performatively as an "other stage," a space of difference and self-division from which uncanny figures of strange familiarity can be reworked. In a much-cited passage from Plath's novel *The Bell Jar,* when editor Jay Cee asks Plath's narrator/surrogate Esther Greenwood to represent herself as a poet for a journalistic photo,[6] Plath projects the image of a young woman savvy in, if nothing else, the ways of the mid-century writing business. Esther Greenwood knows that in celebrity culture, becoming a writer means photographic exposure. But if there are signs that reading and seeing her image potentially intruded on Plath's powers of self-definition, Plath would also prove adept at re-inscribing the surfaces of photographs with her own subversive meanings. In an early poem, "Tale of a Tub," the speaker's apprehension of the surveiling "photographic chamber of the eye" in a lavatory "assault[s] the ego" and exposes the alien wince of the "stranger in the mirror."[7] The recognition that Plath often saw herself through the "third eye" of an objectifying lens (and through different kinds of lenses) should be the beginning, not the end, of our interest in such phototextual constructions. Just as "material modernism" has advanced our knowledge of auras in books that published words alone do not recognize, we are only beginning to take into account the ways in which Plath photographs supplement linguistic meanings.[8]

The Evolution of the Photographic Archive

Scholars working in Plath archives might be forgiven for wondering, "Where are all the Plath photographs? Why are the same images of her reproduced over and over again"?[9] Even if all the published photographs of Plath were locked together in one room, there are not many of them. Given that it is the character of the modern archive to be both overflowing and incomplete, Plath photographs are just as likely to be languishing in the back drawer of a publicity file cabinet, artifacts of the mid-century writers' market, as moldering in a basement flooded from season to season, part of the flotsam and jetsam of personal memorabilia. Yet with photographs, as with other kinds of material texts, the lesson of Carolyn Steedman's provocative meditation on archival knowledge in *Dust: The Archive and Cultural History* is pertinent—the objects "speak" depending on where we find them.[10]

Questions about the politics of representation of Plath photographs—and the myriad narratives that might develop from these "telling objects"—are not well sorted out in what little commentary Plath images have received. While it is not the purpose of this essay to do all that sorting, the most productive way to begin is not with the question of why there aren't more Plath photographs, but rather, given the ones we have, what kind of cultural work do they propose? Along what borders are they arrayed? And how should we read them?

One of the most luminous tales of the modern photographic archive, a precedent for reading Plath photographs, especially photographs of the young Plath, centers on Walter Benjamin's reflection on a photograph of Franz Kafka, taken when the author was about six years of age, in a winter garden landscape that was set up (probably in the photographer's studio) to imitate the tropics. This is a photograph that belonged to Benjamin's private collection, but it is not one that Benjamin chose to reprint, and it was only published later by those who documented his collections. Benjamin's description of that photograph as a "moving testimony" reveals a writer's motive (his own). He explains what he sees as a magical essence that pictures, at their best, give back to a writer's words—the optical unconscious that the camera's eye reveals, but the human eye can't see. That particular photo of Kafka at the age of six, no doubt had its artistic and allusive charms—but Benjamin wants more than to admire the picture, he wants to engage in a kind of literary anthropology, using the snapshot to explore widening circles of identity, history, and memory. Benjamin admires the capacity of the camera's eye to enlarge the myth of the author—and yet he famously draws what some have regarded as an overly sharp distinction between the value of the replicated image in an exhibition (*ausstellungswert*) and cult value (*kultwert*). For Benjamin, the photo from the private album is linked to intimate attachment, and remains under the sign of the auratic.[11]

But can these economies of looking and valuing photographic images, the "preciously private" and the "vulgarly public" be so very fixed and distinct from one another? I refer to Benjamin's reading of the photograph of Franz Kafka for two reasons—because it is a well-known site of divisions I want to complicate in the course of my readings of Plath photographs, and because the particular tropes of winter garden photographs (also taken up by Roland Barthes) offer some appealing possibilities, later on in this essay, for reading one of Plath's significant *Colossus* poems. As a precedent for thinking about exchanges between word and image, however, the separation of the cult value in the family photograph album and the exhibition value in public display, has some obvious problems. First, the vast majority of Plath photographs available to scholars in published form are already drawn from family albums, cards, or letters. Aside from studio portraits by Rollie McKenna, Siv Arb, and several photojournalists, Plath did not live long enough to have many posed photographs for public consumption. Second, despite the emphasis on manuscripts as the most valued possession of literary archives, renewed emphasis on Plath's visual history and visual culture more generally means that Plath photographs are increasingly being thought of as part of, rather than apart from, the "dust" of the archives.

In addition to photographic images of Plath presumed to be taken by Aurelia Plath or Ted Hughes, a number of private collections inviting thematic, historical, and aesthetic considerations have been acquired by "official" Plath archives in recent years. The kind of "evidence" these photographs provide is often ambiguous. A photograph album consisting of several dozen snapshots put together by Gordon Lameyer, one of Plath's boyfriends (assembled by Lameyer after a European tour they took together), is a good example of a collection with an apparent thematic unity that nonetheless presents questions of value and interpretation not easily resolved merely by considering the photographs as little documentaries. If "reading" Plath photographs means considering the triad of the photographer, the photographed subject, and the details of the photograph, then it won't do to read what Plath tells us in her journals alone—that she has set out, at twenty-two, to forge an identity across the Atlantic. The journal won't finally determine whether, for example, to read the casual snapshot of Plath in Paris at the south entrance of Notre Dame (reproduced on the frontispiece of this volume) in late March or early April 1956, her gaze focused at the level of the street, as a minor incident in accidental tourism, a footnote in the history of her visual education, or a souvenir of a relationship gone sour.[12]

Other photographs of Plath might never make their way into official archives at all because they belong to the history of something other than the individual personality. In this category are photographs of considerable cultural interest that are probably not "lost," yet bringing them to light would take some digging that no one has yet managed. For example, Plath's "posture" pictures from her freshman year at Smith College, referenced in *Letters Home,* and presumably somewhere to be found in the Smithsonian collections, belong to the history of William Sheldon's 1950s experiments in somatic body types, and to his planned publication, in the 1950s, of an *Atlas of Women.*[13] If it is ever discovered, the contact sheet with photographs of Plath at a party given for Robert Frost in Boston in 1958, taken by journalist Gary Villett for a *Life* magazine article, might tell us more about the centrality of the camera's eye to changing forms of sociality that transformed the midcentury literary cocktail party into a televised photo op with "star" authors as anchoring personalities. Peter Davison remembers a "lost" *Life* magazine photograph from that party in which, as Davison recalls, the photostrip revealed Plath's hand nervously clutching a cocktail glass over the back of Ted Hughes's head. The absent photograph in Peter Davison's *The Fading Smile,* hints (as does its title) at Plath's positioning ("behind" Hughes) in the politics of the literary gaze.[14]

Pictures at an Exhibition: The Grolier Club, New York

Exhibitions of rarely seen Plath photographs, including those shown at the 2005 Grolier Club exhibit, "'No Other Appetite': Sylvia Plath, Ted

Hughes, and the Blood Jet of Poetry," give added impetus to critical reconsideration of Plath photographic images across several genres of her writing.[15] One of the most compelling and paradoxical features of Plath's photographs now is that, as new audiences become interested in Plath (and in such exhibits), the photographs seem to reach across generational and cultural divides. To suggest that they do so, of course, is to invoke vexed debates about how photographs signify—about their capacity to evoke presence and absence, disclosing or withholding partial, secret, residual meanings, and about their controversial value as scholarly "evidence." The framed and photographed body exists outside Plath's writing as a cultural image and inside her writing as a metaphor of vision and an emblem of cultural reproduction. This is not to say that the written word and the photographic image are equivocal modes of representation for her. The signifying potential of the photographic image for Plath is clearly different from that of the words in a poem, although the two are integrally related.

We can approach some of the nuanced distinctions Plath makes between words and photographic images through her poetic representations of snapshots drawn from her family album. In what is arguably the most famous invocation of a family photograph within the context of her poems—"You stand at the blackboard daddy, / in the picture I have of you."[16]—Plath confirms her place in a long-running tradition from the platonic to the confessional in which the photograph signifies a failed, illicit, or insufficient representation. For her, the family album is a metaphorical locus of struggles, triumphs, and disappointments. Plath suggests the photograph is merely a mechanical "thing"; the photograph can't speak—and so the poet must. And yet the performative rhetoric of the photographic, implied ("look, here it is"), and shudderingly enacted in "Daddy" ("You do not do, you do not do"[17]—as if the shutter won't close) allows for the possibility of the writer's repossession of the power of the camera through the mythologized, primordial "eye" of the artist. It offers the possibility of seeing and imaginatively recovering what was taken away in the moment of the picture-taking.

From within her poems, Plath's camera-style metaphors work in two directions: toward a skeptical resistance to the claims of the photograph as a bearer of truth and authenticity and toward an exploitation of devices through which surrealist traditions retraced the journey of photography from popular culture back into art. Poems such as "Insomniac," where the image of the self is diminished in the recesses of its camera obscura-like box, and "Couriers," where the chemical and physical processes of photographic development are described as flawed and deceptive, as several critics have noted, extend the medium's self-representational powers by disturbing the boundaries of photo-realism and reintroducing the shock of disjointed seeing.[18]

The rhetorical and performative frames of Plath photographs have been enlarged by the opportunity to view them in exhibition settings. At the 2005 Grolier Club exhibit, the arrangement of manuscripts, drafts, holographs, and photographs from the intense years of Plath's and Hughes's lives together inscribed a narrative arc around the room. With each footstep around the circumference of the viewing area, the viewer gained access to Plath and Hughes as literary partners—never the one without the other. Pairings of manuscript and photograph raise questions of considerable interest for scholarly projects that have not been undertaken. One of those projects would have to do with analyzing the struggles for mastery between verbal and photographic representation in Plath's and Hughes's poems.[19] In one family snapshot exhibited at the Grolier Club, a young Ted Hughes, perhaps in his late teens or early twenties, talks back to the photographer; he is seated, apparently for a casual portrait, but he is holding a large mirror that captures the reflection of his sister, Olwyn Hughes, who is behind the camera taking the photograph.[20] The mirror captures the image of the photographer within the two-dimensional space of the photograph and makes us read against the grain of the medium itself. The ghostly appearance of the photographer within the photograph's inner, mirrored frame challenges the whole ontology of the photograph, upending the relationship of mastery implied by the one who "takes" the picture and is normally invisible. At the same time, in the exhibition space, the viewer is set up to regard a playful interchange in which identities are at stake. Is this a first appearance of the poet as "invisible man," one who reaches into the depths of imagination, as Hughes tells us, in *Winter Pollen,* where "understanding has its roots and stores its X-rays?"[21] Is it a moment of surrealist experiment in which *both* photographer and subject collude? Especially for writers who equate the camera's eye with a dangerous disturbance of the boundaries between exterior and interior, as Lynda Haverty Rugg has speculated, the psychic and iconographic dimensions of authorial self-editing in photographs may be related.[22]

"I Am" / "You Are" A Camera

References to double exposures, snapshots, and camera angles layer many of Hughes's and Plath's accounts of memory and invention. In *Birthday Letters,* a coy revisionism centers on the gendered terms of the photograph—around who is "snapped" or who does the "snapping." In a related set of poems, "The Owl" restages the trope of lover who is blinded by seeing through his beloved's eyes; Hughes reinterprets the figure (and reverses the trope) by insisting that the camera is the alien medium through which the beloved looks back at him, but finds his image through a foggy lens: "You were a camera / Recording reflections you could not fathom."[23] In "The Chipmunk," the visual memory of Plath is the "orphan" of the moment of the "flash-still," of a domestic squabble: "retorting to my saying something, / You made a chipmunk face."[24] Displayed against the black-and-white parquet and coffered ceilings of the Grolier Club, alongside drafts and holographs of manuscripts and artifacts of daily life, the images extend insights about Hughes's and Plath's practices of composing and revising drafts of poems on the back sides of each other's manuscripts.

Long before they morphed into literary icons, Plath and Hughes were a writer-photographer pair, sometimes snapping images of each other from what archivist Karen V. Kukil notes is often the same roll of film.[25] Casual photographs Plath and Hughes took of each other, such as the photograph of Plath seated against a low stone wall with her typewriter on her lap in West Yorkshire, or the photographs each took of the other sketching and writing in the course of their travels, confirm the interest each took in witnessing the other's creative processes and in viewing photographic surfaces as drafts for reinscription. The photographic exchanges parallel their literary exchanges. Just as, in composing their manuscripts, Hughes and Plath recyled paper on which one or the other had drafted poems, and lifted lines from each other's poems, so too, images from snapshots are recirculated as material for stories and poems in their travels and domestic life. In his picture-postcard to his brother Gerald of the trip through Yellowstone Park, Hughes offers his version of the bear tearing the rear window from their car in the middle of the night; while still on the trip, Plath found the postcard with a bear's pawprint on it. In her later draft of a short story about the vacationing couple, "The Fifty-Ninth Bear"

(1959), she recycles and rescripts the themes of the snapshots complete with a reference to the rude hand of the bear on the card.

If one kind of phototextual project leads to analyzing the work of the camera eye in reframing the "real" from within Plath's (and Hughes's) poems, another has to do with how photographs of Plath (and Hughes's artistic manipulation of image as memory) function as a medium for Hughes's self-inquisitional postures in *Birthday Letters*. In a recent discussion of Plath photographs, Tracy Brain pointed out that the biographical record is so familiar that one has to fight against arranging Plath poems in a seamless documentary alongside Plath's photographs. We view the Siv Arb photograph of Sylvia Plath with Frieda and Nicholas, Court Green (April 1962),[26] with its triptych of values—mother, children, daffodils (and spontaneous generativity), now canonized in Hughes's poem, "Perfect Light," and it is hard not to leap ahead to the dismal end of story, to images of the trio in "Edge," or when nature runs amok, as in "Totem," where the flies "buzz like blue children / In nets of the infinite."[27] Given how well known the biographical text has become, it isn't surprising that Plath photographs disturb with an excess of the spectral that Ronald Barthes finds in the snapping and stopping of all photographs, an awareness of death— "that the thing has been there."[28] Yet Hughes's critics have been divided on whether Hughes's use of photographic images of Plath position him as a conventional mourner. Jo Gill, for example, argues for a more complex hermeneutics for the speaker in *Birthday Letters*, a speaker who demonstrates frustrated desire in search of direct "truth" or "evidence" of Plath's existence.[29]

One of the most important considerations introduced by the juxtaposition of known, familiar and rarely seen photographs in exhibition is the awareness of how difficult it is to resolve the many photographic images of Plath in a single unified frame of archival transparency or neutrality. Genre matters, especially in ideological recodings of word and image. Hughes's poem "Perfect Light" is generally understood as addressing the April, 1962 Siv Arb photograph for a Swedish magazine that had published her poems; it is a professionally posed photograph modeled on the painterly plein air tradition amid daffodils at Court Green, and it replicates an influential familial image in culture. In Hughes's poem, that image is rendered through another high art genre, the "mother and infant, as in the Holy portrait."[30] But there was another photo blown up in the Grolier exhibit, a casual black-and-white snapshot of Plath smiling into the camera, on a picnic outing at another grassy knoll, Primrose Hill, that puts the themes of "Perfect Light'" in a less naturalized, romanticized perspective. In the Primrose Hill photograph, presumed to have been taken by Hughes, there are similar elements—a hillside, another springtime, mother and child.[31] This blow-up of a 2" × 2" snapshot that Hughes had enclosed in a letter to Gerald Hughes along with its "verso"—Hughes's notation on the back—makes an uncanny double to the photo taken at Court Green, and to images from the second stanza of the poem, "Perfect Light." The black and white photo taken at Primrose Hill does not picture the close-cropped literary garden, magnanimously fruitful with its prospect of flowers; it is a littered space of public ground, pocked with wear.

But because the photographic medium is technologically malleable, unforeseen details jump out when photographs are blown up for the museum. In the Primrose Hill photo, Plath is sitting on the grass, but from an atmospheric perspective (the figure blurs into sky and ground) we can sense a sticky closeness about the air, and the cottony texture of baby things: the pram with a white towel hung over its handlebars; another white towel, perhaps for nursing, tossed over a handbag converted ceremoniously into covering (as Hughes's annotations note) for a champagne bottle. In the blown up version, we can see that the photograph at Primrose Hill, unlike the later "portrait" at Court Green, is taken at a middle distance, and although the light is focused around the body in the more idealized portrait, in the Primrose Hill photo, Plath's white cottony figure is only a pinpoint of light against the dark hillside and the overcast sky that take up most of the picture. The exhibition catalog offers the intriguing suggestion that the occasion for the picnic on Primrose Hill may have been the celebration of the return of page proofs for The Colossus.[32] Instead of thinking of one of these photographs as a holy triptych and the other as the realistic snapshot, it is possible to read these juxtaposed images as two different ways of relating maternity to authorship and generativity. It appears Hughes did not write a poem "about" the Primrose Hill photo; he stood behind the camera to take a picture that renders a less idealized image of the daily work of parenthood and the work of poetry—not an image overlaid upon the setting, as in "Perfect Light," but inclusive of its particulars, mixed up with the landscape's worldly imperfections. Yet when the two photographs and the poem are juxtaposed with the second half of Hughes's poem, (the dark "hill" of the second half itself connecting death to the awful break in time, and the future rushing fatally toward her), the composition of "Perfect Light" appears to pull as much from the camera's eye view of the earlier Primrose Hill landscape as from the posed photograph in the garden at Court Green.

Regions of Memory in Public/Private Frames

> I am going back to the ocean as my poetic heritage and hope to revisit all the places I remember in Winthrop with Ted this summer: Johnson Avenue, a certain meadow on it, our beach and grammy's. Even run-down as it now is, the town has the exciting appeal of my childhood, and I am writing some good poems about it, I think.
> —SYLVIA PLATH, LETTERS HOME, JULY 5, 1958

The remaining pages of this essay make a foray into several kinds of pictures that pass across public/private thresholds, one a journalistic photograph of Boston Common in holiday season that finds its way into a greeting card and a few photos that fill out contexts of some of Plath's scenic constructions of landscape and memory. Themes of time, place, love and death, sound and silence, incursion and catastrophe organize the photographs that are associated with elements of local yet highly mobile regionalism prevalent in Plath's early writing.

The places and spaces in photographs and poems I want to consider here are Eastham, Boston, and Winthrop, a triad of points in Plath's scenic consciousness when she returned to the United States in 1957 to make renewed contact with what she grasped, at first exuberantly, and later uneasily, as a sense of "poetic heritage." That sense of inheritance assumes that memory is accessed by the writer's eye and drawn into a personal and historical significance through landscape, architecture, and photography.

I was born too late to meet Plath in any other realm but that of photographs, simulacra that passed across the threshold between my home and world with all the regularity of the seasons. My mother carried on a correspondence with Aurelia Plath for thirty years, and although the two women were of different generations, their affiliation has always seemed to me like a thumbprint on the margins of literary history. I have respected its privacy. As luck would have it, the photographs that often accompanied cards and letters were never "lost" or missing and censored, nor particularly neglected. However, the photographs I remembered from my childhood have proven to be of a different order altogether from the contexts in which I had come to know Plath's writing as a student and as a scholar. And these image-memorials are also different from those displayed at the Grolier Club, from Plath's and Hughes's album, since the photo album evokes a world, often, largely of girls and women, taken at home or on vacations, sunbathing at the beach, sometimes photographing each other, against the background of daily events in family life.[33]

When I hauled these photographs, clippings, and cards from the 1930s–1950s from my parents' basement many years later, the fact that the photos were not tidily displayed in an exhibition case, but wedged and clumped, together with cards and letters, between the tobacco-brown padded covers of my mother's photo album, or slipping out of the tri-cornered vellum holders pasted onto black construction paper pages, verified their precarious status halfway between the "artistically relevant" and "memorabilia." My mother, who made the album, was not ordering a "literary" life: she was keeping a holiday diary of sorts, in a ritualistic, even feral saving, as if to say, or so it seemed to me, *this is a covenant, it speaks only unto us.* And yet to my surprise, when I consider her loopy scrawling handwriting on the back sides of these photographs I realize that she must have made these inscriptions anticipating they would be read, and so I am conscious of reading between the lines of her annotations and between the borders of archival distinctions that have separated the literary from the personal artifact. Because I had known so much more about Plath from books, the particular objects I have retrieved, especially those already published, have in fact crossed these porous borders a number of times. Some of these photographs that I have seen in print accumulate more "dust" of intimate associations from having been viewed in private contexts; others seem to supplement narratives already densely impacted, therefore adding very little. Still others, such as a few I describe here, seem to acquire fresh interest in relation to poems that have no canonical history. Like the public/

private image-memorials that organized responses to loss in the nine-teenth century, these contemporary artifacts retain their power to organize meaning as they move through realms of cultural and historical memory.[34]

Conscious of album-reading as a modernist literary tradition, I hastened to donate the photographs to a research library, and then considered how these artifacts might be historicized within modern confessional culture and the poetry of the 50s. Other scholars working at the intersections of postmodern culture and its alternatives to realism have filled out these connections. Paul Giles and Thomas Travisano have noticed the relevance of the "camera style" (Giles) and the role of "surviving artifacts" (Travisano) in cementing or disrupting personal and national identifications.[35] But what my mother was not positioned to have understood in the late 1960s when she finished assembling her album, and what I did not appreciate without later having rummaged into the back files of the New Yorker, was that debates about the appropriations of snapshots into published versions of artists' notebooks, memoirs, and plays were also on display in some of the publications that Plath viewed as vital to her artistic aspirations. In the New Yorker, for instance, the "camera style" of the 1950s was part of a discourse on auto/biographical dramas. In his omnibus of plays for 1958, New Yorker drama critic Kenneth Tynan begins a column by announcing a "new genre," "Portrait of the Artist as a Young Camera," revisiting precedents such as Isherwood's Berlin stories, adapted in I Am a Camera, and work by Thomas Wolfe, William Inge and Stanley Berman (Berman's stories of growing up in Worcester, Massachusetts, had been serialized in the New Yorker in the 1950s).[36] Tynan is not a fan of the camera play he reviews, but he recognizes the function of the photograph as a reflective point of awareness for dramatizing incidents from the writer's past. "In play after play," Tynan notes, insertion of the photograph "accompanies the writer on a series of formative strolls down memory lane, the broad highway leading from the wrong side of the tracks to the ante-rooms of Perry and Pulitzer." Tynan speculates that such "camera play," by capitalizing on a new, mass mediated relation between the writer and the audience, replaces an earlier generation of lyricists' "recollections in tranquility."[37]

Sylvia Plath, age four, at Winthrop Beach in eastern Massachusetts, ca. 1937. (Photo courtesy Mortimer Rare Book Room, Smith College, ©Aurelia Schober Plath.)

Aurelia Schober Plath (Sylvia's mother), Dorothy Schober ("Aunt Dot"), and Sylvia near the sea wall at Point Shirley, ca. 1936–37. (Photo courtesy Mortimer Rare Book Room, Smith College, ©Aurelia Schober Plath.)

Sylvia Plath as the young artist, posing with flowers for the camera, Wellesley, Massachusetts. (Photo courtesy Mortimer Rare Book Room, Smith College, ©Aurelia Schober Plath.)

Aurelia Greenwood Schober (Sylvia's grandmother, in the poem "Point Shirley"), Aurelia Schober Plath, and Sylvia, 1933. (Photo courtesy Mortimer Rare Book Room, Smith College, ©Aurelia Schober Plath.)

Sylvia, Wellesley, en route to Cambridge, September 1955.
(Photo courtesy Mortimer Rare Book Room, Smith College,
©Aurelia Schober Plath.)

The view of the beach fr[om]
"Point Shirley" in Plath's
poem. (Photo courtesy P[eter]
K. Steinberg.)

A photo of the house
belonging to Plath's
grandparents at Point
Shirley on the Winthrop
Peninsula of eastern
Massachusetts, evoked i[n]
"Point Shirley, Revisited[.]"
(Photo courtesy Peter K[.]
Steinberg.)

Nauset Light Beach, Eastham, Massachusetts: "The Hermit at Outermost House"

Recent criticism has begun to fill in a picture of Plath's development from an orphic lyricism rooted in national and regional models, which she associated with close descriptions of native landscapes, to a more cosmopolitan geographical imaginary.[38] When Plath revisited places in Cape Cod, Boston, and Winthrop, as early as 1957–58, material features of these locations influenced what her writing could produce; in turn, her memories of places, and quite possibly, photographs themselves, shaped what she perceived. During this period, Plath would likely have come upon an essay in the *Paris Review* by another acquaintance who was experimenting with photographic technologies, the poet W. S. Merwin. In "Flight Home," a version of which would later appear in his essay collection entitled *Regions of Memory*, Merwin wrote about the reencounter with one's native land as a series of flickering memories through which it is discovered that home is already "a place that does not exist."[39] Merwin, and presumably also Plath, had instructions from on high—through the word of Robert Graves—that an American-born writer needed to find his "own poetry," but that "you had to go somewhere completely different before you did it; . . . Americans [had to go] back to America, but the time they were out of America was very important, before they got to see it."[40] Merwin's performative genuflecting in "Flight Home" is agonistic, full of soaring and falling, stabbing and contending against a dark Puritan tradition that he claims already to have thrown off. And for Merwin, as for Plath, a reinvestment in the elemental and particular, repossessing the gaze that looks back from the silvery frames of family photographs and portraits, becomes an essential mode of reinstantiating the subject. Plath's focus on rewriting home places with a sharply critical eye finds a parallel in Merwin's recontextualization of his craft: "Let me find instead a hard eye, proud of having no mercy, needing none, for the thing it loves."[41]

An unmarked nexus connects Plath's "The Hermit at Outermost House" and "Point Shirley" to New England landscape poems such as Merwin's "The Native," where immersion in revising places from the past through pictures and excursions shapes the artist's visual and aural memory.[42] Steven Gould Axelrod argues that Plath's New England poems of the sea are poems of instruction[43]—a common thread is an encounter with otherness that leads to a disappointment that is not fully traceable to the "originating" presence, which often proves alienating or deceptive. It is perhaps the fact that New England rustic Henry Beston, the subject of "The Hermit at Outermost House," was a figure so relatively distant from Plath, already a new England popular cliché, that accounts for this poem's ease with an avuncular, rather than fatherly, figure of heroic struggle. Hughes's notes in *Collected Poems* tell us that Beston was a popular classic;[44] but indeed, the fact that tourist postcard photos of Beston's hut were commonplace in Eastham, pictures complete with the rickety doorsill Plath notices, may have made Beston an easy subject for a poetic exercise. Plath's effort in "Hermit" works from the fixing and freezing of time toward a more fluid form of poetic closure. In "Hermit" she admires, and her rhythms confirm, a blend of Emersonian self-reliance with the images of determined individualism being celebrated by British "angry young men" such as Alan Sillitoe and John Osborne. The last lines of the poem embrace the flux of inner being and natural law.

> He withstood them, that hermit.
> Rock-face, crab-claw, verged on green.
>
> Gulls mulled in the greenest light.[45]

Boston Common

Months after that summer at the cottage near Eastham, while anticipating a year off to write in Boston, Plath announces her intention to begin a new collection of place-centered urban impressions, something between a "sketchbook" and a journal, a new project she at one point calls her "Boston diary"—

> Reading own books. . . . History even. Knowing Boston. Boston diary: taste, touch, street names. Six o'clock rings, belling from the church where all the funerals come. Rooms. Every room a world.[46]

Plath "knows" Boston in perceptual and embodied terms: names, places, geographies, verbal sketches, and snapshots signal emerging styles in the journals of her Boston year. In his last published interview on Plath in 1995, Hughes complicates previous accounts of his and Plath's contrasting styles and methods of working from the Willow Street apartment by considering their relationship to memory work, and he adds a number of reflections on topics of crucial interest to memory systems, mnemonic devices, the problems introduced to the flow of thought by handwriting and graphic systems. Speculating about Plath's writing blocks, Hughes notes her dependency on images, commenting on what he views as her overfocus on objects and description: "Her method was more painterly, mine more narrative, perhaps."[47] He needed to shut out distractions and so papered over his side of their bellied study windows, while she wrote perched "up in the glare" while "Boston clanged / All its atoms below."[48]

It makes sense to view Plath's writing problem—and her determination to return to settings from her early life—as akin to Virginia Woolf's, struggling to tunnel into the mind through images. Not that Plath couldn't remember, but that, especially while undergoing an intensive psychoanalysis that would itself be dependent on analogies between space and the images preserved in the mind, she was steeped in memories as she moved from place to place around the city at street level or observed it from her bird's-eye study window. Having returned from study abroad, she was both in and out of place in a Boston where many of her best-loved places—Scollay Square, for example—were being transformed through postwar urban renewal. Her journals, noting some of these changing circumstances of the city, and frequent trips from Boston to Winthrop, Massachusetts, suggest that the accelerated transformation of Boston further heightened estrangement from places she revisited and had remembered nostalgically. In her movements through space, images from the frozen past were reactivated. Just as Woolf's access to and navigation of the grounds at St. Ives enabled her to write her memory of her mother in *To the Lighthouse*, the regular practices of walking and observation, both from the street and from the bellied study window, helped Plath to bind image to embodiment and reinforced visual pleasure she had long taken in looking and making her own pictures.[49]

"A Winter's Tale"

An insert from the family album, a Christmas clipping from the *Boston Globe*, and a mimeo poem that drifts from a card fill out contexts for another poem with strong regional associations, "A Winter's Tale." Completed in 1959, the poem was first drafted in 1958, a letter tells us, after a long holiday walk from Willow Street off Louisberg Square that took Plath, Hughes, and her mother in a loop around Boston Common, Beacon Hill, and commercial districts. Several holiday photographs accompanied the card, but the newspaper photograph depicts lit squares around the Commons at Christmastime.

This "occasional" poem, as Plath called it, was accepted for publication by the *New Yorker* in 1959 for its holiday issue; it has no record of canonical reading, but its presence in the *Collected Poems* and its mixing of seasonal and parodic tropes raises questions about the slipperiness of the category of the "occasional" in midcentury verse culture. Given Plath's proximity in Boston to Adrienne Rich, another model for this poem might have been Rich's "Landscape of a Star," a poem that Rich had placed in the *New Yorker* and that also works on two levels, as a pastiche, but with serious, socially critical undertones. Rich's poem complicates the position of the speaker, obviously Jewish, who finds herself "no longer sick for home" but leans toward cosmopolitan diffusion:

> Our gifts shall bring us home—not to beginnings
> Nor always to the destination named
> Upon our setting forth. Our gifts compel,
>
> . . . . and lead us in the end
> Where we are most ourselves, whether at last
> To Solomon's gaze or Sheba's silken knees
> Or winter pastures underneath a star,
> Where angels spring like starlight in the trees.[50]

I had read Plath's "A Winter's Tale" in *Collected Poems* before having paged back into my mother's album to unfold the poem, in blue mimeo ink on white paper, accompanied by clippings, tucked into a card. When I read this poem in the edited version (the text is the same), on the page opposite to another red-drenched satire of bourgeois literalism, the sestina entitled "Yadwigha, on a Red Couch, Among Lillies: A Sestina for the Douanier," I marveled that "A Winter's Tale" had received almost no critical attention. The poems are similar in their metrical schemes. Both poems deal with limits to imagination, although "Yadwigha," is more obviously ekphrastic. In the album, the newspaper clipping with a photo of the lit commercial squares around Boston Common, floating out from the UNICEF holiday greeting card in which Aurelia Plath's letter was enclosed, seemed initially out of place in relation to the poem. Rereading the card, I realized that the photo and clipping might have been of a piece, as related motifs, more than just coincidence. The clipping was from a regular holiday newspaper feature, a column written by a local historian with a particular interest in cultural syncretisms—his columns typically included references to classical art and local folkways, but his particular forte was how Bostonians, historically, had celebrated the season.[51] Given that, as Robin Peel has noted, Plath is not a poet of the "headlines" but an absorptive reader who recast fragments from what she read in newspapers, these fragments are part of the picture puzzle of this overlooked poem in Plath's canon.[52]

In an earlier letter to her mother from Yaddo, Plath is working on this poem; in October, she thanks Aurelia Plath for rescuing a poem from her Willow Street apartment, so it can be submitted, first to *Harper's,* then to the *New Yorker:*

> The *New Yorker,* at last, bought the poem you sent me, "A Winter's Tale," for their December 26th issue, which is pleasant. There is a lot more competition for special seasonal occasions like that, and I wrote the poem as a light piece after that pleasant walk you and Warren and Ted and I took last Christmas time around Beacon Hill.[53]

But "light" and "pleasant" is surely not quite the way to describe the opening lines of "A Winter's Tale," with its disjunctive references to pastoral time and modern progress. Even if we don't immediately recognize "A Winter's Tale" as a pastiche of anthems (its tetrameters like those of "America, the Beautiful"), we should be interested in the many ways both its intricate prosody and its imagery exceed the boundaries of the "occasional." In the context of revisionary thinking about cold war surveillance and confessional verse, a red image of threat is wired to an emblem of the nation's confidence.

> On Boston Common a red star
> Gleams, wired to a tall Ulmus

Americana. . . .

Old Joseph holds an alpenstock.
Two waxen oxen flank the Child.
A black sheep leads the shepherds' flock.
Mary looks mild.

Angels—more feminine and douce
Than models from Bonwit's or Jay's

. . . .

Gilt trumpets raise.[54]

The poem's disjunctive disharmonies hinge on its opening representation of a strongly vertical visual image, "Ulmus Americana," for "Dutch elm," in the regional idiom, America's "Liberty Tree"; such strong verticals set a precedent for the totemic figurations in Plath's "Man in Black" and "Daddy." Linguistically cosmopolitan ("Ulmus Americana" puns on her German-American inheritance, with its allusion to the name of a German town, and sends a gutteral echo through the poem), the ominous sentinel seems also a forerunner of the "black yew" of "Little Fugue." From its opening description of the crowning star, the poem explodes a bombshell that is both nuclear ("the red star wired") and domestic. Plath's poem works as pastiche; its critique of consumption and commercialism highlights what Calvin Bedient calls "compulsive optics"[55]—seeing and seeing again, each time with an intensity that works through parodic juxtapositions and heightened visual acuity. "Looks" is the pivotal verb in the poem, for its ambiguity (Mary "appears," Mary's looked-at-ness) captures the ways by which the dynamics of seeing are shaped through socially refracted images. In this poem, the image is manufactured on one side of the store window, and its reality-effects bounced back through reflection on the other: poodle "baking cookies" in Filene's show windows, angels "feminine and douce" in Bonwit Teller. Another motif of the poem is weaving and reweaving. Just as the carolers in the poem weave around the lit squares, commercialism provides Plath an occasion for re-weaving bits of narrative romance into a satirical parade. Small but precise bits of detail are drawn from local architecture and mapping—the "odd violet panes" of glass in Beacon Hill mansions, for example. The ugly crèche sets up a flashpoint to the mimesis of the "waxen" holy family. The lit fuse in this poem is all that is glittering with banality and kitsch, and it is placed in the hands of "Mary milde," one of the first in a long line of Marian icons which Christine Britzolakis has linked to Plath's critique of commodifications of nation and home.[56]

Aurelia Plath was also a literary woman, and indeed, another literary interpretation is available through reading the poem in the context of the Christmas letter in which the home mimeo version of "A Winter's Tale" is enclosed. Aurelia Plath's holiday letter to family and friends—part of correspondence at the Lilly Library—begins with a reference to the "ghosts of Christmas past" and emphasizes the themes of loss in "A Winter's Tale," especially the loss of a daughter, Perdita.[57] The two "ghosts" were Sylvia and Ted, who, by late 1959, when the poem was to be published, were leaving the U.S. for West Yorkshire. Had the publication schedule gone as Plath's earlier letter to her mother anticipated, the mimeo poem and holiday card, dated December 13, 1959, might have preceded the intended publication date of December 26; but in fact the *New Yorker* published the poem on December 12. Thus the home mimeo version enclosed in the holiday card can be seen as a nearly simultaneous, domestic issue. Encased in a holiday greeting card, the more pastoral themes float to the surface. This epistolary version is marked by Aurelia Plath's pride in her daughter's literary accomplishments. As a strategy of converting loss into collecting and editing, it is a mark of things to come twenty years later when *Letters Home* is assembled.

Looking Back: "Point Shirley, Revisited"

> *What is it*
> *Survives, grieves*
> *So, over this battered, obstinate spit*
> *Of gravel?*

If the photographs of Plath's Winthrop leave me with some picture-puzzles about the way they fit or don't fit with the poems, they also leave me considering what is beguiling and strange about them.[58] The predominance of women, especially of small groups of women at Point

Shirley in front of the seawall, their ease and laughter, the strands of hair blowing around, evokes many pleasant associations of a separate, convivial female world. Was the seawall against which the women were photographed the acoustic surround, the first place, against which both voice and gesture became responsively and reciprocally coded? Or is the greatest danger of these photographic images that they only pull us ever closer to the impossible myth of the "intact child-hood"?

What I have come to recognize and appreciate about the scenic consciousness in "Point Shirley" are the ways in which its visual epistemologies presents a version—perhaps an American version—of a "winter garden,"[59] the image that so fascinated Walter Benjamin in gazing at Kafka's photo (where the winter garden is a mimesis in studio), and later also fascinated Roland Barthes, in *Camera Lucida* (a more rustic version, where the winter garden is set in the French countryside). Plath's is a remarkable writing of a winter garden, especially when we consider the speaker's position, reaching back into a child's world, not from the perspective of looking in on the warmth of the glassed-in conservatory, as in the photograph that is Benjamin's subject, with its exotic furnishings, its animals and plants, and its seasonal reversals, but, from a position *outside* the house, in the devastated "sand yard." In that place, radically overexposed to nature, to the "mulish elements" of ice cakes and quahog chips in winter, life forms and garbage of the sea are fused together in torn and bruised yet fascinating forms, including the phallic "thresh-tailed / lanced / shark littering the gernanium bed" and the "salty mash."[60] Functioning in ways similar to a child's imaginary museum, the scene Plath offers does not position us or her speaker to have the luxury of looking and lingering nostalgically, for one of its subjects is the question of how to carry on, how to go on making things in a world where the materials of making are a grim catalog of the rudimentary, "cold gizzards" and the "millstones, root and pith"[61] (from an earlier draft). The "bier" of winter owes much to Lowellian "Massachusetts' low-tide dolor,"[62] as has often been noted, and yet the poem seems to me to owe as much to the epistemology of the photograph and the ways of seeing it proposes. An elegy to her grandmother, "Point Shirley" pictures the return of the dead; the poem is crowded with detail related to the snapping and stopping of time of which all photographs make us mortally aware. In its surplus of detail, the poem offers a kind of bizarrely disordered or dizzying form of light writing—there is almost too much to look at, including the many "whitening" surfaces of things caught in the icy, oceanic wash.[63]

It is impossible to know how much the particular images of the poem, the vernacular architecture of the multi-story New England salt-box with planked-up windows perched off the end of a peninsula between two bodies of water (with stones stuck in its basement foundations), draws from the particular place and the day on which it was composed, or from photographs. From Plath's scavenging of scrapbooks and photos found in letters, we know that, like many migrant artists of the twentieth century, she carried tiny image-memorials with her, photographs and cards. We also know that on January 20, 1959, she revived her memories of Winthrop, as she had on frequent trips back during the Boston year. In one of the many "appendix" notebooks that make up her journal, we see that one draft of this poem appears, as a "listing out" of images, on pages that also feature her drawings. She writes that "Point Shirley, Revisited" was begun on a day trip to Winthrop and that, at a time when her writing was stuck and she hoped to break through to a graphic description of the world, she found it "oddly powerful" to make a poem that was "not so one dimensional."[64] And we know, too, because we can see it in pictures, that the speaker in "Point Shirley" has feet planted in the very places from which Plath herself was photographed, so that her aesthetic consolations are made from *looking back* to the place where the camera's eye had been.

In looking back, several planes of vision are brought into realignment with the speaker's intentions, both to mourn, and yet to recognize what is unmourned, or impossible to mourn—the "it" that survives so persistently. In the poem's spatial, temporal and geographical arrangements, a broad canvas of history and memory are drawn. The poem moves from past to present of the Winthrop peninsula itself, inscribing a summative arc from "Water-Tower Hill to the brick prison" (the prison a reference to a place that had once been an almshouse and refuge for immigrants). In another sweep of vision looking back again, later in the poem, the line of vision splits between Boston's "bloody" suns to the west and the Atlantic to the east, articulating the uneasy identity of the speaker who finds herself somewhere in between.

But since for me it is tempting to read these poems and landscapes in the photographs nostalgically, it took reading through the *punctum* of the photographs, the spec of detail that, as Barthes suggests, wounds and pricks us with sharp awareness, to sense the way that catastrophes of history emerge in "Point Shirley" on a larger scale. Almost by definition the incursions of the sea into the yard, and the household, serve as a punctum from within the poem, since it signals an interruption of visibility, a breach in the clear view of an outside. And the meanings of the poem appear far from merely private, since it is the manipulation of chronology that repositions Plath's grandmother's death so that it coincides with events surrounding the hurricane of 1938, and Hitler's invasion of Austria, when the sounds of the war flew over Winthrop, and trouble spread over the household ("The shingle booms, bickering").[65] Just as the poem suggests the idea that the past contains a riddle (what is "it" that survives *and* grieves, yet remains nameless), the double chronology locates that sheathe of unspokenness in a past that cannot be fully recovered at the surface of the image. Yet unlike Barthes, who in returning to the winter garden in his mother's photograph is reborn through her, Plath does not finally replace history with genealogy and parental intimacy, thereby revising her place in a family story as something that can be restored. Plath's poem would seem to work against such revision, with its insistence that the speaker "comes by / Bones, bones only" and therefore launches herself ("I contrive"),[66] unmentored and unsheltered.

Many critics have not shared my interest in "Point Shirley."[67] But it was only after reflecting on Jacqueline Rose's introduction to a New York Public Library reading in 1997, and following Rose's comments on the gathering storm clouds of war and the amnesias of history in a later poem "Little Fugue," that I began to see how, in "Point Shirley," Plath's speaker begins to inhabit two places at once, fusing history and memory. Refusing the easy gesture of homage, Rose suggested that the audience, in listening to each poet read Plath (Eavan Boland, Jane Miller, and Jorie Graham), consider what is not pictured in the poems—and the histories, the memories, the silences these create. Inviting the audience to "throw back" questions "across the threshold," Rose posed this question about Plath's radical negativities:

What should the woman poet do in the face of a history so monstrous for [those] who have engineered it, that all they can pass on to the daughter making her way into the house of poetry is inaudible—a breach, as it were, in a potential wall of sound? What are the consequences of that silence? For those who lived the history that lies behind it?[68]

This is surely not a question that Plath's poem "Point Shirley" answers, although it is one that it begins to pose, through its work on seeing and silence, and its juxtapositions of maternal and paternal inheritances, against a backdrop in which New England and Europe, great upheavals, love, losses, and amnesias figure. Rose's question reformulates the incursion into the garden as the means by which Plath passes into the house of poetry, amnesias on the horizon here bordering on a deeper past, and the silence of inheritance.[69] By the time Plath makes "The Colossus," she is working with three-dimensional, diorama-like structures that, for all the difficulty of getting their parts "put together," cannot be reduced to a single vanishing point. They allow her to speak through a more open structure, yet to rework another after-image of catastrophe, "clear [ing] / The bald white tumuli of your eyes."[70]

No doubt the America Plath returned to between 1957 and 1959 was not exactly the place she remembered. Making poems and finding a place was difficult—it required looking, framing, perspectivizing. The images and rhythms of "Point Shirley"—and its perpetually unanswered question, "what . . . / Survives, grieves / So?"—belong as much to the codes of the photograph, as a souvenir that cannot fully console, as to the speaker's position in the poem and the terms on which its prolonged questioning becomes unanswerable. Reading "Point Shirley" on the page, there is a space (no thing) around "nothing of home" ("nothing of home / To that spumiest dove"), an insistence, perhaps, that memory is of consciousness and not of souvenirs, or outcroppings swept by disaster. What I find remarkable is that the poem achieves its public "dimension" through a remapping of an ordinary, privately cherished place to which Plath repeatedly submits her rawest talent. The poem begins to fill out Plath's self-created myth of the poet's exceptional powers by looking back in the end from a point out at sea, proceeding on faith that what will return from the breach, what returns from silence and catastrophe, is once again sound, "spewed relics" that "clicker" in the wind, and image, frozen "laundry snapped."[71]

NOTES

I especially thank Marsha Bryant for encouraging inclusion of the subject of Plath photographs in this book and Karen V. Kukil for conversations on the Grolier Club exhibit in 2005, as well as the Grolier Club Program Committee.

1. Mieke Bal, "Light Writing: Portraiture in a Post-Traumatic Age," *Mosaic* 37 (2004): 3.

2. Robin Peel's "Body, Word, and Photograph," *Journal of AmStudies* 40 (2006), 71–95, treats Plath's interests in photographic narrative through visual collage; I extend George Bornstein's *Material Modernism: The Politics of the Page* (New York: Cambridge University Press), 2001.

3. On Plath's "colossal celebrity" and photographs, see Marsha Bryant, "IMAX Authorship: Teaching Plath and her Unabridged Journals," *Pedagogy* 4 (2004): 241–61; Susan R. Van Dyne on the cinematic body of the 1950s, *Revising a Life: Sylvia Plath's Ariel Poems* (Chapel Hill: University of North Carolina Press, 1993), 71–73; and Christine Britzolakis on "The Spectacle of Femininity" in *Sylvia Plath and the Theatre of Mourning* (Oxford: Clarendon Press, 1999), 136–56; on mirror images, transnational identities, and Plath's camera style, see Paul Giles, "'Double Exposure: Sylvia Plath and the Aesthetics of Transnationalism," *Symbiosis* 5 (2001): 103–20.

4. The nomenclature "public private meanings" derives from Marita Sturken, "The Image as Memorial: Personal Photographs in Cultural Memory," in *The Familial Gaze,* ed. Marianne Hirsch (Hanover: University Press of New England, 1999), 193; see also Maggie Humm, *Modernist Women and Visual Cultures* (Rutgers, 2002), 95.

5. Here, and in the importance of photojournalistic identity constructions, I echo Langdon Hammer's "Plath's Lives," *Representations* 75 (2001): 61–88.

6. *UJ*, 155; *BJ*, 83.

7. *CP*, 24.

8. Scholarship on literature, photography, and auto/biography has mushroomed: Roland Barthes, *Camera Lucida: Reflections on the Photograph,* trans. Richard Howard (New York: Hill and Wang, 1981); Walter Benjamin, "Little History of Photography," in *Selected Writing,* vol. 2, *1927–1934,* ed. Michael W. Jennings, Howard Eiland, and Gary Smith (Cambridge: Harvard University Press, 1999), 507–30; Linda Haverty Rugg, *Picturing Ourselves: Photography and Autobiography* (Chicago: University of Chicago Press, 1997); Timothy Dow Adams, *Light Writing and Life Writing: Photography in Autobiography* (Chapel Hill: University of North Carolina Press, 2003); Jay Prosser, *Light in the Dark Room: Photography and Loss* (Minneapolis: University of Minnesota Press, 2005); and Marsha Bryant, ed., *Photo-Textualities: Reading Photographs and Literature* (Newark: University of Delaware Press, 1996). Marianne Hirsch, ed., *The Familial Gaze,* and Hirsch, *Family Frames: Photography, Narrative and Postmemory* (Cambridge: Harvard University Press, 1997), as well as Judith Williamson, "Family, Education, Photography," in *Culture/Power/History: A Reader in Contemporary Social Theory,* ed. Nicholas B. Dirks, Geoff Ely, and Sherry B. Ortner (Princeton: Princeton University Press), 236–44, have been critical to theorizing family archives. Even so

apparently transparent an example of photograph realism as the family album section of *Letters Home* could be said to function paradigmatically to raise complicating questions about the narrative and photographic display. For while the retrospective narrative of *Letters Home* provides an alternative to the dominant narrative of Plath as angst-ridden poet, the inclusion of pages from a scrapbook-journal Plath herself assembled as the inside binding of the first edition of the book introduces an alternative to the retrospective narrative, in which Plath incorporates photos of family, friends, and region to launch a prospective self into the world beyond home.

9. Tracy Brain, *The Other Sylvia Plath* (Edinburgh: Pearson, 2000), 18–29, comments on repetitions of cover photos.

10. Carolyn Steedman, *Dust: The Archive and Cultural History* (New Brunswick, N.J.: Rutgers University Press, 2002), 81.

11. Trans. Lillane Weissberg, "Circulating Images: Notes on the Photographic Exchange," in *Writing the Image after Roland Barthes,* ed. Jean-Michel Rabate (Philadelphia: University of Pennsylvania Press, 1997), 110. Throughout this paragraph, I also rely on Weissberg's translation of Benjamin's writing on the Kafka photo, and its "moving testimony" in "Kleine Geschichte der Photographie," in *Gesammelte Schriften,* vol. 2, bk. 1, ed. Rolf Tiedemann and Hermann Schweppenhauser (Frankfurt am Main: Suhrkamp, 1977), 377.

12. *UJ*, 208; see also Lameyer MSS (Lilly).

13. I am grateful to Jon Lewis for suggesting Ron Rosenbaum, "The Great Ivy League Nude Posture Photo Scandal," *New York Times,* January 25, 1995.

14. Peter Davison, *The Fading Smile: Poets in Boston from Robert Frost and Robert Lowell to Sylvia Plath* (New York: Knopf, 1994), 51–62.

15. "'No Other Appetite,' Sylvia Plath, Ted Hughes, and the Blood Jet of Poetry," an exhibition at the Grolier Club, New York, September 14 to November 19, 2005.

16. "Daddy," *CP*, 264.

17. Ibid.

18. Terry Eagleton in "New Poetry," *Stand* (1971–72): 76, makes the earliest statement on Plath's use of the photographic image in "Couriers"; see also Paul Giles, *Virtual Americas: Transnational Fictions and the Transatlantic* (Durham: Duke University Press, 2002) for an approach to Plath's "camera style" through transatlantic exile and intertextuality, esp. 217–24.

19. See also W. J. T. Mitchell, *Iconology: Image, Text, Ideology* (Chicago: University of Chicago Press, 1986), for a reading of "iconophobia" that may be relevant here (3). Hughes's aversions to being photographed undoubtedly did not extend to poetic collaborations with landscape photographers Fay Godwin in his Pennines sequence, *Remains of Elmet* (London: Faber and Faber, 1979), and P. Keen in the *River* sequence (republished in *Three Books,* Faber and Faber, 1993). For an early exploration of Hughes's use of photographic vision, see also Graham Bradhsaw, "'Flash Vision" in "Ted Hughes and the New Aesthetic," *Cambridge Quarterly* X (1981), 172–78.

20. Detail from Item 25 in *"No Other Appetite": Sylvia Plath, Ted Hughes, and the Blood Jet of Poetry,* ed. Stephen C. Enniss and Karen V. Kukil (New York: The Grolier Club, 2005), 7 (Emory).

21. Hughes, *Winter Pollen* (London: Faber and Faber, 1997), 226.

22. Rugg, *Picturing Ourselves*, 82. For some writers, Rugg argues, sensitivity to the intrusions of reading and viewing photography's power compels "negotiation" between the photograph as realistic representation and as an occulted medium"(a medium in which the "snapping" of a picture is tantamount to having one's identity stolen).

23. "The Owl," *CPTH*, 1063.

24. "The Chipmunk," *CPTH*, 1083.

25. Enniss and Kukil, Item 45, 17 (Smith); Item 83 (Smith and Emory), 33. Karen V. Kukil notes that the bear's "hat" in a storydraft is the same hat featured in the photo taken by Hughes. Conversation with Karen Kukil, November 2006.

26. Ibid., Item 109, 28 (Emory).

27. "Perfect Light," *CPTH*, 1136; "Totem," *CP*, 265.

28. Barthes, *Camera Lucida*, 76.

29. Jo Gill, "'Your story. My story': Confessional Writing and the Case of *Birthday Letters*," *Modern Confessional Writing: New Critical Essays* (London: Routledge, 2006), 72–73. Gill argues that there is a kind of visual excess through which a "lost real" of Plath is represented, but that the self-conscious strategies of Hughes in "Fulbright Scholar" negotiate the modes of confessional representation with more poststructuralist and postmodern orientations to textual truths.

30. *CPTH*, 1136.

31. Item 95, Enniss and Kukil, 40 (Emory).

32. Ibid., 39.

33. Such nostalgia is perhaps echoed in Plath's essay, "Ocean 1212-W."

34. Sturken, "Image as Memorial," 193.

35. Thomas Travisano, *Midcentury Quartet: Bishop, Lowell, Jarrell, Berryman and the Making of a Postmodern Aesthetic* (Charlottesville: University Press of Virginia, 1999), 67; Giles, *Virtual Americas*, esp. 196–97.

36. Kenneth Tynan, "Portrait of the Artist as a Young Camera," *New Yorker*, December 20, 1958, 69–72.

37. Ibid., 69.

38. The debate about just how Plath's transnational identities develop has jumping-off points in Brain, *The Other Sylvia Plath*, 45–59; Paul Giles on "transatlantic transnationalism," 182–224; and Tim Kendall's study of Plath's landscapes, which begins with her Emersonianism, *Sylvia Plath: A Critical Study* (London: Faber and Faber, 2001), 1–24. Kendall outlines a philosophical position on Plath's landscape writing but does not extend it to regional memory or visual culture. See also Sandra Gilbert's "On the Beach with Sylvia Plath," in this volume.

39. W. S. Merwin, "Flight Home," *Paris Review* 17 (1958): 127.

40. From an interview with W. S. Merwin, November 13, 1991, qtd. in Davison, *The Fading Smile*, 95.

41. Ibid., 135.

42. W. S. Merwin, "The Native," *The Drunk in the Furnace* (New York: Macmillan, 1960), 45.

43. Steven Gould Axelrod, *Sylvia Plath: The Wound and the Cure of Words* (Baltimore: Johns Hopkins University Press, 1990), 6.

44. *CP*, 289; Plath's vision of "The Hermit at Outermost House" might have been formed not only through her walks along the beach, but through having seen the numerous photos and drawings of this site near Eastham where she and Ted Hughes had a summer vacation cottage rented for them by Aurelia Plath. Nan Turner Waldron's publication of popular drawings and photographs of the Boston house documents this popular tourist attraction, *Journey to Outermost House* (Bethlehem, Conn.: Butterfly & Wheel, 1996), esp. 23, 30.

45. *CP*, 118.

46. *UJ*, 306.

47. Ted Hughes, "The Art of Poetry LXXI," *Paris Review* 134 (1995): 77; for Hughes's earlier discussion of Plath's relationship to objects, see *JP*, 7; and the BL poem, *THCP*, 1088.

48. *CPTH*, 1088.

49. See Kathleen Connors, "Visual Art in the Life of Sylvia Plath: Mining Riches in the Lilly and Smith Archives," in this volume.

50. Adrienne Rich, "Landscape of a Star" (1953), reprinted in *Christmas at the New Yorker: Stories, Poems, Humor, and Art* (New York: New Yorker Magazine, 2003), 275.

51. Monsignor Francis X. Weiser, *Boston Globe*, December 21, 1958. Weiser's columns drew from his book *Handbook of Christian Feasts and Customs* (New York: Harcourt Brace and World, 1958). "Metropolitan Boston" for December 1, 1958, also shows a special exhibition of crèches at Copley Square.

52. Robin Peel, *Writing Back: Sylvia Plath and Cold War Politics* (Madison, N.J.: Fairleigh Dickinson University Press, 2001).

53. *LH*, 355.

54. *CP*, 86.

55. Calvin Bedient, "Sylvia Plath, Romantic," in *Sylvia Plath: New Views on the Poetry*, ed. Gary Lane (Baltimore: Johns Hopkins University Press, 1979), 10.

56. *LH*, 355. See also Britzolakis, on the cultural crisis of femininity that Plath's poems locate around these iconographies, 135–56.

57. *Letters Home*, unedited correspondence, Plath Mss. IV (Lilly).

58. Hirsch, *The Familial Gaze*, xxiv, reminds us that reading photographs displayed in a family album is incredibly seductive business: "We must recognize both the seductions and deceptions fostered by familial looking." If the warnings about the problem of reading family photographs are true, it is possible that one never construes anything new from them, pulled so far back into familial looking that the conventional codes and ideologies of the photograph become invisible.

59. Barthes, *Camera Lucida*, 90.

60. *CP*, 110

61. Ibid; Plath's draft notes appear in *UJ*, 615.

62. Lowell, foreword to *Ariel* (Faber and Faber, 1965), ix.

63. *CP*, 110.

64. *UJ*, 463.

65. *CP*, 110.

66. *CP*, 111.

67. See Britzolakis, "The Spectacle of Femininity," 194; Axelrod, *Sylvia Plath*, 65.

68. Jacqueline Rose, "A Tribute: Sylvia Plath," *Poetry Society of America Journal*, www.poetrysociety.org (accessed November 2005).

69. *CP*, 110.

70. *CP*, 129.

71. *CP*, 110–11.

MARSHA BRYANT

Ariel's Kitchen

PLATH, *LADIES' HOME JOURNAL*,
AND THE DOMESTIC SURREAL

An unacknowledged page circulates outside of Sylvia Plath's unraveling archive, her published volumes, and critical discussions of her work. But during her lifetime, it gave her poetry one of its widest circulations. Plath noted in her journals that she received $140 for what she called her "first acceptance from *The Ladies' Home Journal* of a poem,"[1] so she apparently intended to place more poetry with the magazine. Titled "Second Winter," this sonnet was originally one of her college prize poems.[2] Plath's appearance in postwar America's bible of domesticity put her in league not only with women poets she weighed as rivals (Edna St. Vincent Millay, Marianne Moore, Phyllis McGinley, and Adrienne Rich),[3] but also with John Ciardi, Richard Eberhart, Donald Hall, Robert Hayden, Randall Jarrell, Galway Kinnell, Maxine Kumin, Theodore Roethke, May Sarton, and William Stafford; all were listed in the magazine's contents pages between 1950 and 1959. Because Plath is hardly the sole canonized poet who appeared in *Ladies' Home Journal* in the 1950s, we cannot discount the suppressed page as an anomaly in the magazine, either. So why has this cultural convergence gone unremarked for so long?

Several reasons spring readily to mind. First, Hughes listed the poem as "Uncollected Juvenilia" in *Collected Poems* but did not include it among his selection of fifty poems written prior to 1956. Second, Plath wrote that her *Ladies' Home Journal* poem "doesn't really count at all for my book,"[4] which removes "Second Winter" from the category of her own "preferred products."[5] Third, Plath's critics tend to discuss

Ladies' Home Journal only in terms of her fiction—including those who rightly interrogate boundaries between academic and popular culture, such as Jacqueline Rose. Fourth, Plath's critique of postwar culture in *The Bell Jar* makes several indictments of domesticity, such as Esther Greenwood's ptomaine poisoning from food prepared in the *Ladies' Day* Food Testing Kitchens (Plath's portmanteau title joins the women's magazines *Ladies' Home Journal* and *Woman's Day*). Fifth, the afterimages of Betty Friedan's *The Feminine Mystique* surely motivate the construction of what Zoë Heller has termed "a fake, *Ladies' Home Journal* Sylvia,"[6] even though critics such as Nancy A. Walker have called into question Friedan's most damning claims about postwar women's magazines. Finally, *Ariel* became Plath's signature work; as Frieda Hughes notes in her introduction to the restored edition, this new voice did not appear in Plath's poetry until 1961.[7]

And yet discounting *Ladies' Home Journal* as an alternative archive for Plath has consequences larger than removing one particular poem—and page—from critical consideration. For as Jacques Derrida has claimed, "archivable meaning is also and in advance codetermined by the structure of the archives";[8] in other words, Plath's official archive both stores her textual remains and restricts our interpretations. Moreover, Derrida argues that an archive attempts "the unity of ideal figuration" by disallowing "any absolute dissociation, any heterogeneity or *secret* which could separate *(secernere),* or partition, in an absolute manner."[9] This phenomenon holds true even when scholars retrieve previously unexamined material from the Plath archive, such as Tracy Brain's suggestive reading of kitchen collages that incorporated magazine advertisements. While recognizing these visual texts would seem to open up new directions for Plath studies, Brain's analysis follows a standard line of reasoning in assuming that Plath would only subvert Madison Avenue's dream kitchen.[10] By implication, the stuff that slick ladies' magazines are made of does not really belong in Plath's aesthetic. But as we shall see, the alternative archive of *Ladies' Home Journal* has the potential to challenge widespread assumptions about Plath, domesticity, and poetry. In fact, the unacknowledged page that houses "Second Winter" enables a recovery of cultural configurations that underwrite what I define as the surreal domesticity of Ariel's kitchen. This page can prompt us to consider not only alternative materials but also new ways of reading.

Derrida reminds us that the word *archive,* a reference historically

traceable to the public custom house, has a domestic etymology, deriving from the Greek word for "a house, a domicile."[11] If *domesticity* is
the linguistic root of the archive and the defining vision of *Ladies' Home
Journal,* it has a more vexed relation to Plath. Rather than rooting or
defining her, domesticity strikes most interpreters of Plath as a catalyst
for conflict. We see this in Christine Jeff's film *Sylvia,* when the frustrated heroine confesses to Ted, "I sit down to write, I get a bake
sale."[12] In fact, Plath's critics tend to see the everyday world of cooking
and cleaning as diametrically opposed to her writing—especially her
poetry. For her detractors, such as film reviewer Anthony Lane, Plath's
baking is a welcome exception to her presumed self-absorption; his
review of *Sylvia* relishes the heroine's "scrumptious" cakes and wishes
she had aspired toward culinary rather than literary greatness.[13] Plath's
early defender, A. Alvarez, did not initially recognize the poet he had
published because she looked "like a young woman in a cookery advertisement"; he felt that housewifery "effaced" her true self.[14] If Alvarez
saw domesticity as a false front for a genuine poet, more recently
reviewer Cristina Nehring finds it a dubious means of rehabilitating
Plath's pathological image.[15] Indeed, when Kate Moses appeared on the
recent *Biography* program about Plath, she ironically reflected how the
poet is often hailed as "the original domestic goddess" who "out-
Martha'd Martha Stewart."[16] Alluding to America's current (and compulsive) doyenne of domesticity erases neither Plath's extreme reputation nor domesticity's pejorative sense. We are still left with the
polarity that Heller articulates in her review of *Unabridged Journals:*
namely, that "banal rituals of domestic life" allowed Plath "brief connections with a material reality outside her fevered head."[17] Seen
strictly through biographical lenses, domesticity becomes an unam-
biguous, therapeutic, and normalizing space outside of Plath's troubled
psyche. Diane Middlebrook offers a notable exception to this trend,
arguing that Plath "viewed cooking as a practice that advanced her aim
of developing a writing style grounded in womanly experience."[18] Here
Plath's domesticity is neither escapist nor compulsive, but a set of skills
that complements the art of writing.

It is the *discursive* level of domesticity that most interests me here,
rather than Plath's cooking. For postwar domesticity includes not only
housewifery and food preparation but also their intersections with
artistic discourses and the supernatural, the ways that food and appliances were advertised, technologies of the all-electric dream kitchen,

and practices of female consumership. In recovering the heterogeneous meanings of domesticity in *Ladies' Home Journal,* I view this discourse as intersecting rather than conflicting with Plath's poetry. Rather than follow a traditional interpretive model of direct influence, I will argue for the kind of cross-media relationships revealed through cultural studies. As Patrick Brantlinger explains, this approach "locates the sources of meaning not in individual reason or subjectivity, but in social relations, communication, cultural politics."[19] Plath explained to her mother that *Ladies' Home Journal* provided her with "an Americanness" she felt compelled "to dip into,"[20] and she subscribed to the magazine during her final years in England. As Walker notes, such magazines "reflected an ongoing debate about how domesticity could and should be defined,"[21] and so the tensions that most concern me here lie within this discourse rather than within Plath's life or psyche. My alternative archive draws us to Ariel's kitchen, not Plath's.

Poems, Percolators, and Potatoes

We can begin to access this repository through the page of *Ladies' Home Journal* that houses "Second Winter."[22]

By reading the poem alongside the other materials on the page, we can complicate three recurring claims about Plath: that her poetry conflicts with postwar domesticity, that her writing subverts women's magazines, and that the *Ariel* poems mark a complete break from her earlier poetry. In the layout of the "Second Winter" page of *Ladies' Home Journal,* Plath's poem is off center, surrounded by the continuation of a story ("Miracle in Radlands") and dwarfed by a half-page advertisement for Coffeematic. The text of "Second Winter" occupies approximately the same space as the percolator, and the layout truncates Plath's lines so that their sonnet form is not apparent. One might conclude prematurely that Plath's poem does not belong in this popular archive. And yet the story, advertisement, and poem all contribute to a complex construction of domesticity that mixes the natural with the mechanical, the mundane with the mythic. All three texts situate romance within seasonal cycles and modern technology, and all three rely on some mythical element to effect a change in the relationship. In the story, an unhappy rural housewife has lost faith in her husband and in her mail order arriving before Christmas. Her desperate letter to the

MIRACLE IN RADLANDS

CONTINUED FROM PAGE 46

and full-breasted as on their wedding day. Now she avoided the old-fashioned swinging mirror mounted on her dresser in their bedroom.

Life at Crystal Junction, the first seven years when Sam worked for the railroad, had not been a picnic. But there were neighbors and the children had playmates.

Sam Custer was born a rancher, the dust and sunlight of the plains in his blood stream. A bitter disagreement with his father had driven him to the railroad. Then, with a little cash saved, they had bought the run-down Slaker place and Sam's dream of a ranch of his own had come true.

Five years. Five years of dust and drought, of cattle disease, of the wells' drying up, of dawn-to-midnight toil, of a pitiful income and a mounting debt; a fourth child coming still-born into the harsh light of a July noon with only Mac Eagle's wife to help.

And now—two days to another Christmas, their sixth since coming to the valley.

"There will be a change for the better, a turning," Sam had said. "We'll have a turning, a sign. It can't always be this way, Lorena. Then we'll know things are to be better."

That was his faith, Sam's faith.

She asked herself now what the words meant and felt she did not know. Had she ever known?

She hated herself, not for her own loss of faith, but for what her despair had done to Sam. He was a strong man. But a man can't stand alone forever.

Sam no longer talked about a turning. Suddenly she realized it. Not since autumn had he talked that way. His dream was shattered, blasted, and because hers had died long before, she had not seen his go. That was the meaning of the look in her son's eyes. The lad had caught the subtle change in his father before even she had guessed it.

She opened her eyes to stare at the table. On these plain boards she had sat the previous evening, writing the letter to Bishop's:

The President of G. G. Bishop Co. Denver, Colorado

Dear Sir: December 5, this month, I sent a Christmas order to your company. I enclosed 29.33 in cash to pay for the order and mailing cost. We have not received the package and we have heard nothing from your company about our order. Since we have received no reply from you I am wondering if the order was lost. I don't know what to think. We have a very small income and this is all the money we have to spend for Christmas. In case you can do anything about this I am enclosing another list of our order.

Bishop's special talking dolls, with extra sets of dresses, Cat. No. SC 1260. . . . $8.47
Battery-powered model Ford car, Cat. No. AC 32. . . . . 3.28
Bishop's stainless-steel Timemaster wrist watch, style 56, Cat. No. EJ 1222 . . . 6.23
Alton's world atlas, in color, Cat. No. CA 14622. . . . . 2.98
Nylon lady's sweater, pink, Size 36, Cat. No. US 42 . . . . 7.12
Total . . 28.08
Postage . . 1.25
$29.33

I do hope that you will find the order with our money and that the presents will arrive by Christmas.
Yours truly,
MRS. SAMUEL CUSTER
Custer Ranch
R.D. 1, Radlands Valley
Crystal Junction, Colorado

The crawling, jerky freight that carried Lorena Custer's airmail, special-delivery letter from Crystal Junction to Fort Lorson ran only an hour ahead of the snow from out of the northwest. By morning all flights within a thousand miles had been canceled. So the letter in its lumpy mail sack transferred to a slow passenger and freight and limped and slid on to Denver, another hundred miles.

Now it was Tuesday night. The glistening city on the hills lay under a vast blanket of crystal feathers, and traffic was running slowly when it ran at all. The mail at the post offices was piled waist high and tired clerks worked the night through to sort it.

On Wednesday, after lunch, on the tenth floor of G. G. Bishop's, in the executive offices, George Geoffrey Bishop, Jr., sat at his pool-table-sized desk beneath the portrait of his father, barking into a telephone.

The son was young to run an enterprise as fabulous as this one. But old G. G. had quit early. He wanted to travel, hunt in Africa.

In the war—the one before Korea—young George had turned in something of a record, flying the Hump from India to China. The "flying Bishop," they called him. His fierce blond mustache and his dress-parade shoulders reminded junior executives that there was a kind of military command right here on Third Avenue. G. G., Jr., ran things as if he were still supplying the boys with ammo and gas in Hengyang and Kunming.

In three hours now it would be Christmas Eve. Like the thousand or so employees at Bishop's, George Geoffrey was trying to finish up by four P.M. As the phone on his desk rang, a secretary carried in an armful of packages and laid them on his desk. They were tied around with a cord.

He clamped a hand over the phone. "Those packages weren't to be wrapped," he barked.

She replied steadily, "They aren't, sir, that's just the underwrapping. I have the wrapping and trim here for you."

He took up the phone. It was his mother, reminding him of the dinner date he and Cynthia, his wife, had with them for Christmas Eve.

"Come early, George," she told him. "Your father is looking forward to tonight. I'll help you wrap the gifts." His mother's voice tinkled off merrily.

As he was on his way down the hall, the packages swinging on their stout cord and his coat flung jauntily over his shoulders, another secretary clattered over the marble, calling to him.

"Mr. Bishop, a letter just came I thought you should see. I —"

He took the letter and went rapidly on—past the full-sized stuffed Santas which marked every corner of the floor's giant toy shop, then down the elevator and through the

"Second Winter" page from *Ladies' Home Journal*®, December 1958. (Used with permission of the publisher.)

SECOND WINTER

By SYLVIA PLATH

department store president is delayed by heavy snow, arriving late on Christmas Eve. But the president's wife prompts him to make a daring airplane delivery of gifts and a stuffed Santa. Thus the miraculous transforms the heroine's consumer misfortunes into a parable of female consumer power, completing the seasonal sales cycle and renewing her marriage. In the advertisement, the Christmas buying season enables a blending of traditional romance and Coffeematic's mechanized brewing, as we see in the contrast between the woman's lacy attire and the percolator's metallic gleam. Moreover, the couple's beaming faces and intertwined coffee cups smooth over any potential conflicts that domestic technologies introduce to gender relations, such as the one Plath recorded in her journal the year before: "Ted using coffee percolator wrong, making poisonous brew, milk boiling over, mislaying percolator directions."[23] The proliferation of household gadgets called into question the traditional "maleness" of technical knowledge, but Coffeematic sutures this tension with the invisible processes of its automatic "Flavor-Selector." In her later poem "Words heard, by accident, over the phone," Plath uses the verb "percolate" to distill the tensions brought on by the speaker's inadvertent discovery of an affair, which she compares to "foreign coffee" that is "thick" and "sluggy." Here technology disrupts domesticity, breaking up the relationship and interfering with household tasks: "O god, how shall I ever clean the phone table?"[24] While Plath employs the percolator and telephone to trouble rather than nurture marriage relations, her construction of domesticity often intersects with advertising's use of household appliances to configure romance.

In "Second Winter" Plath depicts a late freeze as both failed romance and nuclear winter. The poem's imagery moves outside the home, but not outside the discourse of postwar domesticity. "Second Winter" links discursively with the other materials on the page because it brings postwar technologies to bear on both nature and normative heterosexuality. Initially Plath figures the "greening bud" in natural terms, then fuses these images with metaphors of munitions and pyrotechnics: "the seed / Prepares to strike through stubborn shell and launch / Bright fireworks of flowers."[25] There is an element of surreality in Plath's flowers that anticipates the strangely mouthed and flickering poppies in *Ariel*; in the archive of *Ladies' Home Journal*, Plath's flaming flowers intersect with the reproduction of Salvador Dalí's *The Lorelei* in the January 1959 issue. Mythic elements enter the poem when the thwarted flower is about to "flame in a phoenix ecstasy of wings"; Plath also uses the phoenix image in the culmination to her *Ariel* poem "Lady Lazarus." As the poem turns into its final quatrain, Plath overlays its natural imagery with cold war resonance:

> Suddenly the traitor climate turns
> . . . .
> While sun is frozen in a crown of thorns.[26]

Like the fused image of radiant poppies, this figuration of the "frozen" sun as crucified Christ activates levels of meaning that interconnect Plath, "high" culture, cold war politics, and *Ladies' Home Journal*. Edith Sitwell, who had appeared in the popular magazines *Life* and *Time,* played on sun/Son in her postwar poems about atomic warfare; Plath knew Sitwell's work and taught it at Smith. In the late 1950s, Plath considered Sitwell and Marianne Moore to be "the ageing giantesses & poetic godmothers" of women poets."[27] The nuclear dimension of Plath's second winter also intersects with the "climate" of the cold war. Despite Friedan's claims that magazines like *Ladies' Home Journal* kept readers "shut out of the larger world,"[28] the editorial for September 1956 addressed the threat of "atomic explosions" causing mutations and genetic damage.[29] In March 1950, Gladys Taber weighed in on the nuclear arms race in her "Diary of Domesticity" column: "I can't help feeling if we continue to experiment with dropping atom bombs, we may upset the earth's natural balance sufficiently to lose everything we need to maintain life."[30]

We cannot simply argue that "Second Winter" subverts *Ladies' Home Journal.* As we have seen, Plath's poem intersects with the odd mixture of mythical, technological, and romantic meanings that underpin the magazine's discourse of domesticity. Moreover, the magazine did not have the degree of transparency that Friedan ascribed to it in 1963. Rose has offered valuable insights to what she terms the magazine's "internal strain" and "ideological ambiguity,"[31] such as stories and articles that call into question idealized marriage and motherhood. One such article—"Cruelty in Maternity Wards"—Rose finds in the same issue that archived "Second Winter," yet she does not mention Plath's poem. Rose's approach proves especially useful in enabling topical links between the magazine and Plath's fiction; indeed, we could connect the piece on maternity wards with Plath's critiques of medicalized childbirth in *The Bell Jar* and her story "Sweetie Pie and the Gutter Men."[32]

My own approach hinges more on aesthetic convergences that arise from the poet's and magazine's related combinations of disparate materials, and these cannot always be explained in terms of ideological contradiction. Plath's fiction may tend to pit art and domesticity against one another, but like *Ladies' Home Journal* her poetry often integrates them. I find that the magazine's ambiguities are better understood in terms of Henri Lefebvre's theory of the everyday. Inspired by postwar French women's magazines,[33] Lefebvre saw in them a microcosm of an expansive everyday life that permeated postwar culture: "It is a world where triviality does not exclude the extraordinary, where the physiological does not exclude high culture, where the practical does not exclude the ideal, and where these aspects never become disconnected."[34] Mythic meanings as well as strangeness inflect the "extraordinary" dimension of both Lefebvre's everyday and what I am terming the domestic surreal. In her kitchen poems especially, Plath shared with *Ladies' Home Journal* an ability to sustain this degree of domestic heterogeneity. High culture contributes to this project, a phenomenon reflected in the December 1958 issue as a whole. The color and arrangement of the food pictured in the homemaking article "I Love to Eat . . . But I Hate to Cook" resemble the reproduction of André Bauchant's painting *(The Flower Boat)* on the next page; in fact, the author of the piece remarks, "I always design a meal as carefully as I do a canvas."[35] The magazine's suggestions for Christmas gifts include reproductions from museum gift shops. In short, Plath's sonnet is hardly the only high-culture signifier in *Ladies' Home Journal*.

Nor is it the only poem. Throughout the 1950s *Ladies' Home Journal* included a poetry department on its contents page. This practice distinguished the magazine not only from rivals such as *Good Housekeeping*, but also offered a lucrative venue for poets who were working their way into the literary canon. Granted, not all of the magazine's poetry had high literary quality; poetry editor Elizabeth McFarland also published sentimental verse. And yet the *Journal* often bested more literary magazines in its attention to women poets, which complicates assumptions that its format was not conducive to women artists, or that it assumed what Friedan termed a "brainless" readership.[36] May Sarton's poems appeared in the *Journal* five times in the 1950s. The issue with "Second Winter" also included Phyllis McGinley's "Office

Party."[37] Although Plath dismissed her as a writer of "light verse" who had "sold herself,"[38] McGinley had broken into the *New Yorker* early in her career and would win the Pulitzer prize in 1961.[39] (W. H. Auden, one of Plath's literary idols, wrote the foreword to McGinley's prize volume.) The August 1956 issue included Rich's "Lullaby" and Moore's "Blessed Is the Man." In its prominent layout of Moore, the magazine notes the text's occasion as that year's Phi Beta Kappa poem for Columbia University.[40] Moore's poem "Boston" appeared in *Ladies' Home Journal* one month after "Second Winter." Thus we cannot claim that the magazine required its women poets to adhere consistently to the standard domestic topics of romance and motherhood.

The divergent ways that poetry figured into the *Journal's* discourse of domesticity help us understand the aesthetics of Ariel's kitchen. Two articles on women poets in the kitchen linked literary and culinary arts in a time period when the reigning school of poetry was, as Middlebrook puts it, "ornately formal, allusive, academic: what Robert Lowell called 'cooked.'"[41] It was also a time of decorative cooking and food sculptures; as with the New Critical aesthetic, form was paramount to demonstrating a polished technique. In her January 1960 article "Cooking to Me Is Poetry," McGinley presents "the poetry of the domestic arts" as an acquired repertoire of skills demanding "the same talents as writing good verse—taste, imagination and the patience to take pains." What interests me about this comparison is the aesthetic behind it; McGinley posits both cooking and poetry as rules-bound enterprises grounded in an apprenticeship to form. For example, she notes that mashed potatoes demand "a dexterous hand" while fried eggs require "a light one" so that the latter yields "a perfection of formed white and gently quivering yolk."[42] Only when a cook has mastered these forms can she advance to hollandaise sauce. McGinley maintains a taste for "old-fashioned" cooking and offers recipes with detailed instructions. Friedan errs in claiming such articles on women artists "deny the vision, and the satisfying hard work involved in their stories, poems, and plays."[43] McGinley's article and the accompanying photograph of her cutting vegetables neither glibly diminish her literary accomplishments nor falsely elevate kitchen cookery. Rather, they promote a model of creativity that intersects with both professionalized homemaking and literary standards. For example, *Betty Crocker's Picture Cookbook* included this breezy verse about maintaining proper proportions: "Cooking success is up to you! / If you'll take pains to measure true, / Use *Standard* cups and spoons all the way. / And then level off—it'll always pay!"[44] In her *Ariel* poem "A Birthday Present," Plath invokes such culinary conformity with her signature use of triple repetition: "Measuring the flour, cutting off the surplus, / Adhering to rules, to rules, to rules."[45]

In "Poet's Kitchen," a February 1949 article on Millay and remodeling, *Ladies' Home Journal* invokes the sonnet as a principle of design rather than a rigid set of rules, integrating its aesthetics and mental discipline with a more heterogeneous sense of domestic order. The opening paragraph notes that this denizen of Mount Parnassus "washes dishes and scours the pots and pans" in her newly modernized kitchen that is "Polished as a sonnet . . . Light as a lyric."[46] Contrary to Friedan's characterization of this piece, we do not see Millay cooking or doing housework; in fact, she appears in none of the "before" and "after" kitchen photographs. According to Friedan, the article denies the poet's "private vision of mind or spirit" through a false domestication,[47] but its author, Gladys Taber, notes that Millay's husband does the cooking and that she is "one of the greatest poets of our day."[48] Indeed, *Ladies' Home Journal* published a condensation of Millay's autobiography and several of her sonnets in October 1952; the contents page deems her poetry "valued and enjoyed by all the English-speaking world."[49] For Taber, the poet's redesigned kitchen reflects her "disciplined mind" that could both compose sonnets and "attack the details of living as swiftly and accurately";[50] in other words, Millay's new domestic arrangements reinforce rather than detract from her artistry. Plath's journals often express the desire for a similar integration, as we see in this passage from 1956: "I would like a life of conflict, of balancing children, sonnets, love and dirty dishes; and banging banging an affirmation of life out on pianos and ski slopes and in bed in bed in bed."[51] Here the young poet imagines a harmony of energizing tensions similar to New Criticism's lyric ideal, and yet her rhetoric invokes both Friedan's sense of conflict and Taber's sense of balance.

In 1958 Plath was still sorting out the relationship between her poetry and domesticity. "Poems, Potatoes" argues that unlike words, potatoes and stones provide materials for the culinary artist and sculptor that *open* rather than foreclose creative possibility. By contrast, the speaker claims, a line of poetry proves hard and inflexible in her hand like a weapon, because it manifests itself at the expense of latent words and meanings that remain inchoate:

> The word, defining, muzzles; the drawn line
> Ousts mistier peers . . . murderous,
> In establishments which imagined lines
>
> Can only haunt.[52]

Plath's domestically freighted poem claims literary kinship with academic pieces like Wallace Stevens's "No Possum, No Sop, No Taters." She also mixes terza rima and a closing quatrain to venture beyond the limited flexibility she achieved with heavy slant rhyme during this period. Plath also grows more flexible in considering how to make potatoes the stuff of poetry; they will "hiss" in her *Ariel* poem, "Lesbos."[53]

In seeking to move beyond the poetry/domesticity opposition in my analyses, I find Taber's work for *Ladies' Home Journal* especially useful for rethinking their relationship. For Taber, "poetry is an integral part of living, never an ivory-tower kind of art," and so it infuses her vision of domesticity. Her "Poet's Kitchen" article quotes often from Millay and delights in the poet's ability to recite Catullus over the kitchen sink. Taber finds in Millay's "deep turquoise" floor a translation of "the color of the sea she loves and writes about."[54] Taber was well known to *Journal* readers for her column "Diary of Domesticity," which ended in 1958. These pieces would sometimes extol the importance of the fine arts—especially poetry—for bringing beauty to daily life. In the February 1950 issue, for example, Taber quoted not only from Millay but also from Shakespeare, Keats, de la Mare, and Yeats.[55] Less frequently, Taber would contribute short articles on design that, like the Millay piece, promoted an ideal kitchen that was both convenient and aesthetically pleasing. In short, Taber's poetics of domesticity blurred boundaries between high culture and housework to an even greater extent than McGinley's cooking advice; Millay at her sink remains the consummate sonneteer. Finally, Taber sees a "fairy tale" element in the sonnet-kitchen's new range and percolator; their "automatic performance" integrates popular and literary culture, and fuses the magical with the mechanical.[56] Such resistance to rigid hierarchies and categories opens up domesticity to the kinds of possibilities that culminated for Plath in her vibrantly surreal kitchen scenes. In *Ladies' Home Journal* surreality proves most apparent in its advertising.

Levitating Housewives and Mechanical Marriage

My key term, the *domestic surreal,* refers to a postwar American construction of domesticity that Plath tapped in her *Ariel* poems. Although parts of *Ariel* portray negative images of domesticity, such as "a stink of fat and baby crap,"[57] Plath does not simply transform the dream kitchen into a nightmare. *Ariel's* kitchen opens up domesticity in the ways I have been discussing, but adds an intensity charged by strange combinations of housewifery with the supernatural and mechanical. Marjorie Perloff has termed this aesthetic "Plath's peculiar ability to fuse the domestic and the hallucinatory,"[58] but I find it more everyday than peculiar. As I have argued elsewhere, the advertisements in *Ladies' Home Journal* prove especially relevant to Plath's late style because their undercurrent of surreality transforms domestic space into a hyperbolic site of wondrous appliances and mythic beings.[59] Through the domestic surreal, Plath fashions an aesthetic that links to the male modernism she admired while recalibrating to postwar paradigms its construction of domesticity and gender. Her strangely animated household appliances (such as the tentacled telephone in "Words, heard by accident") also anticipate the defamiliarized domesticity of Craig Raine and other "Martian" poets in Britain.[60]

Plath's ekphrasis poems from Giorgio de Chirico attest to her early interest in the surrealist movement, but there are crucial differences between this modernist aesthetic and the domestic surreal. While surrealist images of household objects privilege form over function, the domestic surreal merges these values into consumable forms such as food sculpture and appliance design. Surrealists viewed domesticity as insipid in and of itself, seeking to liberate household objects from functionality so that they "ascended to a new level," as Marina Vanci-Periham writes of Man Ray. In *The Gift,* for example, Ray transformed a common flatiron into a startling art object by attaching a row of carpet tacks to its bottom.[61] The surrealist aesthetic removes household objects from the feminized domicile and places them in the transcendent, male-curated gallery. Plath revises this tendency in the opening lines of *Ariel,* which figure the home as a "drafty museum."[62] Thus the domicile becomes an alternative site for aesthetic display. In the domestic surreal, household objects—and housewives—can become marvelous through the quotidian tasks they perform.

Instead of moving beyond the everyday like surrealism, the domestic surreal contains both transcendence and transformation within it. Lefebvre's postwar critique of surrealism found the movement false because its aesthetic "belittle[s] the real in favour of the magical and the marvellous"—qualities that he claims operate "only on the level of everyday life."[63] While Plath does not share Lefebvre's aim of transforming postwar society along Marxist lines, she does effect an everyday surreality that sometimes functions as a site for critique. Both writers, as well as *Ladies' Home Journal,* presented everyday life as "rich in surprises, inhabitable and densely inhabited";[64] in other words, the everyday could be strange in and of itself. Lefebvre's gender biases surely shape his sense that the everyday is "muddled" and "murky," and yet his characterization of it in terms of postwar women's magazines bears striking similarities to the heterogeneous domesticity that Plath brought into her *Ariel* poems: "Cookery becomes a fairyland and fantastic stories are like recipes in a magic cookery book, flanked by articles on fashion and stories about the romantic agonies of a famous star or an oriental princess."[65] This odd mixture of seemingly disconnected ingredients imbues domesticity with surreality and ambiguity, making it aesthetically interesting for Plath.

In *Ladies' Home Journal* we see domestic transcendence most clearly in the figure of the levitating housewife. Often her eyes are closed, and her expression conveys an unconscious bliss that renders ambiguous her degree of control over her domestic labors. In a 1957 ad for Jet Bon Ami spray cleaner, the housewife can "fly through housework" with outstretched arms like an airplane; her miraculous horizontal levitation allows her to float through the den, bathroom, and kitchen. A 1958 ad for Junket Quick Fudge Mix depicts a jet-propelled housewife hurling through the air with a tray of treats. A 1955 ad for River and Carolina Rice figures an aproned housewife as a domestic Hermes with winged pumps. We see a more delirious vision of domestic transcendence in a 1956 ad for Baker's Angel Flake coconut: "Everybody's Going Coconutty." A pair of cake wings transports this housewife through the clouds, startling a bird. Still, her ascent remains within the everyday world of kitchen magic.

Plath's ascending speakers tend to retain a degree of normativity similar to the levitating housewives in magazine advertisements. In *Ariel,* the delirious speaker of "Fever 103°" anticipates a flight past the world of bed sheets and chicken soup into the sky with cherubim; the imagery plays as much on the domestic surreal as the Assumption of

Detail from Jet Bon Ami ad in *Ladies' Home Journal*®, October 1957.
Courtesy of Faultless Starch/Bon Ami Co.

Mary. The speaker of Plath's title poem ascends into a sun she figures as a cauldron; this culminating image can signify a "cookpot of poetry," to borrow Middlebrook's evocative phrase.[66] Even the "red hair" of the mythical Lady Lazarus suggests, at one level, a domestic transformation powered by miracle products like Miss Clairol.[67]

Mechanical imagery also becomes surreal in Plath's vision of domesticity. We can better understand this everyday transformation by comparing three images of sewing machines: a surrealist assemblage, an advertisement in *Ladies' Home Journal,* and Plath's poem "An Appearance." In *The Enigma of Isidore Ducasse,*[68] Ray renders a sewing

Detail from ad in *Ladies' Home Journal*®, March 1955. Courtesy of the manufacturer. Carolina Rice and River Rice are registered trademarks of Riviana Foods Inc.

machine into a mysterious object by wrapping it in wool cloth and tying it with rope. Thus household objects can become beautiful only if they are dislocated and defamiliarized in a surrealist artist's hands. The advertisement for the Elna Automatic plays on surrealism with its Magritte-inspired caption—"This is not a machine." Under the Elna's mechanical arm, a Lilliputian wife hangs homemade draperies next to a dress she has sewed, and the caption continues further below: "it's the world's greatest home-maker!" This fusion of women with machines and dolls also intersects with surrealism, but the Elna's functionality embellishes rather than denies its extraordinary beauty. Even with its "Magic Brain" and "magic discs," the Elna does not transcend domesticity.[69] *Magic,* in fact, proves a key word in the lexicon of the domestic surreal, operating along the mechanical/mythic spectrum that animates the dream kitchen. In *Ladies' Home Journal*'s advertising, housewives could enlist supernatural assistance with the Magic Chef range, S.O.S. "Magic Scouring Pads," and the "blue-magic action" of Blue Dutch Cleanser. When Linda Wagner-Martin argues that "the magic" of *Ariel* arises when "domestic events are transformed by art,"[70] she ignores those magical properties of postwar domesticity that Plath incorporated into her poems.

The image of the sewing machine proves central to Plath's surreal love poem "An Appearance"; its title suggests the blending of supernatural and material elements that we find in Ariel's kitchen. Written in April 1962, this poem is, as Frieda Hughes notes, one of Plath's earliest "in the distinctive *Ariel* voice."[71] The poem's speaker is a husband who voices astonishment at a wife he describes as a refrigerator, a typewriter, and a watch. When this mystified man shifts to describing the nature of love, he figures it as the action of a sewing machine:

> Is this love then, this red material
> Issuing from the steel needle that flies so blindingly?
> It will make little dresses and coats,
>
> It will cover a dynasty.[72]

Plath's tropes of redness, blindness, and a pierced heart play on romantic imagery, recalling her macabre valentine in the earlier "Two Views of a Cadaver Room." But here she does not need to depart from domesticity to make love strange—a quality that also distinguishes this poem from the surrealist movement. The poem's key verb, *issuing*, links the cloth flowing under the needle with the couple's future progeny, which will be clad in the housewife's creations. Thus Plath mechanizes not only the woman but also romance and heterosexual reproduction; the male lover is woven into "this red material" and becomes part of the poem's mechanical processes.

Women were not the only mechanical spouses in the domestic surreal. An advertisement for Gibson refrigerators presented this major kitchen appliance as a model husband, a "Good Provider" whose thoughtfulness and adaptability will enrich the housewife's life. This particular ad from July 1950 appeared in a magazine that Plath also considered a market for her stories, *Good Housekeeping;* the copy pushes appliance purchasing into surreal territory: "It's like getting MARRIED—you should get well acquainted first!" Comparison shopping becomes analogous to weighing the differences among eligible men; after all, "you and it are going to live and work together for a good many years."[73] As the prime consumers for the home, housewives exercised considerable buying power. Between 1945 and 1950, Elaine Tyler May points out, "consumer spending increased 60 percent, but the amount spent on household furnishings and appliances rose 240 percent."[74] Juliann Sivulka notes that in the 1950s, "the adman's obsession with the female consumer intensified" as he courted the American housewife on behalf of manufacturers.[75] We see this romance in a pitch for Philco refrigerators that appeared in *Ladies' Home Journal* the same month as the Gibson ad: "Everything to Catch a Woman's Eye."[76] Thus the rhetoric of the efficient housewife-consumer had more agency than surrealism's mechanical woman. Plath experimented with the idea of animating appliances and switching roles in 1958. In notes for a story, "Changeabout in Mrs. Cherry's Kitchen," she imagines that "shiny modern gadgets" and appliances have become "overspecialized" and wish to perform other tasks. Drawing on the domestic surreal, Plath planned to have "fairies or equivalent" come at midnight to effect the "change-about" so that the refrigerator can store clothes, the dishwasher can cook, and the iron can make waffles. "Complex, perhaps, but possible?" Plath wondered.[77] Indeed, how far can one push the boundaries of personification, functionality, and gender roles in the postwar dream kitchen while maintaining its legibility? Plath would work out these issues in Ariel's kitchen.

Like "An Appearance" and the Gibson ad, Plath's poem "The Applicant" uses housewifery to normalize kitchen craziness. Rather than seeing Magritte as the inspiration for Plath's mechanical housewife as does Sherry Lutz Zivley,[78] I see more likely intersections with the rhetoric of advertisements for household appliances. Plath explained in her BBC broadcast of 1962 that "The Applicant" portrays a "marvelous product" pitched by "a sort of exacting super-salesman."[79] Indeed, her housewife-machine combines all the requisite nurturing and technological abilities into a "living doll" that "works," offering the convenience of one-stop shopping for a feminized male consumer of household goods.

While Plath effects a change-about in the housewife's form, she alters the eligible man's gender. The applicant-groom takes on female functionality through appliance shopping. Ironically, the salesman turned marriage broker faults the applicant for not being needy *enough*, as if pushing the relentlessness of Rosser Reeves's Hard Sell technique past the point of sale. Initially he refuses to deal:

> First, are you our sort of a person?
> Do you wear
> A glass eye, false teeth or a crutch,
> A brace or a hook,
> Rubber breasts or a rubber crotch,
>
> Stitches to show something's missing? No, No? Then
> How can we give you a thing?[80]

This applicant's need for wholeness seems excessive; indeed, Plath's images of surgery and gender-bending prosthetics present a freakish image of young men on the marriage market. Plath reinforces the applicant's incompleteness by ending each of these opening stanzas with a sentence that enjambs the next stanza. In fact, the only autonomous stanza is the final one, in which the salesman wraps up his pitch for the housewife-machine with the proposal to "marry it, marry it, marry it."[81] Here Plath's penchant for triple repetitions coincides with Reeves's masterful pitches for miracle products. Such an ad appeared in the December 1958 issue of *Ladies' Home Journal*, promising Anacin's "Fast Fast Fast" relief to housewives suffering from nervous tension. Plath's applicant apparently needs a similar miracle because the salesman commands him to "Stop crying." He has lost control of himself like a beset housewife, thus effecting a "change-about" in masculinity.

Toward a Topography of the Domestic Surreal

In the topography of the domestic surreal, the housewife inhabits a colorful, electrified, and animated household full of strange happenings—especially in the kitchen. Vibrant colors brighten plastic housewares, linoleum, appliances, upholstery, even toilet paper. Karal Ann Marling notes that in the fifties, "color was an extra, a mark of futuristic technology at work . . . in a thousand unimaginable rainbow-hinted hues."[82] Plath's "polished lozenges of orange linoleum" in "Lesbos" pale in comparison to the crazy colorations of duo-tone and plaid patterns advertised in women's magazines. In the gaudy ecstasy of America's dream kitchen, this excess of color could rival the garish palette of the era's Technicolor films, a comparison Plath makes in *The Bell Jar*. At the *Ladies' Day* kitchen, Esther Greenwood envisions the process of food photography as preparing "lush double-page spreads of Technicolor meals." At the theater she describes excess color as a visual onslaught: "Everybody in a Technicolor movie seems to feel obliged to wear a lurid costume in each new scene and to stand around like a clotheshorse with a lot of very green trees or very yellow wheat or very blue ocean rolling away for miles and miles in every direction."[83] More surreal than the painterly discourse of food preparation, this oversaturation of color parallels the jarring ways that domesticity can permeate Esther's world.

Electricity powers the "very large charge" of the domestic surreal and Ariel's kitchen. While Plath's critics tend to ground the poetry's high voltage in the poet herself, I see more parallels with the often strange ways that electricity figured into the discourse of postwar domesticity. The apex of modern American living, household electricity seemingly activated an invisible army of electric servants that did everything from percolating coffee to toasting bread. Thus household labor was neither fully human nor mechanical, but a mixture of both. In *Ladies' Home Journal*, the "Live Better Electrically" ad campaign promoted a supercharged domesticity that transformed kitchen work from "Roughing It!" to "Just Wonderful!"[84] In a television commercial, the campaign depicted a nuclear family dancing spasmodically through their appliance-laden home to an ecstatic song: "What a thrill to be so free, when you live better electrically." A commercial for PG&E showed the mythical Reddy Kilowatt—a personified lightning bolt—jumping from suburbia's electrical outlets.[85] The circuitry in Plath's poems often proves more volatile than Madison Avenue's ideal. For example, the speaker of "Lesbos" perceives a "fluorescent light wincing on and off like a terrible migraine" in the addressee's kitchen. In "An Appearance" the husband senses that his refrigerator-wife has "blue currents" and a smile that "annihilates" him. In "Elm" the speaker declares: "My red filaments burn and stand, a hand of wires."[86] Although Plath questioned the postwar dictum to "live better electrically," she draws from its techno-mythological discourse to increase the intensity of her poems.

Animation was also crucial to the topography of the domestic surreal, not only in the form of appliances and gadgets but also mythic beings. For example, *Ladies' Home Journal* advertising for Presto pressure cookers presented the secret conversation of range-top ware: "Said the Pot to the Kettle . . . 'What in the world is *that?*'" The December 1958 issue with Plath's poem includes an ad for green beans featuring an animated Mr. Blue Lake, "the Aristocrat of the green bean family."[87] This visual style, which often combines cartoonish and photographic images, intersects with an unstable boundary between the real and the fantastic that drives the domestic surreal. Roland Marchand's observations about earlier American advertising also prove relevant in situating such postwar kitchen ads: their "'re-personalization' of life" entailed "a tacit recognition of an unvanquished public propensity for animism—the belief that all objects are alive."[88] Such animations allow space for the supernatural in an increasingly technological society, and in the domestic surreal they often suture mechanical and mythic dimensions. In postwar advertising strange beings inhabited or visited the housewife's kitchen—including the Minute Minder Man in Lux appliance timing devices, Elsie the Borden Cow, and the Jolly Green Giant. In *Ariel* as in the ads, women experience the most delirious domesticity when they are the sole companions of these supernatural beings. In "A Birthday Present," for example, Plath's speaker perceives a haunting presence: "When I am quiet at my cooking I feel it looking."[89] Paradoxically, such strange companions manifest themselves only when the housewife performs her everyday labor.

Plath's poem "Cut" opens up a seemingly unstoppable blood jet of the domestic surreal. In an unpublished letter to her mother from 1960, she justified a gift subscription to *Ladies' Home Journal* as a vital source: she wrote of "needing" a "constant flow of Americana to enrich my blood!"[90] There is a tendency to read Plath's "blood jet" metaphor in strictly confessional terms.[91] But I find that the vibrant discourse of postwar domesticity proves as pertinent to Plath's stylistic excess as the idea of *l'écriture féminine* in red ink. For "Cut" presents a cascade of jarringly mixed images in a "red plush" of domestic delirium:

> What a thrill—
> My thumb . . .
> The top quite gone
>
> . . . .
> Little pilgrim,

The Indian's axed your scalp.
Your turkey wattle
Carpet rolls

Straight from the heart.
. . . .
Out of the gap
A million soldiers run,
Redcoats, every one.[92]

"Little pilgrim" echoes John Wayne, while the Indian and redcoats invoke the violence of American history. Yet even these male figures are grounded in domesticity. The opening line taps the rhetoric of ads promising the "thrill" of home appliances, while the "pink fizz" and "pill" suggest household medicines. The speaker cuts her thumb while peeling an onion and the blood becomes a carpet. Hysterical and historical, violent and witty, graphic and theatrical, the poem strikes me as an over-the-top exercise in metaphor making that resists the confessional bent of the earlier maternity poems "Metaphors" and "You're." Langdon Hammer asserts that the title "Cut" refers to "an imperative directed at the poet herself, giving her instructions for writing."[93] I see a doubleness in this kind of "cutting" because it refers not only to the removal of superfluous elements, but also to the opening that releases the domestic surreal into Plath's signature poems.

Ariel's kitchen can propel its speaker into a kind of ecstasy charged by the unstable boundaries of postwar domesticity. Ultimately it is this quality, rather than Plath's life or psyche, that most distinguishes her domestic poems from those of peer American women poets. Plath departs from the domesticity of Rich's "Snapshots of a Daughter-in-Law," although both poets bring an edginess to kitchen scenes. For Rich, literary and domestic experience prove as adamantly separated as the coffeepot that bangs into the kitchen sink. In her poem "chiding" angels urge the daughter figure to look beyond the kitchen window. Culminating in the image of Simone de Beauvoir's helicopter woman, this poem seeks a high-flying femininity that escapes domestic confinement.[94] In Plath's *Ariel* poems transcendence does not rise *above* domesticity, but *within* it—only then can their speakers experience domestic delirium. We can also distinguish the topography of Ariel's kitchen from that of Anne Sexton's domestic poems. In "Self in

1958" Sexton employs the surrealist motif of the mechanized doll-woman, but this figure proves the only strange element in "the all-electric kitchen."[95] Ultimately Sexton's poetic kitchen is more intimate than Plath's and more connected to the female body (kitchen walls become a vagina in "Housewife"). Ariel's kitchen distills a fuller range of the postwar domesticity that shaped women's magazines: the mundane and the surreal, the technological and the mythic, the personal and the cultural.

Considering *Ladies' Home Journal* as an alternative archive for Plath offers several advantages. It has open access. It puts Plath squarely into the cultural mainstream instead of the psychological extreme. It enables interpretations that move beyond the linearity of direct influence to consider the more radial configuration of cultural relationships. Moreover, this archive is immune from the kind of intersubjective haunting that often produces necrophilic narratives of Plath critics and readers. Instead of Plath's ghostly presence, we may encounter a "Ghostess" who vanishes into the kitchen after hosting a meal.[96] If *Ladies' Home Journal* shares with standard archives the psychic level of meaning that Derrida attributes to them, it does not house Plath's subjectivity but rather what Paula Bernat Bennett calls "the intersubjective framework of the public sphere."[97] And in the 1950s, domesticity was a part of this sphere—from Nixon and Khrushchev's Kitchen Debates to corporate America's Betty Crocker and television's Ozzie and Harriet. As a primary storehouse for America's dream kitchen, *Ladies' Home Journal* preserves Plath's aesthetic in ways that prompt cultural rather than biographical interpretations. Everyday understandings of Plath, *Ladies' Home Journal,* and domesticity show that her writing is not only a corpus to be archived, but also an archive of the domestic surreal.

NOTES

1. *UJ*, 365.
2. Paul Alexander, *Rough Magic: A Biography of Sylvia Plath* (New York: Penguin, 1991), 157.
3. *UJ*, 360.
4. Ibid., 365.
5. Langdon Hammer, "Plath's Lives: Poetry, Professionalism, and the Culture of the School," *Representations* 75 (Summer 2001): 71.
6. Zoë Heller, "Ariel's Appetite," review of *The Unabridged Journals of Sylvia Plath*, in *The New Republic*, December 18, 2000, 30.

7. *AR*, xii.

8. Jacques Derrida, *Archive Fever: A Freudian Impression*, trans. Eric Prenowitz (Chicago: University of Chicago Press, 1996), 18.

9. Ibid., 3.

10. Tracy Brain, *The Other Sylvia Plath* (London: Longman, 2001), 92.

11. Derrida, *Archive Fever*, 2.

12. *Sylvia*, dir. Christine Jeffs (Focus Features, 2003).

13. Anthony Lane, "Young Blood," review of *Sylvia*, dir. Christine Jeffs, *New Yorker*, October 20, 2003, 206–7.

14. A. Alvarez, *The Savage God: A Study of Suicide* (New York: Random House, 1972), 6.

15. Cristina Nehring, "Domesticated Goddess," *Atlantic Monthly*, April 2004, 126.

16. Ilana Trachtman, prod. and dir., *Sylvia Plath* (Working Dog Productions, A&E *Biography* Series, December 27, 2004).

17. Heller, "Ariel's Appetite," 30.

18. Diane Middlebrook, *Her Husband: Hughes and Plath—A Marriage* (New York: Viking, 2003), 90.

19. Patrick Brantlinger, *Crusoe's Footprints: Cultural Studies in Britain and America* (New York: Routledge, 1990), 16.

20. *LH*, 433.

21. Nancy A. Walker, *Shaping Our Mothers' World: American Women's Magazines* (Jackson: University Press of Mississippi, 2000), 16.

22. This poem is not to be confused with "Prologue to Spring," which Stephen Tabor also lists under "Second Winter" in his *Sylvia Plath: An Analytical Biography* (Westport, Conn.: Meckler, 1987).

23. *UJ*, 301.

24. *CP*, 202–3.

25. Sylvia Plath, "Second Winter," *Ladies' Home Journal (LHJ)*, December 1958, 143.

26. Ibid.

27. *UJ*, 360.

28. Betty Friedan, *The Feminine Mystique* (1963; New York: Dell, 1983), 248.

29. Dorothy Thompson, "Radioactivity and the Human Race," *LHJ*, September 1956, 11.

30. Gladys Taber, "Diary of Domesticity," *LHJ*, March 1950, 137.

31. Jacqueline Rose, *The Haunting of Sylvia Plath* (Cambridge: Harvard University Press, 1991), 175.

32. *JP*, 143.

33. Kristin Ross, *Fast Cars, Clean Bodies: Decolonization and the Reordering of French Culture* (Cambridge: MIT Press, 1995), 79. Ross notes that the cofounder of *Elle*, which was especially influential on Lefebvre, had worked for several U.S. magazines and thus brought an American look to this exemplar of French women's magazines.

34. Henri Lefebvre, *Critique of Everyday Life*, vol. 2, trans. John Moore (1961; London: Verso, 1991), 81.

35. *LHJ*, December 1958, 64.

36. Freidan, *Feminine Mystique*, 65.

37. Phyllis McGinley's poem "Calendar for Parents" appeared in the February 1952 issue of *LHJ*, "A Scientific Explanation of Monday" in March 1954, and "The Landscape of Love" in February 1959.

38. *UJ*, 360.

39. McGinley's Pulitzer volume was *Times Three: Selected Verse from Three Decades with Seventy New Poems* (New York: Viking, 1960).

40. *LHJ*, August 1956, 101.

41. Diane Wood Middlebrook, introduction to *Coming to Light: American Women Poets in the Twentieth Century*, ed. with Marilyn Yalom (Ann Arbor: University of Michigan Press, 1985), 7.

42. Phyllis McGinley, "Cooking to Me Is Poetry," *LHJ*, January 1960, 66–67.

43. Friedan, *Feminine Mystique*, 57.

44. *Betty Crocker's Picture Cookbook* (1950; facsimile edition Minneapolis: Macmillan and General Mills, 1998), 7.

45. *CP*, 206.

46. Gladys Taber, "Poet's Kitchen," *LHJ*, February 1949, 56.

47. Freidan, *Feminine Mystique*, 53.

48. Taber, "Poet's Kitchen," 56.

49. *LHJ*, October 1952, 3.

50. Taber, "Poet's Kitchen," 183.

51. *UJ*, 225.

52. *CP*, 106.

53. Ibid., 227.

54. Taber, "Poet's Kitchen," 185.

55. Gladys Taber, "Diary of Domesticity," *LHJ*, February 1950, 149.

56. Taber, "Poet's Kitchen," 57.

57. *CP*, 227.

58. Marjorie Perloff, "Icon of the Fifties," *Parnassus* 12–13 (1985): 283.

59. Marsha Bryant, "Plath, Domesticity, and the Art of Advertising," *College Literature* 29, no. 3 (2002): 17–34.

60. In "A Martian Sends a Postcard Home," for example, the telephone becomes an alien life form.

61. Marina Vanci-Perahim, ed., *Man Ray*, trans. Willard Wood (New York: Harry N. Abrams, 1998), 17, 6.

62. *A*, 1.

63. Henri Lefebvre, *Critique of Everyday Life*, vol. 1, trans. John Moore (1946; London: Verso, 1991), 110, 115.

64. Lefebvre, *Critique of Everyday Life*, 2:81.

65. Ibid., 84.

66. Diane Wood Middlebrook, "What Was Confessional Poetry?" in *Columbia History of American Poetry*, ed. Jay Parini and Brett C. Millier (New York: Columbia University Press, 1993), 645.

67. *CP*, 247.

68. Ducasse is better known as the symbolist poet Le Comte de Lautrémont.

69. *LHJ*, April 1955, 211.

70. Linda W. Wagner-Martin, *Sylvia Plath: A Biography* (New York: St. Martin's, 1987), 227.

71. *AR*, xii.

72. *CP*, 189.

73. *Good Housekeeping*, July 1950, 34. The Gibson ad in the February issue of *Ladies' Home Journal* lacked this personification.

74. Elaine Tyler May, *Homeward Bound: American Families in the Cold War Era* (New York: Basic Books, 1988), 165.

75. Juliann Sivulka, *Soap, Sex, and Cigarettes: A Cultural History of American Advertising* (Belmont: Wadsworth, 1998), 265.

76. *LHJ*, July 1950, 60.

77. *UJ*, 304.

78. Sherry Lutz Zivley, "Sylvia Plath's Transformations of Modernist Paintings," *College Literature* 29, no. 3 (2002): 43.

79. *CP*, 293.

80. Ibid., 221.

81. *CP*, 222.

82. Karal Ann Marling, *As Seen on TV: The Visual Culture of Everyday Life in the 1950s* (Cambridge: Harvard University Press, 1994), 220; *CP*, 228.

83. *BJ*, 21, 34.

84. *LHJ*, May 1957, 45.

85. Johnny Legend, producer, *Commercial Mania* (Rhino, 1986).

86. *CP*, 227, 189, 192.

87. *LHJ*, April 1956, 115; December 1958, 119.

88. Roland Marchand, *Advertising the American Dream: Making Way for Modernity, 1920–1940* (Berkeley and Los Angeles: University of California Press, 1985), 358.

89. *CP*, 206.

90. Quoted in Brain, *Other Sylvia*, 49.

91. Catherine Thompson, Moses, and Brain go so far as to qualify it as menstrual blood, which Brain also perceives in "Cut" (77). Moses cites Thompson's research into Plath's menstrual cycles in the second part of her article for Salon.com, published on June 1, 2000.

92. *CP*, 235.

93. Hammer, "Plath's Lives," 80.

94. Adrienne Rich, *The Fact of a Doorframe: Poems Selected and New 1950–1984* (New York: Norton, 1984), 35, 38.

95. Anne Sexton, *The Complete Poems of Anne Sexton* (1981; Boston: Houghton Mifflin, 1999), 155.

96. *LHJ*, July 1956, 127.

97. Paula Bernat Bennett, *Poets in the Public Sphere: The Emancipatory Project of American Women's Poetry, 1800–1900* (Princeton: Princeton University Press, 2003), 5.

LYNDA K. BUNDTZEN

Poetic Arson and Sylvia Plath's "Burning the Letters"

⊞

Only they have nothing to say to anybody. I have seen to that.
　　　　　　　　　—SYLVIA PLATH, "BURNING THE LETTERS"

*What was in those manuscripts, the one destroyed like a Jew in Nazi
Germany, the other lost like a* desaparecido?
　　　　　　　　　—STEVEN GOULD AXELROD, "THE SECOND DESTRUCTION
　　　　　　　　　OF SYLVIA PLATH"

*Sticks and stones may break your bones, but words can never
harm you.*

In his foreword to *The Journals of Sylvia Plath,* Ted Hughes confessed to
destroying one of Sylvia Plath's "maroon-backed ledgers" and losing
another. They "continued the record from late '59 to within three days
of her death. The last of these contained entries for several months, and
I destroyed it because I did not want her children to have to read it (in
those days I regarded forgetfulness as an essential part of survival). The
other disappeared."[1] As Steven Gould Axelrod's comparison of Plath's
missing journals to a Jewish victim of the Holocaust shows, many critics regard Hughes as committing an act of desecration worse than
Hitler's burning of the books. Indeed, Hughes's handling of Plath's
work has aroused endless critical fury, and he has responded in myriad
ways—at times with scorn, defensively, at others with cool detach-
ment, as if he were only her editor.[2] In a piece titled "Sylvia Plath and
Her Journals," Hughes refers to himself as "her husband" when he

describes the destruction and disappearance of the final two journals and even says, "Looking over this curtailed journal, one cannot help wondering whether the lost entries for her last three years were not the more important section of it. Those years, after all, produced the work that made her name. And we certainly have lost a valuable appendix to all that later writing."[3] Hughes the editor criticizes Hughes the husband for an unnecessary appendectomy on Plath's corpus.

Acts of textual violence or abuse, if so they might be called, were, as it turns out, habitual in the Plath-Hughes marriage, although Plath was customarily the perpetrator. Plath's biographers describe more than one incident in which Plath destroyed her husband's work, and Plath's "Burning the Letters" is about one of those times, when she pillaged and burned the contents of Hughes's study. A more covert form of sabotage and vandalism is apparent only when one views Plath's manuscripts at Smith College's Mortimer Rare Book Room. Smith paid for one corpus when it bought Plath's manuscripts but received tattered remnants of another body of work—that of Ted Hughes. Many of her final poems are written on his backside, so to speak: Plath recycles old manuscripts and typescripts by Hughes, and often she seems to be back talking, having the last word in argument. The friction between these two bodies is palpable at times, as text clashes with text, and one intuits Plath's purposeful coercion and filleting of Hughes's poems and plays as she composes. Even some of Plath's phrases—"The tongue stuck in my jaw. // It stuck in a barb wire snare"[4] and her obsession with "hooks" ("The air is a mill of hooks")[5]—may well allude to Hughes's sometimes indecipherable handwriting, clotted with a thicket of curlicues, hooks, flourishes, and, like barbed wire, backward, snarelike strokes. These allusions often suggest how a tongue, a feminine voice, finds itself stuttering to express itself in the presence of a stronger masculine one: "Ich, ich, ich, ich."[6]

If Plath's "rare" body is skillfully re-membered for public viewing and scholarly dissection, Hughes's seems at times hopelessly dismembered, scattered, and disordered. Her words are on top and one peeks at the other side, often finding her ink has bled through, indelibly splotching and staining Hughes's work. One cannot help but interpret Hughes's book cover for *Winter Pollen*, his 1994 collection of critical essays (some of them on Plath), in light of this practice by his wife. His photograph on the cover is defaced on one side with Plath's manuscript for "Sheep in Fog," covering him from pate to cheek to chin—an acknowledgment of how thoroughly he has been "overwritten" (humbly "effaced") by his wife? how hopelessly his own immortal body of work is inscribed/entombed with that of his wife?

One of the more striking moments of simultaneous entanglement of textual bodies and of marital violence occurred in Plath's composition of "Burning the Letters." According to *The Collected Poems*, it was the only poem written during the month of August 1962, when marital discord was moving toward the Plath-Hughes decision to separate. At Smith, there are six heavily reworked drafts of the poem before a final typed copy dated August 13.[7] Then, more than a month passed before Plath composed "For a Fatherless Son" (its title speaks for itself), dated September 26, 1962, the poem that initiated a phenomenal outpouring of creativity. By the end of October, Plath would have composed twenty-seven poems, among them some of her most famous: "Ariel," "Daddy," "Lady Lazarus," the bee poems. Against this later achievement in October, "Burning the Letters" appears paltry, both as an odd blip on the flat line of poetic activity for August, and because it seems so thoroughly embedded in biographical circumstance, unlike the poems she was about to write, where personal grievance is raised to the level of myth. Unlike these October poems, too, Plath did not intend to include "Burning the Letters" in her version of *Ariel*, and although she sent it off to the *New Yorker* and the *Hudson Review*, it was not published until 1973 in the collection of poems titled *Pursuit*, a limited edition of one hundred copies by the Rainbow Press.[8]

"Burning the Letters" is halting in its rhythms, enervated in its tone, and misshapen on the page, its unwieldy verse paragraphs alternating very long lines—"They would flutter off, black and glittering, they would be coal angels"—with short, blunt assertions—"They console me."[9] Though it certainly fits Ted Hughes's category of "personally aggressive" poems, it also sounds weary and flat, as in its opening line of explanation, "I made a fire; being tired," repeated a few lines later as an excuse: "Love, love, . . . I was tired."[10] Instead of the incendiary rage that fuels a poem like "Lady Lazarus," here Plath is just fed up with feeling stupid, like a "Dumb fish" mocked by

> . . . the white fists of old
> Letters and their death rattle
>
> . . . .
> What did they know that I didn't?[11]

"Burning the Letters" is, I believe, important precisely because of its cru-
dities, its poetic awkwardness, and, further, because these deficiencies
constitute an attack on her poet-husband Ted Hughes's aesthetic principles. It is, to my mind, a "slash and burn" poem, clearing the poetic playing field to make room for the type of poems she would compose for *Ariel*.

What is, perhaps, surprising is that all of the biographies and
memoirs describe the incident commemorated in "Burning the Letters"
more vividly than the poem itself, which has a deliberative, even plodding quality. In early July, while Ted Hughes was away from the Court
Green home in Devonshire he shared with Plath and their two children, she invaded his attic study, gathered assorted papers and "stuff,"
and burned them. According to Susan Van Dyne, as Plath describes the
act in her first draft, it is motivated by a desire to overcome "feelings of
isolation or helplessness with claims of control and authority. For
example, in the first draft the speaker complains, 'There was nobody
for me to know or go to. / So I burned the letters & the dust puffs & the
old hair.'"[12] The tone is one of exasperation and vicarious control, as if
to say, "Even if you are not around, I can take possession of your
things." The most vivid account available is Clarissa Roche's, in her
memoir, "Sylvia Plath: Vignettes from England." Roche was not a witness but Plath's confidante in November, after Plath and Hughes had
separated and he had left her and the children in Court Green. Roche
retells the incident as she remembers hearing it from Plath:

[W]hen the moon was at a certain stage, she had skimmed
from his desk "Ted's scum," microscopic bits of fingernail par-
ings, dandruff, dead skin, hair, and then, with a random handful of papers collected from the desk and wastebasket, she had
made a sort of pyre in the garden and around this she drew a
circle. She stepped back to a prescribed point, lit the fire with
a long stick of a torch and paced around, incanting some
hocus-pocus or another. Flames shot up toward the moon, and
smoke sketched weird shapes in the mist. Then fragments of
letters and manuscripts fluttered like moths, hovered and,
after the heat abated, floated to the ground. One charred piece
settled at Sylvia's feet. It had been reduced to an ash save for a
corner. She picked it up and by the light of the moon read
"A———," the name of a friend. Sylvia now knew the woman
with whom Ted was having an affair.[13]

Here, the incident sounds like Plath meant to cast a spell, to exorcise a demon. Whether Plath embellished what happened in order to entrance Roche, who also describes Plath as a witty raconteur, or whether Roche is the source of these spellbinding details, we still have the poem, and "Burning the Letters" has none of this quality of a witch's ritual being performed. In fact, many of Plath's revisions have the effect of taming the potential melodrama in the incident.

Other evidence for what happened is slight. Aurelia Plath, visiting her daughter from June 21 to August 4, leaves no account of the incident immortalized by the poem. Nor do the letters of Plath to her mother after she concluded her visit refer to this episode. Biographers have supplied other details, the sources for which seem vague. In her 1987 biography, Linda Wagner-Martin places the incident on July 10, following Plath's interception of "a mysterious phone call for Ted" and another act of violence:

> [W]hen Ted's conversation was over, she tore the telephone wires from the wall. She turned her rage inward as she stoically, blankly, dressed Nick and carried him to the car. Leaving Frieda with Aurelia, she drove the twenty-five miles to [her friends] the Comptons'. When she arrived, both Elizabeth and David were worried about her behavior; distraught, she wept and held on to Elizabeth's hands, begging "Help me, help me." . . . Sylvia fed Nick and the two of them spent the night in the Comptons' living room.[14]

The following day, Plath is described as returning home, and in the evening, she made a pyre of Hughes's "letters, drafts of work, and papers, and the manuscript of what was to have been her second novel, the book about her great love for Ted."[15] Biographers Ronald Hayman and Paul Alexander agree with this order of incidents, although Alexander claims there were at least three bonfires that summer: one destroying a novel conceived as "the sequel to *The Bell Jar*," a second when she burned all of Aurelia's letters to her ("upwards of a thousand"), and then the third, the burning of papers from Hughes's attic study.[16] Anne Stevenson oddly reverses the chronology, claiming that the phone incident occurred after the burning of the letters, and also refutes the notion that Plath burned anything of her own: "There is . . . no documentary evidence that such a novel existed."[17] What provoked Plath to burn Hughes's papers is left so murky in Stevenson's narrative that it makes no sense at all:

> On July 9 she and her mother drove to Exeter for a day's shopping. On the way home Sylvia exulted, "I have everything in life I've ever wanted: a wonderful husband, two adorable children, a lovely home, and my writing."
>
> Days later, while Ted was in London, she invaded his attic study, hauled down what papers she could find—mostly letters—and made a bonfire in the vegetable garden. The mother watched, appalled.[18]

The phone incident then occurs "Soon after the bonfire."[19] To this, Ronald Hayman adds that Aurelia "was holding Nick and trying to keep Frieda inside the house" and "did her best to stop Sylvia from starting a bonfire."[20]

Perhaps the best evidence for when Plath knew for certain who her rival was comes in a poem earlier than "Burning the Letters": "Words Heard, by Accident, Over the Phone," composed on July 11, 1962. One line reads, "Now the room is a hiss," suggesting the whispered intimacies between Hughes and the "other woman," but also Assia's name. The words in this poem are clearly feces: "They are plopping like mud" from "the bowel-pulse" of conversation, and the phone is itself a "muck funnel."[21] In the first draft for "Burning the Letters," words are set on fire—"lit"—and become a vehicle for revenge and purgation, and while "letters" in Plath's title refers directly to Hughes's personal correspondence, her delight in destruction extends to words and letters—to writing itself.

The first draft of "Burning the Letters" begins on a page topped by three crossed-out lines from an early version of "Stings," a poem about an incident in June when Plath's bees began attacking—"zinging"— Hughes. On the back is the typescript for Hughes's poem "Toll of Air Raids," which may well have been chosen for its analogy to the air attack of the bees. Plath's last line for this version of "Stings" warns her "love" that he is trapped in the bees' aerial assault as if he were in a "cat's cradle." Cat's cradle is a little girl's game, and the sense here is of girls' flying fingers happily weaving and "zinging" back and forth like stinging bees, with Hughes caught in the middle, tangled in knots of string.[22] Better than a "cat's cradle" stinging her unfaithful husband will be the revenge of Plath's poetic suttee in the poem she is about to compose. Both Hughes's papers and letters from Assia will fuel this fire.

After a false start of two lines she crosses out, Plath arrives at her title, "Burning the Letters." Though discarded, these lines show that her inspiration comes directly from the distinctive character of Hughes's handwriting and its predilection for deceptions and mockery, evidence that he is a liar. Eventually, these lines will evolve into a final form: "And here is an end to the writing, / The spry hooks that bend and cringe, and the smiles, the smiles."[23] Hughes's handwriting, which I described earlier in similar terms, is here conceived as a series of springlike hooks, with bending and cringing backward strokes. More important, though, than its physical appearance is the sense of smirking duplicity attributed to Hughes's writing. Coupled with the substitution of Hughes's textual body for his actual body in the vengeance she imposes, this makes Plath less the witchy voodoo queen of Roche's memoir than a vulgar harridan who has decided to invade the writing garret of her brilliant poet-husband. She has had enough of his linguistic sophistry, and enough of the high culture it represents. The reverse of the third page of draft 1 is a typescript for Hughes's poem "A Fable," and the first line reads, "A man brought to his knees in the desert."— what Plath would probably like to do to Hughes.

Van Dyne argues that Plath oscillates between representing herself as Hughes's victim and his victimizer in "Burning the Letters," that she "fails to resolve whether the burning words in her 'little crematorium' are more dead than alive or whether she murders or is herself ghoulishly tormented by 'letters <crawling> spidering <like hands> <by hooks and hands> on a skin of white.'"[24] My own sense of Plath's phrasing in the earlier drafts for "Burning the Letters" is that she conceives of his writing as a body on which she inflicts pain, and that her poem is itself a crematorium from which there is no escape. He desperately tries to wriggle free—"by hands & hooks" or "hand over hand" to crawl out of the way of the fire. But the butt of her rake stirs the fire and unfists the crumpled papers so that everything will burn in "my little crematorium." While Hughes is out of reach physically, and Plath can neither subjugate nor humiliate him in person, then, she does have access to his poetic body and may wound it.

On the reverse of the second page of Plath's first draft of "Burning the Letters" is what Van Dyne describes as "one of [Ted Hughes's] most famous statements of his own poetics, 'The Thought-Fox.'"[25] "Burning the Letters" is similarly inhabited by a fox, but one that must be read as an anti-thought-fox. Plath's fox helps to make her case for the poetic efficacy of shrieks—the animal's death cry as immortal utterance:

> A red burst and a cry
> That splits from its ripped bag and does not stop
> With the dead eye
> And the stuffed expression, but goes on
> Dyeing the air,
> Telling . . .
> What immortality is. That it is immortal.[26]

While this immortal "music" is not exactly, indeed, exactly not the "full-throated ease" of Keats's nightingale, Plath is making a similar if cruelly perverse claim for the fox's cry as transcendent expression, superseding the efficacy of the printed word. She is turning a purposely deaf ear to poetic lyricism in favor of something crude and sensational.

Plath's immortal fox challenges what she derides as Hughes's poetic taxidermy—"the dead eye / And the stuffed expression" of his "The Thought-Fox."[27] Her ink bleeds through onto his poem, "dyeing" it with her fox's agony, spilling onto his page and sullying its silent beauty. More attuned to literary convention, Hughes's poem contrarily invokes solitude and silence as the moment of poetic inspiration. He opens:

> I imagine this midnight moment's forest:
> Something else is alive
> Beside the clock's loneliness
> And this blank page where my fingers move.[28]

Plath's handwriting also mars Hughes's "neat prints into the snow" and thereby defies her husband's poetic authority. Her mockery of his "thought-fox" is evident in "stuffed expression," nastily implying that Hughes's poem, his creation of a fox, is a stuffy and bombastic little piece with about as much life as one of Norman Bates's birds. Her own fox is immortal because of its pain, and, by extension, Plath makes a case for private anguish as the basis for her new poems. She stakes the immortality of her verse on the sincerity, the authenticity of its feeling, on the impact of a *cri de coeur*. One discarded line from her first draft baldly exclaims her sense of being abandoned by him, left completely "loveless."

The aesthetic alternative in Hughes's poem is that the poet reveals nothing about himself except as a poet. "The Thought-Fox," to the extent that it has a content, is about all those elements prized by T. S. Eliot, Ezra Pound, or W. H. Auden, Hughes's own poetic mentors: the impersonal voice, the crafting of sensuous images, the cultivated representation of the poet as a mind that creates and not a man who suffers. "The Thought-Fox" is one of those tricky little self-reflexive pieces about the process of creating the poem's writing of itself. The title suggests its cerebral origin, and when we come to the final stanza—

> Till, with a sudden sharp hot stink of fox
> It enters the dark hole of the head.
> The window is starless still; the clock ticks,
> The page is printed.[29]

—we suddenly realize that the whole poem celebrates the imagination's ability to evoke an animal's presence in language. All of the animal's foxy grace redounds to the brilliance and concentration of the poet who created it—even, perhaps most of all, its "sudden sharp hot stink." The fox's "neat prints into the snow" magically become the poet's writing on the blank whiteness of the page at the end. Voilà! A poem has been made. In her first draft for "Burning the Letters," Plath responds in kind, with a writerly gesture: the cry of the fox is merely a splash of red ink in clear water. By draft 3, however, the cry is independent of ink and paper, standing apart as simply a "red burst," and now it is the poet's blood, not ink, that implicitly stains the white page.

The youthful Hughes leaves himself open to the charge of smugness in the way he boasts about "The Thought-Fox." Indeed, one cannot help but speculate that Plath chose to attack this poem precisely because of the way Hughes invested it with claims to poetic immortality. On October 6, 1961, a year earlier, in the first of a series of BBC broadcasts designed for schoolchildren on how to write poetry, Hughes read the poem as part of a lesson titled "Capturing Animals." While he begins with childhood memories of trapping animals, as Hughes warms to his subject, we know he will end with the idea of "capturing" as an artist captures the essence of animals, the essence of *fox,* as it were, to use a "stuffed expression." He highly prizes his achievement in this poem:

> If I had not caught the real fox there in the words I would never have saved the poem. I would have thrown it into the wastepaper basket as I have thrown so many other hunts that did not get what I was after. As it is, every time I read the poem the fox comes up again out of the darkness and steps into my head. And I suppose that long after I am gone, as long as a copy of the poem exists, every time anyone reads it the fox will get up somewhere out in the darkness and come walking towards them.
>
> So, you see, in some ways my fox is better than an ordinary fox. It will live for ever, it will never suffer from hunger or hounds. I have it with me wherever I go. And I made it. And all through imagining it clearly enough and finding the living words.[30]

It is hard not to read the final lines of Plath's "Burning the Letters" as throwing down the gauntlet, as spattering the blood/ink of her fox, the hunted and truly captured animal, onto Hughes's rigorously artificed fox and thereby defying his intellectual and, yes, "high" culture version of literary immortality with something literal, real, and downright low. Her emphatic "This is what it is like," followed by the extended trope of the fox torn by hounds, and then the repetitive "What immortality is. That it is immortal," is flat-out assertion, insistently stomping on Hughes's subtlety, his cleverness, his literary sophistication. Unlike Hughes, she does not mean to dazzle with her brilliance, nor to condescend as to a child. As she explains earlier in the poem, "I am not subtle."[31]

"Burning the Letters" was initially interpreted either as super-subtle in its meaning or as a grossly literal representation of an actual incident. It was either extraordinarily encoded with allusions to "moment[s] of breakthrough or enlightenment" in Zen Buddhism or simply negligible in the context of the literary value of Plath's later *Ariel* poems.[32] I would argue that its subtlety—or perhaps "cunning" is a better word—paradoxically depends on its literal-mindedness, its insistence that textual and real bodies are the same: "I open the pages, white wads that would save themselves. / Spirit after spirit gives itself up!"[33] and later, "I flake up papers that breathe like people."[34] Plath knew, I believe, that her fox was not the product of sophisticated thinking about what constitutes poetic immortality. She means to be both coarse and low in her fury, and not a poet so much as a woman scorned, invading the man's study, destroying his "property," burning her husband's letters: "So I poke at the carbon birds in my housedress." Violating all sense of propriety, she is consoled with having snuffed out both his words and the words of others' writings to him: "they have nothing to say to anybody. / I have seen to that." The detail of the housedress makes her the "little woman," not the rival poet-wife, and the *so there!* implicit in her satisfied assertions is meant as a retort to the condescensions she has suffered. She is cleaning house, and it's about time:

> And at least it will be a good place now, the attic.
> At least I won't be strung just under the surface,
> Dumb fish
>
> . . . .
>
> Riding my Arctic
> Between this wish and that wish.[35]

Even the self-demeaning metaphor here seems appropriate, as if a housewife were trying to challenge her poet-husband with less than perfectly realized artistic form. To paraphrase, "At least now I won't be treated like some dumb fish waiting, even hoping, to be caught, looking for a lure, a sign, from you, upstairs in the attic, while I live in cold uncertainty down here." In draft 1, the arctic imagery was explicitly linked to Hughes's inattentiveness as a husband and elaborated to demonstrate his cold estrangement from her—Plath's sense of being taken for granted. The metaphor in this poetic and marital situation also suggests his "higher" state of being, his clear atmosphere, his warm and ambient space, while she lives beneath his feet, a subhuman fish in a state of arctic suspension.

One can only speculate as to why Plath chose not to include this poem in her version of *Ariel*. My own suspicion is that she knew it was too low and too antiliterary in many ways. Of all the late poems, the body of this poem is the one most dependent for its meanings on knowledge of others' bodies. It is, as Freud might say, anaclitic in the way it leans on the writing-body of Hughes and Assia Wevill's embodiment as burning paper. The frustrated desire in pyromania is also apparent in Plath's urge to play with the fire and to reach in and touch these paper bodies:

> My fingers would enter . . .
> They melt and sag, . . .
> *Do not touch.*[36]

The lines describing Assia confound her sexual and textual bodies, the sound of her voice and name with its signature:

> And a name with black edges
>
> Wilts at my foot,
> Sinuous orchid
> In a nest of root-hairs . . .
> Pale eyes, patent-leather gutturals![37]

In the image of the hairy orchid, Assia's crumpled and burning letter (invaginated folds of paper) resembles female genitals, and the hissing is both her name and the sound of the fire. In draft 1, page 3, Plath misspells "gutturals" as "gutterals" (a Freudian slip?), alluding to Assia's German accent and also suggesting that it belongs to a guttersnipe. As for Hughes, the poem celebrates an act of poetic arson and scorns Hughes's writing at every level—from its physical appearance to its poetic pretensions—as dissembling, pompous, and useful only as recycled scrap for her own poetic process.

According to Anne Stevenson, this was not the first time Plath systematically went about destroying her husband's poetic property. In a fit of jealous rage, she vandalized Hughes's work as an act of "preemptive revenge"[38] for a liaison that never materialized except in her fantasy. Stevenson reports that Hughes was interviewed for "a series of children's programs" early in 1961 (ironically, the same ones described above and including "Capturing Animals") by a woman producer with "a lilting Irish voice, which Sylvia instantly associated with flaming red hair and lascivious intentions."[39] When Hughes was late returning, and based only on the sound of the producer's telephone voice, Plath created a scene of carnage. All of his work in progress, his play, poems, notebooks, even his precious edition of Shakespeare, had been torn into small pieces, some "reduced to 'fluff.' "[40]

The Shakespeare is described as "his most treasured book," and Stevenson goes on to claim that "Ted could neither forget nor forgive this desecration."[41] The language suggests that Plath's crime was not directed only at her husband, but at culture—a "desecration" of an artist's work in progress, of a rare book, of Shakespeare. As in "Burning the Letters," Plath insists on venting her fury on textual bodies, literalizing poetry as a substitute victim for her husband, whom she would probably like to tear into, reduce to fluff.

This incident not only haunts "Burning the Letters" but also seems to haunt Hughes. Writing to Anne Stevenson about this episode in *Bitter Fame,* Hughes expresses regret for not asking her to delete "one phrase in particular":

> When Sylvia's destruction of my papers etc. has been described, it is said "this could never be forgotten or forgiven," or words to that effect.
>
> The truth is that I didn't hold that action against [Sylvia]—then or at any other time. I was rather shattered by it, and saw it was a crazy thing for her to have done. But perhaps I have something missing. She never did anything that I held against her. The only thing that I found hard to understand was her sudden discovery of our bad moments ("Event," "Rabbit Catcher") as subjects for poems. But to say I could not forgive her for ripping up those bits of paper is to misunderstand utterly the stuff of my relationship to her. It is factually untrue, in other words. So in the future, in any new edition or translation, I would like to have that phrase cut out. Let the episode speak for itself.
>
> All those fierce reactions against her—which she provoked so fiercely—from people who thought, perhaps, sometimes, that they were defending me—were from my point of view simply disasters from which I had to protect her. It was like trying to protect a fox from my own hounds while the fox bit me. With a real fox in that situation, you would never have any doubt why it was biting you.[42]

Hughes's reluctance to understand Plath's "sudden discovery of our bad moments" as poetic ore to be mined reflects his later editorial choices when he put *Ariel* together, deleting virtually all of the poems from Plath's own version of *Ariel* that were explicitly about their bad moments. Yet Hughes also appears to be acknowledging Plath's fox in "Burning the Letters" here—conceding to its eloquence as poetic statement and its immortality over that of his own thought-fox. Perhaps this is a belated apology for the earlier hubris in the boast that he has "captured" the fox by giving it the permanence of art in his poem. In his 1961 BBC talk, Hughes says, "An animal I never succeeded in keeping alive [after capturing it] is the fox."[43] This is prelude, of course, to the claim he will then make that poetry is the better strategy for "keeping alive." A real fox, however, defies poetic sophistry. It desperately wants to escape and, in the frenzy of its capture, will not abide its own survival, its own salvation, especially not at the hands of its captor. Its desperation and ferocity speak for themselves—as do Sylvia Plath's.[44]

While Ted Hughes steadfastly refused interviews by biographers of Plath, he was not entirely silent. Prior to 1998 and the publication of *Birthday Letters,* Hughes would occasionally publish a poem that provided an intimate glimpse into his relationship to Plath or Assia Wevill. In a 1995 poem published in the *New Yorker,* "The Error," he provides chilling evidence that Plath's fire of July 1962 continued to burn and to inflict pain. The overall conceit of the poem is that Plath's "grave opened its ugly mouth" and spoke to Assia, but that she made an "error in translation":

> You must have misheard a sentence. You were always mishearing
> Into Hebrew or German
> What was muttered in English.[45]

The fire that yields up the name of Assia Wevill to Plath—"The name of the girl flies out, black-edged, like a death card"[46]—eventually swallows up the woman herself, described as having "selflessly incinerated yourself / In the shrine of [Plath's] death."[47] He "watched [Assia] feeding the flames," and once again, her life is as crumpled paper:

> Six full calendar years—
> Every tarred and brimstone

Day torn carefully off,
One at a time, not one wasted, patient
As if you were feeding a child.[48]

Six years after Plath's suicide, Assia Wevill killed herself and her daughter by Hughes, Shura, in a similar way to Plath, by gas and carbon monoxide asphyxiation. A discarded line from "Burning the Letters" personifies the earth as savoring "the taste of ashes," and following as it does "a name with black edges" that "Wilts at my foot,"[49] one cannot help but hear—or mishear—the pun on Assia in "ashes." As Plath goes on to boast, she is salting the red earth with these ashes.

NOTES

1. Ted Hughes, foreword to *The Journals of Sylvia Plath*, ed. Ted Hughes and Frances McCullough (New York: Dial, 1982), xiv.

2. In a 1971 letter to the *Observer* addressing A. Alvarez's criticism of how Plath's poems were published, Hughes defended himself by attacking Plath's audience. He claimed to "feel no obligations whatsoever" to either academics or Plath's fans, whom he regards scornfully as sensation seekers: "The scholars want the anatomy of the birth of the poetry; and the vast potential audience want her blood, hair, touch, smell, and a front seat in the kitchen where she died. The scholars may well inherit what they want, some day, and there are journalists supplying the other audience right now. But neither audience makes me feel she owes them anything." See Ted Hughes, "Publishing Sylvia Plath," in *Winter Pollen: Occasional Prose*, ed. William Scammell (New York: Picador, 1994), 164.

3. Ted Hughes, "Sylvia Plath and Her Journals," in *Winter Pollen*, 177–78.

4. *CP*, 223.

5. Ibid., 268.

6. Ibid., 223.

7. The first draft with a date on it is the third, dated August 12. Drafts 1 and 2 might have been started earlier, closer to the date of the incident described, which biographers place in July.

8. Plath's own collection of poems for her version of *Ariel* is at Smith's Mortimer Rare Book Room with a title page and table of contents. With the publication of *The Collected Poems* in 1981, editor Ted Hughes made this earlier, "authorized" version of *Ariel* known in his notes (*CP*, 295). For an analysis of Plath's *Ariel* versus the volume collected by Ted Hughes and published in 1965 in Great Britain and 1966 in the United States, see Marjorie Perloff, "The Two Ariels: The (Re)Making of the Sylvia Plath Canon," *American Poetry Review* 12, no. 6 (1984): 10–18.

"Burning the Letters" appears in a collection designed for the Rainbow Press by Leonard Baskin. The Rainbow Press was run by Olwyn Hughes, sister to Ted Hughes. *Pursuit* is a rather peculiar collection, including juvenilia composed before 1956, but also poems of 1962 originally intended by Plath for her version of *Ariel*:

"Dark Wood, Dark Water" (1959); "Resolve" (1956); "Temper of Time" (juvenilia); "The Shrike" (1956); "Faun" (1956); "The Lady and the Earthenware Head" (1957); "Pursuit" (1956); "Doomsday" (juvenilia); "Words Heard, by Accident, Over the Phone" (July 11, 1962); "Stings [2]" (July or August 1962); "Spider" (1956); "The Fearful" (November 16, 1962); "The Rival [2]" (July 1961); "A Secret" (October 10, 1962); and "Burning the Letters" (August 13, 1962). The title poem was written shortly after Plath met Hughes and is about her sexual attraction to him. "Words Heard, by Accident, Over the Phone," "Stings [2]," "A Secret," and "Burning the Letters" are also about Hughes, his infidelity, and their marital problems, making *Pursuit* a volume that documents the history of their relationship. "A Secret" is the only poem originally intended by Plath to be in her version of *Ariel*.

9. *CP,* 204.

10. As Hughes describes "[t]he *Ariel* eventually published in 1965," it "was a somewhat different volume from the one she had planned. . . . It omitted some of the more personally aggressive poems from 1962, and might have omitted one or two more if she had not already published them herself in magazines—so that by 1965 they were widely known." See Ted Hughes, "Collecting Sylvia Plath," *Winter Pollen,* 172–73. Most of the "personally aggressive" poems Plath planned to include were directed at Hughes: "The Rabbit Catcher," "A Secret," "The Jailer," "The Detective," "The Other," "The Courage of Shutting-Up," "Purdah," and "Amnesiac."

11. *CP,* 204.

12. Susan R. Van Dyne, *Revising Life: Sylvia Plath's "Ariel" Poems* (Chapel Hill: University of North Carolina Press, 1993), 37.

13. Clarissa Roche, "Sylvia Plath: Vignettes from England," in *Sylvia Plath: The Woman and the Work,* ed. Edward Butscher (New York: Dodd, 1977), 85.

14. Linda Wagner-Martin, *Sylvia Plath: A Biography* (New York: St. Martin's Press, 1987), 208. For a more detailed account of this conversation with the Comptons, see Elizabeth Sigmund, "Sylvia in Devon: 1962," in Butscher, *Sylvia Plath,* 104.

15. Wagner-Martin, *Sylvia Plath,* 208.

16. Paul Alexander, *Rough Magic: A Biography of Sylvia Plath* (New York: Viking-Penguin, 1991), 286. Alexander cites an interview with Clarissa Roche as contradicting her earlier statement that Assia's name was revealed in the fire: "Plath told Roche that the name 'Dido' was written on the charred scrap of paper, not 'A——,' as appeared in Roche's memoir. . . . According to Roche, Butscher changed the name . . . to make the scene more dramatic" (378–79). If so, then Plath did as well in "Burning the Letters," because "patent leather gutturals" alludes to Assia Wevill's German accent, and "Sinuous orchis" fairly hisses out her name.

17. Anne Stevenson, *Bitter Fame: A Life of Sylvia Plath* (Boston: Houghton, 1989), 251.

18. Ibid., 250.

19. Ibid., 251.

20. Ronald Hayman, *The Death and Life of Sylvia Plath* (London: Heinemann, 1991), 161.

21. *CP,* 202–3.

22. The visual image is similar to one in "Gulliver" (*CP,* 251): "The spider-men

have caught you, // Winding and twining their petty fetters, / Their bribes—/ So many silks."

23. *CP*, 204.

24. Van Dyne, *Revising Life*, 37.

25. Ibid., 9.

26. *CP*, 205.

27. *THCP*, 21.

28. Ibid.

29. Ibid.

30. Ted Hughes, *Poetry in the Making: An Anthology of Poems and Programmes from Listening and Writing* (1969) (London: Faber, 1982), 20–21.

31. *CP*, 204.

32. Judith Kroll, *Chapters in a Mythology: The Poetry of Sylvia Plath* (New York: Harper, 1976), 276, note 37. See Kroll's elaborate reading of the fox's immortality as reflecting that Plath "was more than superficially acquainted with Hinduism and Buddhism. (Her familiarity with these literatures was confirmed by Ted Hughes, in conversation)" (275–77 n. 37). My reading directly contradicts Kroll's in the sense that Kroll chooses to elevate what I describe as the literal-mindedness of the poem to an extraordinary symbolic height. I am also skeptical of the way in which Hughes authorizes her reading of the poem, which may be seen as his defensive strategy for obscuring the wounds Plath inflicts on his "The Thought-Fox." Jon Rosenblatt's dismissive commentary appears in *Sylvia Plath: The Poetry of Initiation* (Chapel Hill: University of North Carolina Press, 1993), 107.

33. Sylvia Plath, "Burning the Letters," draft 1 (Smith), 2; qtd. Van Dyne, 37.

34. *CP*, 204.

35. Ibid.

36. Ibid.

37. Ibid., 205.

38. Stevenson, *Bitter Fame*, 206.

39. Ibid.

40. Ibid. According to a note in *Bitter Fame*, "This account is from Dido Merwin, to whom Hughes confided it in the autumn of 1962, after his breakup with Sylvia," 206.

41. Ibid., 206.

42. Ted Hughes to Anne Stevenson, quoted in Janet Malcom, *The Silent Woman: Sylvia Plath and Ted Hughes* (New York: Knopf, 1994), 143.

43. Hughes, *Poetry in the Making*, 19.

44. One of the stranger essays in Hughes's collection *Winter Pollen* is "The Burnt Fox" (1993), an account of a dream Hughes claims to have had as a student reading English at Cambridge in the early 1950s. While trying to write one of his weekly critical essays, he falls asleep and is visited by a figure that was at the same time a skinny man and a fox walking erect on its hind legs. "It was a fox, but the size of a wolf. As it approached and came into the light I saw that its body and limbs had just now stepped out of a furnace. Every inch was roasted, smouldering, black-charred, split and bleeding. Its eyes, which were level with mine where I sat, dazzled with the intensity of the pain. It came up until it stood beside me. Then it spread its hand—a human hand as I now saw, but burned and bleeding like the rest

of him flat palm down on the blank space of my page. At the same time it said: 'Stop this—you are destroying us.' Then as it lifted its hand away I saw the blood-print, like a palmist's specimen, with all the lines and creases, in wet, glistening blood on the page" (9).

One senses allegory at work, the medieval scholar-dreamer visited by a figure representing the English canon and warning him that his critical pedantries are "destroying" literature. The anticritical sentiment echoes Hughes's scorn for "the hundred thousand Eng Lit Profs and graduates who . . . feel very little in this case [about Plath's life and death] beyond curiosity of quite a low order, the ordinary village kind, popular bloodsport kind, no matter how they robe their attentions in Lit Crit Theology and ethical sanctity" (see letter to Stevenson in Malcolm, *Silent Woman,* 141). The same "bloodsport" is rending the body of Hughes's fox-man. In addition, though, one is tempted to read this as yet another self-derisive allusion to "The Thought-Fox," an animal that also comes at night, leaving not its bloody handprint behind on the blank page but the neat prints of the poem's writing. The self-derision may also extend to a comparison once again with Plath's bleeding fox in "Burning the Letters," making its appearance in the charred ruins of her husband's letters.

45. *THCP*, 795–96.
46. Ibid., 796.
47. Ibid., 796.
48. Ibid., 796.
49. *CP*, 205.

DIANE MIDDLEBROOK

Creative Partnership

SOURCES FOR

"THE RABBIT CATCHER"

⊞

In 1965, when Ted Hughes edited and published the manuscript of *Ariel* that he had found among Sylvia Plath's papers after her suicide, he added poems that she had apparently not intended to include— some of the last poems she wrote before her death—and omitted poems that Plath had designated for inclusion. One of the poems he excluded was "The Rabbit Catcher," a poem written in May 1962 that forecast the end of their marriage.

In 1981, in his introduction to Plath's *Collected Poems*, Hughes explained his editorial decisions: he thought Plath might well have gone on revising and reorganizing the book herself, had she lived; and he had deliberately withheld a number of "the more personally aggressive poems" because he thought they might be "too hard for the reading public to take."[1] In the spirit of making a full disclosure, he printed the table of contents Plath had provisionally established for the book she planned to title *Ariel* in his notes to *Collected Poems,* and he included in the body of the text the poems he had previously omitted, placing them in the chronological order of their composition.

Collected Poems received a Pulitzer Prize, an honor rarely awarded a deceased author. But the editorial intervention Hughes revealed in his introduction to the book created a critical uproar, largely because by the time *Collected Poems* appeared, the *Ariel* Hughes published had achieved canonical status in American poetry. Arguably, Hughes's decision to include Plath's very last poems had strengthened his edition of *Ariel* artistically; he might have escaped censure had he given the book a different title: *Poems 1961–1963*, for example. But by the time *Collected Poems* was published, Hughes had sold his legacy of Plath's papers to be archived at Smith College, where scholars were able to study them; and the feminist movement had produced a number of influential commentators who felt deeply possessive of Plath's work and outrage at what they suspected to be Hughes's subversion of Plath's artistic purposes. He had put plenty of evidence in the hands of his critics. Hostility to Hughes over the editing of *Ariel* persisted throughout his lifetime.

In 2004, six years after Hughes's death, their daughter, Frieda Hughes, commissioned *Ariel: The Restored Edition*, as a kind of remedy. It was not, strictly speaking, the book that would have been made of the manuscript Plath left on her desk. This *Ariel* reproduced not only the sequencing Plath envisioned, but the manuscripts of the poems themselves, along with six drafts of the title poem. And in a foreword to the book, Frieda Hughes defended her father's editorial decisions back in 1965. She argued that Hughes was protecting Plath, and others, by withholding some of the poems; and she quoted him as telling her, "I simply wanted to make the best book I could."[2]

In a letter to Plath's biographer Anne Stevenson, written immediately after the publication of *Bitter Fame* in 1990, Hughes acknowledged a more complex motivation for excluding certain poems from *Ariel,* including "The Rabbit Catcher." Plath, he said, "never did anything I held against her," with a single exception: "her sudden discovery of our bad moments . . . as subjects" for poems.[3] Plath's anger had made her willing to expose their private life to public scrutiny. Although Hughes didn't mention this in his letter to Stevenson, Plath had previously submitted "The Rabbit Catcher" to their mutual friend Al Alvarez for publication in the *Observer,* and Alvarez accepted it (he pronounced it "flawless").[4] As it happened, the poem didn't get published during Plath's lifetime, but what Hughes saw as Plath's disloyalty still rankled with him for years after her death.

During all those years, it turns out, Hughes had never been merely Plath's editor and executor. He had remained deeply attached to the earliest relationship they formed with one another, which predated even their marriage: a creative partnership conducted in a context of incessant dialogue. When working side by side with Plath, Hughes said, he often felt he was drawing on "a single shared mind"[5] that each accessed by telepathy. After her death, he continued to draw on that sense of possessing a special access to her attention. In 1998, he published *Birthday Letters*, a volume of verse epistles addressed to Plath. His aim when writing them, he said, was to speak plainly to her, in privacy, and recapture the "intimate wavelength"[6] of communication they had shared during their years together. He had been writing these poems for twenty-five years, he said, without an intention of publishing them.

In *Birthday Letters*, Hughes permitted himself to reenter his own memories of the bad moments. *Birthday Letters,* too, contains a poem titled "The Rabbit Catcher": Hughes's critique of, and meditation on, Plath's version of the occasion on which she recognized their relationship was at an end. No poem by Sylvia Plath or Ted Hughes is more dense with literary resonance than the poems they titled "The Rabbit Catcher." Taken together, this antiphonal pair of poems provides a laboratory for understanding the creative partnership Plath and Hughes had formed during the years of their marriage, and the crisis they were undergoing during that fateful month of May 1962, when Plath wrote her "Rabbit Catcher."

The rabbit or hare had begun evolving a private meaning in Plath's work from the outset of her relationship with Hughes. Back in 1956, during the first months of falling in love with Hughes, Plath inaugurated a practice of coding responses to his work in her own work-in-progress. An early example is "Ode for Ted," in which the rabbit makes its first appearance ever in Plath's poetry:

> From under the crunch of my man's boot
> Green oat-sprouts jut;
> He names a lap-wing, starts rabbits in a rout.[7]

Plath enclosed the poem in a rapturous letter to her mother in April 1956 in which she described romantic idylls with Hughes in the countryside that inspired a flow of poems: "They come from the vocabulary of woods and animals and the earth that Ted is teaching me."[8]

It was a vocabulary that Hughes's poetry drew on, too, as Plath had discovered in Hughes's published writing even before she met him in the flesh. A poem by Hughes titled "The Casualty" describes an airman tumbling from a burning plane into a field; an inquisitive hare

hops up, quizzical, hesitant,
Flattens ears and tears madly away and the wren warns.[9]

"The Casualty" was one of the poems that Hughes published in an issue of *Chequer*,[10] a Cambridge college magazine that had also accepted some of Plath's poetry shortly after she arrived to study English literature on a Fulbright fellowship. Plath's journal indicates that she had memorized Hughes's "The Casualty" and "Law in the Country of the Cats"[11] before attending a launch party for another little college magazine—as a seduction strategy, she memorized lines by several of the Cambridge poets she had hoped to meet and impress that night. Her journal describes the way she quoted the poems to their authors at the party.[12] And as the world knows, it was Hughes she captivated: by accosting him, teasing him, and—after he kissed her, hard—biting him until blood ran down his cheek.

Plath's romance with Hughes glorified his rough masculinity; it is not irrelevant that the rabbit in "Ode for Ted" occupies a line in which the rhyme sound is provided by a boot. The other Hughes poem that Plath had memorized—"Law in the Country of the Cats"—was overtly violent:

When two men meet for the first time
    . . . [they] outright hate each other . . .
Not as bully-boy and delicate boy, but
As dog and wolf because their blood before
They are aware has bristled into their hackles, . . .[13]

At the end of "Law," one of the men has brained the other and rushes to turn himself in to the police: "'I did it, I.'" (Hughes was ironically and without attribution alluding to the old folk ballad "Who Killed Cock Robin?") Plath found it thrilling to quote those words back to Hughes at the party. She recorded the moment in her journal: "I started yelling again about his poems and quoting . . . and he yelled back, colossal . . . . His poem 'I did it, I.' Such violence, and I can see how women lie down for artists. The one man in the room who was as big as his poems, huge, with hulk and dynamic chunks of words; his poems are strong and blasting like a high wind in steel girders."[14]

The poetry of D. H. Lawrence was an obvious influence on "Law in the Country of the Cats"; the works of Lawrence were fundamental to a literary education in those days. Lawrence called this kind of instinctive aggression "blood consciousness." However, Hughes's work reflected not only his fealty to Lawrence's ideas, and to the animal poems in which Lawrence celebrated animal instincts, but also to Hughes's own rearing in the Calder Valley of West Yorkshire, and specifically to the influence of his brother.

Hughes claimed that his earliest memories involved learning about animals from his brother, Gerald, who was ten years his senior. Early every morning, Gerald picked up his rifle and made the rigorous climb up a steep hillside out of the valley onto the surrounding moors to hunt small game. Gerald began taking his little brother, Ted, on these morning raids as soon as he was sturdy and nimble enough to collect the animals Gerald shot: crows and magpies, rabbits and rats and weasels. "I had to scramble into all kinds of places,"[15] fetching the animals for Gerald, Hughes later recalled. Under Gerald's tutelage Hughes acquired the eye of a naturalist, alert to the smallest movement of any creature in a landscape. Hughes claimed that forever afterward he could glance out of a train window at the passing farmland and at once spot the ears of hares sticking out of the corn.[16]

The brothers wove around this morning ritual an elaborate, literary fantasy: they were primeval natives roaming the moors; the pursuit and slaughter of game was an ongoing epic saga. This idyllic period of Hughes's life had ended abruptly in 1938 when the family moved to Mexborough, a coal-mining town in South Yorkshire. Shortly afterward, Gerald left home and found a job as a gamekeeper on a big estate in Devon. But imparting merely practical knowledge was not the lasting influence of Gerald on Ted Hughes. In interviews Hughes pointed to Gerald's mentorship as having provided him with a second mentality, literally another organ of perception that Hughes associated with his creativity.[17] That early phase of Hughes's upbringing retained its force in his psyche and prepared him, in late adolescence, to be deeply influenced by Robert Graves's theory of poetic inspiration, *The White Goddess*. Graves took the view of an anthropologist, observing that poetry has a religious function in society: it keeps alive the primordial myths and ancient rituals that affirm man's animal instincts. A true poet, therefore, writes from the wild, uncivilized depths of his mind, according to Graves. In Hughes's case, because the loss of Gerald's companionship in 1938 was so complete and sudden, their relationship remained intact in his memory as an ideal. And it gave him an origin story to tell, about a lost paradise inhabited only by animals and boys, engrossed by a kind of wildness that seemed natural and innocent. This was some of the history that shaped Hughes's character years before he met Sylvia Plath, and would contribute to the conflicts underlying their separation.

Hughes and Plath married in June 1956, and took off for a summer in Spain, where both intended to get on with their writing. Hughes planned to invest some of his working hours writing a book of animal fables for children. In a letter to his brother, Hughes said he expected the fables to supply them with lots of cash. Sylvia was lucky for him, he said. In a letter to her mother Plath let it slip that they expected to sell the fables to Walt Disney.[18] Eventually, a version of the book Hughes began writing on their honeymoon was published with the title *How the Whale Became and Other Stories*.

One of the stories in that collection is titled "How the Hare Became." Did Hughes write it in Spain? Maybe so, maybe not. But something prompted Plath to decide that they must celebrate Hughes's birthday that August, in Spain, with a feast of rabbit stew.

Plath apparently had never cooked a rabbit before. Her journal tells how she prepared herself, by taking a nap in the afternoon, then drinking strong hot coffee before approaching the stove—"like a surgeon before a difficult new operation to be performed for the first time."[19] The source of Plath's recipe was Irma Rombauer's *The Joy of Cooking*. The page facing the recipe for rabbit stew showed two rubber-gloved hands skinning a rabbit; very likely, this image was the prompt of Plath's reference to the surgeon. Rombauer's "Rule for Making Gravy for Stews" requires vegetable stock, but Plath, in her practical American way, substituted packets of condensed soup and a can of peas. Hughes helped out by adding the glass and a half of wine that Rombauer regarded as optional—"the French use wine,"[20] noted Rombauer, whose home was Missouri. Plath, who had grown up in Massachusetts, was avidly adopting European ways herself.

Plath and Hughes worked together on the birthday stew; sharing domestic work was a feature of their partnership from the beginning of their marriage. The resulting stew was "delectable,"[21] Plath noted, and Hughes took enough interest in its preparation that he was able later that year to reproduce it for a Sunday dinner at his family home in Yorkshire. Hughes wrote to Plath—who was back in Cambridge at the time—a detailed account of how he hunted and shot the rabbit, and then how he followed her method in cooking it, except that he put in too many packets of soup mix and got a stiff rather than a succulent result.[22] There was one additional difference in their methods of preparing the stew, of course: Plath shopped for her rabbit at a butcher's stall and bought it gutted and skinned. Hughes flushed his rabbit out of the brush, then shot, skinned, and dismembered it.

As Plath's poem "Ode for Ted" indicates, Plath idealizes Hughes's predatory familiarity with animals: it was one of the traits that affiliated him with D. H. Lawrence in her mind. Plath's college journals show that as a young woman she had acquired her sexual ideology by reading Lawrence's novels. During 1958–59, the first year that Plath and Hughes allocated to becoming professional writers, they were living in Boston, and Plath was attempting to write a novel herself, to be titled *Falcon Yard*. Its theme would be her romance with Hughes at Cambridge, and she turned repeatedly to Lawrence for inspiration—to be "itched and kindled,"[23] as she put it. She spent a whole day reading *Lady Chatterley's Lover*, "with the joy of a woman living with her own gamekeeper," she wrote in her journal. "Why do I feel I would have known and loved Lawrence—how many women would feel this & be wrong!"[24]

All of these details were in the background in May 1962 when Plath formulated the imagery of "The Rabbit Catcher." Since September 1961, Hughes and Plath had been living in the Devon countryside, where they had bought a dilapidated house, Court Green, in order to escape the high cost of living in London and to make room for their growing family. Their daughter, Frieda, had been born in April 1960, and Plath was in her third trimester of pregnancy by the time they moved to Devon; in January, she would deliver their son, Nicholas. Meanwhile, Plath's fantasy of "living with her own gamekeeper" had become a reality: after they moved to Devon, Hughes supplemented their food supply by fishing and by hunting rabbits, as their letters and Plath's annotated diaries show.

Setting up the household at Court Green and planting a garden required incessant efforts from both Hughes and Plath throughout the autumn and winter. By May, their enormous labors had paid off, and they were feeling sociable. They began inviting London friends down to Devon for weekend visits of literary conversation. And Plath had returned to writing. In March, she had rapidly produced a thirty-minute radio play about three women in a maternity ward, which she sold immediately to the BBC;[25] in April, her poem "Tulips" had been published in the *New Yorker*; the U.S. edition of her poetry book *The Colossus* was due out on May 14. After every morning's work, she showed Hughes what she had written. He wrote to Plath's mother in early May, "Sylvia is beginning to produce some really permanent poetry."[26]

But within the ongoing tight compatibility of their creative partnership, a change was shaping that spring, a change that began to surface in Plath's poems. April and May 1962 are the dates in Plath's *Collected Poems* in which can be witnessed the sudden, unaccountable emergence of her late style: "Elm" (April 19), "The Rabbit Catcher" and "Event" (both May 21), and "Apprehensions" (May 28). In this handful of poems, Plath's talent has evolved into Plath's genius: the extreme, clenched, concision of metaphorical thought traveling in short stanza bursts. Thematically, her poems are increasingly focused on the instability of love, and emotionally they are saturated with dreadful knowledge into which the speaker of the poem is required to travel, as to a destination. "I know the bottom," Plath writes in the opening line of "Elm":

> I know it with my great tap root:
> It is what you fear.
> I do not fear it: I have been there.[27]

This is the matrix from which emerges the startling directness and energy of the "Rabbit Catcher":

> It was a place of force—
> The wind gagging my mouth with my own blown hair, . . .
> There was only one place to get to . . . .
> And the snares almost effaced themselves—
> Zeros, shutting on nothing, . . .
>
> I felt a still busyness, . . .
> . . . hands round a tea mug, dull, blunt,
> . . . .
> How they awaited him, those little deaths![28]

Plath wrote "The Rabbit Catcher" following the weekend visit of Assia and David Wevill to the Hugheses' home in Devon; it is often considered as autobiographical evidence that Plath had discovered Hughes's sexual interest in Assia Wevill. But there is quite good evidence that in May 1962 Plath felt nothing, yet, toward Assia Wevill stronger than her usual uneasiness about the proximity to Hughes of a good-looking woman. Lynda Bundtzen is surely correct in the speculation, based on careful study of Plath's manuscripts, that "The Rabbit Catcher" is not about sexual jealousy but is "about the way marriage enthralls a woman's creativity."[29] Quite specifically, it is about how Plath's creativity has been enthralled by marriage to the man she identified with D. H. Lawrence. "The Rabbit Catcher" is obviously a response to a couple of poems by Lawrence, "Rabbit Snared in the Night" and "Love on the Farm."[30] In "Rabbit Snared in the Night," Lawrence's first-person speaker has just removed a live rabbit from a snare:

> Yes, bunch yourself between
> my knees and lie still.
> Lie on me with a hot, plumb, live weight
> heavy as a stone, passive,
> yet hot, waiting.
>
> . . . .
> It must have been *your* inbreathing, gaping desire
> that drew this red gush in me; . . .
> It must be you who desire
> this intermingling of the black and monstrous fingers of
>   Moloch
> in the blood-jets of your throat.
>
> Come, you shall have your desire
> since already I am implicated with you
> in your strange lust.[31]

In "Love on the Farm," the point of view is that of a wife greeting her husband as he arrives home after hunting game:

> He flings the rabbit soft on the table board . . .
> And caresses me with his fingers that still smell grim
> Of the rabbit's fur! God, I am caught in a snare!
> I know not what fine wire is round my throat;
> I only know I let him finger there
> My pulse of life. . . .[32]

In her own poem, "The Rabbit Catcher," Plath seizes on Lawrence's first-person, present-tense use of sexual metaphors, and also his use of the domestic setting; but she locates everything in a wife's point of view with Plath's whole memory behind it, in which D. H. Lawrence and Ted Hughes are indistinguishable from one another. She cleverly imagines a back story for the dramatic scenes Lawrence narrates in "Rabbit Snared in the Night": an ordinary man sitting at a kitchen table, his hands circling a warm mug of tea as if it were a throat, before venturing into the night to inspect his snares.

It was Ted Hughes who put into Plath's hands those poems about the erotic pleasure of hunting rabbits, when he presented her with the three-volume set of Lawrence's poetry in February 1960, to celebrate the signing of the contract for her own first book of poems, *The Colossus*.[33] By 1962, Plath had also read and admired Hughes's story "The Harvesting,"[34] a surreal, violent fantasy refracted through the mind of a farmer watching a reaping machine reduce to stubble a field where a large hare will soon be flushed into the path of his gun—a brilliant insider's account of the killer instinct. This privileged knowledge of the way hunting and killing inform her husband's creativity finds anguished expression in the closure of "The Rabbit Catcher." The "snare" in her poem is, among other things, her own mind, capturing in this reference to Lawrence's rabbit catcher an insight into the content of her husband's hidden fantasy life:

> And we, too, had a relationship . . .
> Pegs too deep to uproot, and mind like a ring
> Sliding shut on some quick thing,
> . . . killing me also[35]

Her own gamekeeper. Had a relationship. As far back as they go, Plath has been drawn to the potential for cruelty in Hughes; yes, she has had a relationship to that, too, as we know from her journal. If her husband shares traits with Lawrence's rabbit catcher, she shares the erotic position of the creature he has snared. These are psychological structures—"pegs too deep to uproot."

But "The Rabbit Catcher" is not a poem about their now-unsettled domestic life, though jealousy and dissatisfaction may have jarred loose the emotions in the poem. *Had a relationship.* She had begun the process of stripping D. H. Lawrence's sexual ideology from her imagination's core; the process has begun that will lead to the poem "Daddy." (Lawrence: "Look! We have come through"; Plath: "Daddy, we're finally through.") "The Rabbit Catcher" is as much a poem about her dread of losing her love for Hughes as it is about her hostility to the literary masculinity she used to idealize. The pathos of that phrase "killing me also" is an elegy for everything that had to be outgrown in her femininity to acquire such clarity, such mastery within the medium of the distinctive poetic method and subject matter that would make her name.

The poem titled "The Rabbit Catcher" that Hughes placed in *Birthday Letters* is in dialogue with this very aspect of Plath's poem: its resistance to him, and where it was coming from. According to Hughes's poem, on the actual day commemorated in the poem, Plath was enraged by the sight of the snares and ripped them out of the ground; he saw the gesture as acknowledgment of a deep difference between them, nothing to do with rabbits. Hughes writes,

> What had I done? I had
> . . . Trailed after like a dog, . . .
> And I found a snare.
> . . . Without a word
> You tore it up and threw it into the trees.
> In those snares
> You'd caught something.[36]

In most of the poems of *Birthday Letters*, Hughes has a ready explanation for Plath's behavior. "The Rabbit Catcher" is an exception. In this poem, he has questions; in this poem, he experiences his own strangeness, through empathy with her fear and despair. It, too, is a long poem, but here is its core:

> Had you caught something in me,
> Nocturnal and unknown to me?[37]

The answer (not in the poem) is yes. In 1962, Hughes was about to make one of those developmental growth spurts that go on occurring in adulthood and reveal aspects of the character that have long been in formation but haven't yet asserted themselves. He was about to evolve the adult version of the secretive dual existence that had been a feature of his boyhood and adolescence. He said in an interview, "Up to the age of seventeen or eighteen, shooting and fishing and my preoccupation with animals were pretty well my life, apart from books. I also played with my town friends every evening, . . . kicking around the neighborhood. But weekends I was off on my own. I had a double life."[38]

"Nocturnal," then, but not a night life. Rather, the solitary pursuit of something dark, primitive in himself, "something . . . unknown." Shortly after the Wevills' visit, Hughes began meeting Assia Wevill on his frequent business trips to London. And sometime that summer or fall he began writing a radio play for the BBC in which he secreted allusions to their affair: a complicated story about a man who is driving to a sexual liaison when he sees a rabbit in the road and accelerates in order to kill it; on arrival in the city he sells the dead animal for two shillings and buys two roses for his mistress.[39] The play was broadcast on January 23, 1963, and Plath had ears to hear; she snipped those roses and planted them in her poem "Kindness"—the manuscript is dated February 1, 1963—again echoing D. H. Lawrence's "Rabbit Snared in the Night," specifically, Lawrence's phrase, "the blood-jets of your throat":

> The blood jet is poetry,
> There is no stopping it.
> You hand me two children, two roses[40]

In Plath's private retort to the private message she found in Hughes's play, the rabbit/hare has acquired exchange value: they were playing an obsessive game of tag with one another's images.

Precisely this kind of exchange informs Hughes's dialogue with Plath's "Rabbit Catcher" in *Birthday Letters*. Back in May 1962, his imagination had deserted Plath, just as her imagination was deserting him. There is no evidence that Hughes had been sexually unfaithful to Plath before this time; but falling in love with Assia Wevill inaugurated a practice that he pursued for the rest of his life: the creation, alongside his marriage, of a kind of inner game preserve. Had Plath foreseen this turn his life was going to take, "caught" something in him that even he couldn't discern? Not just that he would enter into an adulterous affair with Assia Wevill, but that his life as an artist henceforth would require his wife's acceptance of the "nocturnal" impulses to which his deepest inspiration was attached? True North in Hughes's libido was the position of predator, imprinted in those stealthy exits from the claustrophobic family home in Mytholmroyd, which was dominated by his mother, out and up onto the moors with his brother. Escaping from the domain of actual women, the brothers wrote themselves into a complicated fantasy life that licensed voyeurism and violent capture. And Hughes himself was a shrewd analyst of the role predation played in his creativity. In a letter to a scholar who was preparing an essay on ethical questions raised by Hughes's way of writing about fishing for sport, he was completely straightforward about the kind of allure that fishing, for example, held for him. He pointed to Jung's observation that psychotherapy served as a holding space for human contact with primitive impulses and added, "Think of the many extreme ways in which 'civilized' individuals do keep something of that contact," as in "hectic bouts of adultery."[41] By the time he published "The Rabbit Catcher" in *Birthday Letters*, Hughes could bring to bear on Plath's poem a good deal of just such relevant myth and history.

Hughes's "Rabbit Catcher," however, is not a plea to be forgiven. Instead, it registers his retrospective recognition that he and Plath had reached, simultaneously, the end of their apprenticeships as poets. In actual life, their romance had ended; the presence of their children had reorganized the emotional dynamics of their household; and the tight, hot intimacy of their sexual bond had been replaced by uncomfortable awareness of irreconcilable differences. In their creative partnership, Plath had finally outgrown the usefulness of the D. H. Lawrence figure in her education, and Hughes had finally grown into the legacy of his early training as a hunter. The consequence for each of them, as a married couple and as artists, would be a separation.

And though Plath's mastery of her subject matter—their "bad moments"—cannot help but disturb him, he cannot help but admire, in his own "Rabbit Catcher," the work of art she made of it, either. The expressive power that rises up in this pivotal poem in Plath's work, and in her as its author, expresses an imagination alone with its own wildness, in the inner "place of force" where poetry is made. That aspiration had equal importance in each of them and had been the foundation of their creative partnership. It was what Hughes treasured in Plath to the end of his life.

NOTES

1. *CP*, 15.
2. *AR*, xvi.
3. Ted Hughes to Anne Stevenson, in Janet Malcolm, *The Silent Woman* (London: Picador, 1994), 143.
4. A. Alvarez to Sylvia Plath, July 24, 1962 (Smith).
5. "Poets in Partnership," *Two of a Kind*, Hughes and Plath interviewed by Owen Leeming for the BBC, recorded January 18, 1961, 1/5, British Library (SA).
6. Enclosed in a letter of Hughes to Keith Sagar, June 16, 1998. The letter was addressed to Hughes's German translators (British Library); *Her Husband*, 276.
7. *CP*, 29.
8. *LH*, 238.
9. *THCP*, 42.
10. *Chequer* 7, no. 2 (1954): 17.
11. Plath says she quoted "most dear unscratchable diamond" (*UJ*, 211), which is a phrase from "The Casualty," and "I did it" (*UJ*, 212), a phrase from "Law in the Country of the Cats." The latter poem was untitled when first published.
12. *UJ*, 211–12.
13. *THCP*, 41.
14. *UJ*, 212.
15. Ted Hughes, "Capturing Animals," in *Winter Pollen: Occasional Prose*, ed. William Scammell (New York: Picador, 1995), 11.
16. Thomas Pero, "So Quickly It's Over" (interview with Ted Hughes), in *Wild Steelhead & Salmon* 5, no. 2 (1999): 1.
17. "Poets in Partnership," 1/4; *Her Husband*, 74.
18. Plath to Aurelia Plath, August 10, 1956 (Lilly).
19. *UJ*, 258.
20. Irma S. Rombauer and Marion Rombauer Becker, *The Joy of Cooking*, illustrated by Ginnie Hofmann (New York: Bobbs-Merrill, 1953), 413.
21. *UJ*, 258.
22. Hughes to Plath, October 6, 1956 (Lilly).
23. *UJ*, 337.
24. Ibid.
25. *Three Women*, dir. Douglas Cleverdon, recorded August 2, 1962, broadcast August 19, 1962, repeated September 13, 1962, and June 9, 1968. All on BBC Third Programme, British Library (SA).
26. Hughes to Aurelia Plath, May 14, 1962 (Lilly).
27. *CP*, 192.
28. Ibid., 193–94.
29. Lynda Bundtzen, *The Other Ariel* (Amherst: University of Massachusetts Press, 2001), 49.
30. Marjorie Perloff identified "Love on the Farm" as a source for Plath's "The Rabbit Catcher" in "The Two *Ariels*: The (Re) Making of the Sylvia Plath Canon," in *Poetic License: Essays on Modernist and Postmodern Lyric* (1984; Evanston, Ill.: Northwestern University Press, 1990), 186.

31. D. H. Lawrence, *The Complete Poems of D. H. Lawrence*, ed. Vivian de Sola Pinto and Warren Roberts (Harmondsworth: Penguin, 1977; repr. 1994), 240–42.

32. Lawrence, *Collected Poems*, 43.

33. Linda Wagner-Martin, *Sylvia Plath: A Biography* (New York: Simon and Schuster, 1987), 170.

34. "The Harvesting," in *Wodwo* (London: Faber and Faber, 1967), 86–96.

35. *CP*, 194; *Her Husband*, 169.

36. *THCP*, 1136–37.

37. Ibid., 1138.

38. Drue Heinz, "Ted Hughes: The Art of Poetry, LXXI," (interview), *Paris Review* 134 (Spring 1995): 59.

39. *Difficulties of a Bridegroom*. The title refers to a mystical narrative on alchemy that had stimulated Hughes for many years. The play was broadcast on the BBC Third Programme January 21, 1963, rebroadcast February 9, 1963.

40. *CP*, 270.

41. Terry Gifford, "'Go Fishing': An Ecocentric or Egocentric Imperative?" in *Lire Ted Hughes New Selected Poems, 1957–1994*, ed. Joanny Moulin (Paris: Editions du Temps, 1999), 145.

KATE MOSES

Appendix

THE ORAL ARCHIVE

⊞

This list includes and updates all documentable recordings made by Sylvia Plath, as well as information on their broadcasts and commercial releases where applicable. Stephen Tabor's *Sylvia Plath: An Analytical Bibliography* (London: Mansell, 1987) offers an earlier, less comprehensive listing of archived material.

1. A reading at a radio station in Mt. Holyoke, Massachusetts, on April 16, 1955. The station was probably WMHC, the Mt. Holyoke college station. Although Plath mentions this recording session in a letter to her mother dated April 16, 1955, according to Stephen Tabor, WMHC has no archival copy of this tape and it has not been located elsewhere.

2. A reading for the Woodberry Poetry Room, Lamont Library, Harvard University, at Fassett Recording Studio in Boston, November 1957. Though Plath mentions this recording in a letter to her mother dated November 28, 1957, the Woodberry Poetry Room has no record of this recording in its catalog.

3. A reading and interview with Lee Anderson in Springfield, Massachusetts, on April 18, 1958. Recorded at the request of Lee Anderson for the Archive of Recorded Poetry and Literature, Library of Congress. Ted Hughes was present at this session. Audiotape located in the collections of the Recorded Sound Reference Center, Library of Congress, Washington, D.C.; The Lee Anderson Collection of Recorded Poets, Yale Collection of Historical Sound Recordings, Yale University Library, New Haven, Connecticut; and Mortimer Rare Book Room, Neilson Library, Smith College, Northampton, Massachusetts.

Anderson's interview is interspersed between readings. Poems read are "Black Rook in Rainy Weather," "The Earthenware Head" ("The Lady and the Earthenware Head"), "Departure of the Ghost" ("The Ghost's Leavetaking"), "The Disquieting Muses," "Battle-Scene from the Comic Operatic Fantasy The Seafarer," "On the Decline of Oracles," "Poem for Paul Klee's 'Perseus': The Triumph of Wit Over Suffering" ("Perseus: The Triumph of Wit Over Suffering"), "On the Difficulty of Conjuring Up A Dryad," "November Graveyard," "Sow," "Spinster," "On the Plethora of Dryads," "All the Dead Dears." The interview has not been commercially released. The poems "Black Rook in Rainy Weather," "November Graveyard," "Sow," "On the Difficulty of Conjuring Up A Dryad," "On the Plethora of Dryads," "All the Dead Dears," "Departure of the Ghost" ("The Ghost's Leavetaking"), "Battle-Scene from the Comic Operatic Fantasy The Seafarer," and "Poem for Paul Klee's 'Perseus': The Triumph of Wit Over Suffering" ("Perseus: The Triumph of Wit Over Suffering") have been commercially released on The Voice of the Poet: Sylvia Plath (Random House AudioBooks, New York, 1999, ed. J. D. McClatchy).

4. A reading for the Woodberry Poetry Room, Lamont Library, Harvard University, recorded at Fassett Recording Studio in Boston, June 13, 1958. Ted Hughes read eleven of his own poems at this joint session. The master audiotape is cataloged in the collection of the Woodberry Poetry Room, Harvard College Library, Cambridge, Massachusetts. After Plath's brief introduction ("This is Sylvia Plath reading her poems—June thirteenth, nineteen fifty-eight"), the poems read are "Black Rook in Rainy Weather," "Departure of the Ghost" ("The Ghost's Leavetaking"), "Mad Maudlin" ("Maudlin"), "Sow," "November Graveyard, Haworth" ("November Graveyard"), "Mussel Hunter at Rock Harbor," "On the Plethora of Dryads," "The Moon Was a Fat Woman Once" ("Thin People"), "The Disquieting Muses," "Nocturne" ("Hardcastle Crags"), "Child's Park Stones," "Spinster," "The Earthenware Head" ("The Lady and the Earthenware Head"), "On the Difficulty of Conjuring Up a Dryad," and "All the Dead Dears." With the exception of "The Disquieting Muses" and "Spinster," all of these poems have been commercially released. "Black Rook in Rainy Weather," "Mussel Hunter at Rock Harbor," "Mad Maudlin" ("Maudlin"), "Sow," and "All the Dead Dears" are included on The Poet's Voice (Harvard University, Cambridge, 1978); the remaining poems are included on Sylvia Plath Reading Her Poetry (Caedmon, New York, 1977) and Sylvia Plath Reads

(Caedmon/HarperCollins, New York, abridged and remastered re-release 1999; © BBC Enterprises, Ltd.).

5. A reading for the Woodberry Poetry Room, Lamont Library, Harvard University, recorded at Fassett Recording Studio in Boston on February 22, 1959. The master audiotape is cataloged in the collection of the Woodberry Poetry Room, Harvard College Library, Cambridge, Massachusetts. After Plath's brief introduction ("This is Sylvia Plath reading her poems on February twenty-second, nineteen fifty-nine") the poems read are "Full Fathom Five," "Departure," "I Want, I Want," "Green Rock, Winthrop Bay," "On the Decline of Oracles," "Lorelei," "Moonrise," "Watercolor of Granchester Meadows," "The Bull of Bendylaw," "Frog Autumn," "The Hermit at Outermost House," "The Goring," "Ouija," "Snakecharmer," "The Beggars of Benidorm Market" ("The Beggars"), "Sculptor," and "Point Shirley." All these poems have been commercially released. Included on *Sylvia Plath Reads* (Caedmon, New York, abridged and remastered rerelease 1999) are "Green Rock, Winthrop Bay," "On the Decline of Oracles," "The Goring," "Ouija," "The Beggars of Benidorm Market" ("The Beggars") and "Sculptor." *The Poet's Voice* (Harvard University, Cambridge, 1978) includes all the remaining poems.

6. A reading for the BBC series *The Poet's Voice,* episode entitled "New Poetry," recorded at the BBC studios in London between October 26, 1960, and November 19, 1960. Broadcast on November 20, 1960. Plath mentions her plan to record at the BBC in letters to her mother dated October 26 and October 28, 1960, but does not specify the date of the recording. An audiotape copy of this recording may exist in the BBC Sound Archive via the National Sound Archive, British Library, London, but it was not found during a search conducted in November 2000. Plath reads two poems, "Candles" and "Leaving Early." Both poems were released commercially on *Sylvia Plath Reading Her Poetry* (Caedmon, New York, 1977). "Candles" is included on *Sylvia Plath Reads* (Caedmon, New York, abridged and remastered rerelease 1999).

7. A joint reading and interview with Sylvia Plath and Ted Hughes for the BBC series *Two of a Kind,* recorded at the BBC studios in London on January 18, 1961. Interview conducted by Owen Leeming. Broadcast with the episode title "Poets and Partnership" on January 31, 1961, and in "extended version" on March 19, 1961. An audiotape copy of this recording is located at the National Sound Archive, British

Library, London. An audiotape copy of the transcript of the interview and reading is located in the Manuscripts Room, British Library, London. At the culmination of the interview Plath reads the poem "Mushrooms." The interview has not been published or commercially released, though several sound clips were included on the video documentary *Voices & Visions*. Plath's reading of "Mushrooms" is included on *Sylvia Plath Reads* (Caedmon, New York, abridged and remastered rerelease 1999).

8. A joint reading with Marvin Kane of Sylvia Plath's poems, with commentary by Plath, for the BBC Third Programme series *The Living Poet*, recorded at the BBC studios in London on June 5, 1961. Broadcast with the episode title "Sylvia Plath" on July 8, 1961. An audiotape copy of this recording is located at the National Sound Archive, British Library, London. Plath reads, with introductory commentary, "The Disquieting Muses," "Spinster," "Parliament Hill Fields," and "The Stones" (from "Poem for a Birthday"). Marvin Kane reads "Sleep in the Mojave Desert," "Suicide Off Egg Rock," "You're," "Magi," and "Medallion," with Plath introductory commentary on "Spinster," "You're," "Magi," and "Medallion." Plath's readings, without introductions, of "The Disquieting Muses," "Spinster," "Parliament Hill Fields," and "The Stones" have been commercially released on *Sylvia Plath Reads* (Caedmon, New York, abridged and remastered rerelease 1999).

9. An interview for the BBC Home Service series *A World of Sound*, recorded at Plath's home in North Tawton, Devonshire, on April 10, 1962, and August 20, 1962. Interview conducted by Marvin Kane. Broadcast with the episode title "What Made You Stay?" on September 7, 1962. An audiotape of this recording is located at the National Sound Archive, British Library, London. This interview has not been published or commercially released.

10. A reading of the essay "A Comparison" for the BBC series *The World of Books*, recorded at the BBC studios in London June 25–27, 1962. Broadcast on July 7, 1962. No available recording known. An audiotape copy of this recording may exist in the BBC Sound Archive via the National Sound Archive, British Library, London, but it was not found during a search conducted in November 2000. The recording of "A Comparison" has not been commercially released. The essay was published in Sylvia Plath's *Johnny Panic and the Bible of Dreams: Short Stories, Prose and Diary Excerpts* (New York: Harper and Row, 1978).

11. A reading of "The Surgeon at 2 A.M." for the BBC Third Programme series *The Poet's Voice,* recorded at the BBC studio in London on August 10, 1962. Broadcast on August 24, 1962. An audiotape copy of this recording may exist in the BBC Sound Archive via the National Sound Archive, British Library, London, but it was not found during a search conducted in November 2000. This recording has been commercially released on *Sylvia Plath Reads* (Caedmon, New York, abridged and remastered rerelease 1999).

12. A reading of "Berck-Plage" for the BBC program "The Weird Ones," recorded at the BBC studios on October 29, 1962. Broadcast on November 4, 1962. An audiotape copy of this recording may exist in the BBC Sound Archive via the National Sound Archive, British Library, London, but it was not found during a search conducted in November 2000. This recording was commercially released on *Sylvia Plath Reading Her Poetry* (Caedmon, New York, 1977).

13. A reading and interview for the BBC, the British Council and the Woodberry Poetry Room at Harvard University, recorded at the BBC studios in London on October 30, 1962. Interview conducted by Peter Orr. An audiotape copy of this recording is located at the National Sound Archive, British Library, London. Orr's interview with Plath is followed by her readings of "The Rabbit Catcher," "Ariel," "Poppies in October," "The Applicant," "Lady Lazarus," "A Secret," "Cut," "Stopped Dead," "Nick and the Candlestick," "Medusa," "Purdah," "A Birthday Present," "Amnesiac" ("Lyonnesse" and "Amnesiac" read as one poem), "Daddy," and "Fever 103°." The recording of the interview has not been commercially released, though sound clips from it were included in the video documentary *Voices & Visions.* It was published in *The Poet Speaks—Interviews with Contemporary Poets Conducted by Hilary Morrish, Peter Orr, John Press and Ian Scott-Kilvert,* ed. Peter Orr (London: Routledge and Kegan Paul, 1966). All of the poems have been commercially released. The record album *Plath* (Credo Records, Cambridge, Massachusetts, 1976) includes all of the poems from this session, as does the audiocassette *Focus on Sylvia Plath* (Center for Cassette Studies, North Hollywood, California, n.d.), though both of these releases are now rare. *The Voice of the Poet: Sylvia Plath* (Random House AudioBooks, 1999) includes eight of the fifteen poems: "Ariel," "The Applicant," "Lady Lazarus," "Nick and the Candlestick," "Purdah," "A Birthday Present," "Daddy," and "Fever 103°."

14. A review of the anthology *Contemporary American Poetry,* edited by Donald Hall, for the BBC Third Programme series *New Comment,* recorded live at the BBC studios on January 10, 1963. An audio-tape copy of this recording is located at the National Sound Archive, British Library, London. This recording has not been commercially released or published.

CONTRIBUTORS

Janet Badia is Associate Professor of English at Marshall University. She is coeditor of *Reading Women: Literary Figures and Cultural Icons from the Victorian Age to the Present* (University of Toronto Press, 2005). She is completing a book entitled *Sylvia Plath, Anne Sexton, and the Mythology of Women Readers.*

Tracy Brain is Senior Lecturer in English and Creative Studies at Bath Spa University, United Kingdom, where she directs the Ph.D. in Creative Writing Programme. She is the author of *The Other Sylvia Plath* (Pearson, 2001). Her essays on Plath also appear in *The Cambridge Companion to Sylvia Plath* (ed. Jo Gill, Routledge, 2006) and *Modern Confessional Writing* (ed. Jo Gill, Routledge, 2006).

Marsha Bryant is Associate Professor of English at the University of Florida. She is the author of *Auden and Documentary in the 1930s* (University of Virginia Press, 1997) and editor of *Photo-Textualities: Reading Photographs and Literature* (University of Delaware Press, 1996). Her recent essays on Plath have appeared in *College Literature* and *Pedagogy.*

Lynda K. Bundtzen is the Herbert H. Lehman Professor of English at Williams College. She is the author of two books on Sylvia Plath: *Plath's Incarnations: Woman and the Creative Process* (University of Michigan Press, 1983), which was awarded the Alice and Edith Hamilton Prize by the University of Michigan Press; and *The Other Ariel* (University of Massachusetts Press, 2001). A new paperback edition of *The Other Ariel* (Sutton Publishing, UK, 2005) has been published with a new introduction, taking into account the publication of *Ariel: The Restored Edition.*

Kathleen Connors directed the Sylvia Plath 70th Year Commemoration and Literary Symposium at Indiana University (2002) and curated "Eye Rhymes: Visual Arts and Manuscripts of Sylvia Plath," an exhibition sponsored by the School of Fine Arts Gallery and the Lilly Library at Indiana University and the Mortimer Rare Book Room at Smith College. With Sally Bayley of the University of Oxford, she is codirector of the 75th Year Symposium at Oxford, and coeditor of *Eye Rhymes: Sylvia Plath's Art of the Visual* (Oxford University Press, 2007).

Sandra M. Gilbert is Professor Emerita of English at the University of California, Davis. She is past president of the Modern Language Association and a member of the American Academy of Arts and Sciences. She authored a study of D. H. Lawrence's poetry (*Acts of Attention*) and is coauthor (with Susan Gubar) of *The Madwoman in the Attic* (Yale University Press, 1979) and the three-volume series *No Man's Land: The Place of the Woman Writer in the Twentieth Century* (Yale University Press, 1988–94). She is coeditor (with Susan Gilbert) of *The Norton Anthology of Literature by Women.* Her writing on traditions of elegy and mourning includes an edited anthology, *Inventions of Farewell: A Book of Elegies,* and her recent critical study, *Death's Door: Modern Dying and the Ways We Grieve* (W.W. Norton, 2006). She is also the author of prose memoir, *Wrongful Death* and of seven books of poetry, most recently *Belonging: Poems* (Norton, 2005). Among other awards for her poems, she has won the Paterson Prize, the John Ciardi Award for Lifetime Achievement in Poetry, and the American Book Award.

Anita Helle is Associate Professor of English at Oregon State University. She is editor of *The Unraveling Archive: Essays on Sylvia Plath* and of "American Poetry 1940s to the Present" for *American Literary Scholarship* (Duke University Press, 1996–99). Her recent writing on Plath, archives, and twentieth-century poetry appears in *The Norton Anthology of Theory and Criticism: A Reader* (W. W. Norton, 2007) and the *Oxford Handbook of Elegy* (2008).

Ann Keniston is Assistant Professor of English at the University of Nevada, Reno. Her book, *Overheard Voices: Address and Subjectivity in Postmodern American Poetry* was published by Routledge (2006); a volume of poems, *The Caution of Human Gestures,* appeared in 2005 from David Roberts Books.

Diane Middlebrook is a professional writer, and formerly a Professor of English at Stanford University. Her *Anne Sexton, A Biography* (1991) was a finalist for the National Book Award and for the National Book Critics Circle Award. Her most recent book, *Her Husband: Hughes and Plath—a Marriage* (2003), is the biography of their creative partnership. Middlebrook lives in San Francisco and London, where she was recently elected as a Fellow of the Royal Society of Literature, and was made an Honorary Fellow of Christ's College, Cambridge. In 2004, she served as Chair of the Panel on Non-Fiction, for the National Book Award in the USA. She is currently working on a biography of the Roman poet Ovid.

Kate Moses is the author of *Wintering: A Novel of Sylvia Plath* (St. Martin's, 2003), winner of the Janet Hedinger Kafka Prize and the Grand Prix des Lectrices de Elle (2005). She is also coeditor (with Camille Peri) of the anthologies *Because I Said So: 33 Mothers Write about Children, Sex, Men, Aging, Faith, Race and Themselves* (Washington Square, 2005) and *Mothers Who Think: Tales of Real-Life Parenthood* (Washington Square, 1999), winner of an American Book Award.

Robin Peel is Principal Lecturer in English at the University of Plymouth in the United Kingdom. He is the author of *Writing Back: Plath and Cold War Politics* (Fairleigh Dickinson/Associated University Presses, 2002) and *Apart from Modernism: Edith Wharton, Politics, and Fiction before World War I* (Fairleigh Dickinson/Associated University Presses, 2005) . He is currently working on a study of Emily Dickinson and science, thus continuing the study of writers with strong Massachusetts links.